stamped below.

Celebrity and Power

Celebrity and Power

Fame in Contemporary Culture

P. David Marshall

University of Minnesota Press

Minneapolis / London

Published by the University of Minnesota Press
111 Third Avenue South, Suite 290, Minneapolis, MN 55401-2520
Printed in the United States of America on acid-free paper

Library of Congress Cataloging-in-Publication Data

Marshall, P. David.
   Celebrity and power : fame in contemporary culture / P. David
 Marshall.
      p.   cm.
   Includes bibliographical references and index.
   ISBN 0-8166-2724-X (hc : acid-free paper)
   ISBN 0-8166-2725-8 (pbk. : acid-free paper)
   1. Celebrities—United States—History—20th century.   2. Fame—
Social aspects—United States.   3. Celebrities—History—20th
century.   4. Fame—Social aspects.   5. Popular culture—United
States—History—20th century.   6. Popular culture—History—20th
century.   I. Title.
E169.04.M366   1997
306'.0973—dc20   96-31522

The University of Minnesota is an equal-opportunity educator and employer.

To Erin, Robert, and Theo

Contents

Preface

Vignette 1: In 1993, the long fallen and somewhat ridiculed Soviet/Russian leader Mikhail Gorbachev visits Ottawa and a throng comes out to "see" the man. Radio stations pull in experts to comment on the phenomenon: Why Gorbachev? Why is there this pop star treatment, where the audience cranes to see, to almost touch the person, the clothing?

Vignette 2: O.J. Simpson, the football star, film actor, and sports commentator, creates a massive media frenzy in Los Angeles as he avoids arrest for the brutal slaying of his ex-wife and a young man. Saturation coverage in the United States transforms the event into something internationally significant. O.J. eventually surrenders, not only to the police but also to his new celebrity status as fallen hero and courtroom defendant in the public consciousness.

In contemporary culture, there are obvious sites of power that people can readily identify. Legislative assemblies and government bureaucracies are institutions that represent power clearly for the news media and the populace. Large national and multinational corporations also figure as institutional power centers. The media themselves have often been perceived as powerful in their capacity to shape and frame the messages and representations of particular cultures.

In this book I try to shed some light on a less definable form of power that operates in contemporary culture. In the public sphere, a cluster of individuals are given greater presence and a wider scope of activity and agency than are those who make up the rest of the population. They are allowed to move on the public stage while the rest of us watch. They are allowed to express themselves quite individually and idiosyncratically while the rest of the members of the population are constructed as demographic aggregates. We tend to call these overtly public individuals *celebrities*. In this book I attempt to address the concept and function of the celebrity, with the general objective of detailing how power is articulated through the celebrity.

Celebrities are not powerful in any overt political sense; some may possess political influence, whereas others exercise their power in less politically defined ways. To understand the power of the celebrity requires a different set of tools and a different sense of how power is organized in society, and parts of this book are devoted to the reconceptualization of how one might understand celebrity power. I will investigate the cultural and political potency of the celebrity by investigating how the celebrity structures meaning, crystallizes ideological positions, and works to provide a sense and coherence to a culture. Celebrity status operates at the very center of the culture as it resonates with conceptions of individuality that are the ideological ground of Western culture. Moreover, the celebrity as public individual who participates openly as a marketable commodity serves as a powerful type of legitimation of the political economic model of exchange and value — the basis of capitalism — and extends that model to include the individual.

The concept of the celebrity is best defined as a *system* for valorizing meaning and communication. As a system, the condition of celebrity status is convertible to a wide variety of domains and conditions within contemporary culture. Thus, the power of celebrity status appears in business, politics, and artistic communities and operates as a way of providing distinctions and definitions of success within those domains. Celebrity status also confers on the person a certain discursive power: within society, the celebrity is a voice above others, a voice that is channeled into the media systems as being legitimately significant.

In identifying a system of celebrity that may have a certain ideological consistency, I am not suggesting that the figure or sign of the celebrity is coherent. The celebrity can be described only as an ambiguous sign in contemporary culture that inscribes within and between its various formations a tension of signification. In one sense, the celebrity represents success and achievement within the social world. Contemporary culture has conferred on certain individuals we call celebrities or stars the public stage and renown. The recognition and public fame are part of the act of celebrating their importance and significance. In some generally agreed-upon way, they have earned their position of fame. We grant time for a film star like Tom Cruise to speak extensively on television and in magazine articles not only about his work but about himself, his feelings, and whether his various actions both on- and off-screen are good and moral. Alternatively, Sean Connery, the former James Bond, is now venerated as Henry Fonda, Katharine Hepburn, and Jimmy Stewart before him. They all have become part of an untouchable constellation of film celebrities who are seen to deserve their position because of their ability.

In another sense, the celebrity is viewed in the most antipathetic manner. The sign of the celebrity is ridiculed and derided because it represents the center of false value. The success expressed in the celebrity posture is seen as success without the requisite association with work. Disparaging remarks about individual celebrities are legion: in the original Madonna incarnation, her voice was believed to be electronically enhanced — she couldn't "really" sing; Andie MacDowell is a wonderful blank face that allows the directors and editors to *make* her act; or New Kids on the Block, a singing group looked at more closely later in this book as a case study, are simply a fabricated commodity. Thus, there is no substance to the sign of the celebrity, and without that embedded significance, the celebrity sign is entirely image. To use a Marxian metaphor to describe the vacuity of the sign of the image lacking materiality and productivity, the celebrity sign is pure exchange value cleaved from use value. It articulates the individual as commodity.[1]

The celebrity sign effectively contains this tension between authentic and false cultural value. In its simultaneous embodiment of media construction, audience construction, and the real, living and breathing human being, the celebrity sign negotiates the competing and contradictory definitions of its own significance. The cementing character of the negotiation is the basic and essential authenticity that a "real" person is housed in the sign construction. In a cultural sense, the celebrity is one form of resolution of the role and position of the individual and his or her potential in modern society. The power of the celebrity, then, is to represent the active construction of identity in the social world. Studying the celebrity offers the reader of culture a privileged view of the representative forms of modern subjectivity that pass through the celebrity as discourses. What follows in the succeeding chapters is a discussion of the role and position of the celebrity in contemporary culture. Ultimately, I attempt to provide a conclusion about the kind of power that is expressed in and through the celebrity sign.

Because of the ambiguity of the celebrity, its form of power is difficult to discern. In the following chapters, I define its power in terms of its capacity to house conceptions of individuality and simultaneously to embody or help embody "collective configurations" of the social world. In popular culture, these collective configurations are called *audiences*. It is the social power of the audience that identifies the type of social power the celebrity expresses. Fundamentally, it is a power that is unstable in terms of each individual sign, but consistent as a system. For this reason it is useful to think of the power of the celebrity in terms of a system that constructs and deconstructs the social world in terms of temporal and transforming audiences.

The organization of the book parallels this configuration of celebrity power. The first chapter deals primarily with the way certain authors have expressed the power of the individual in terms of leadership and notoriety. This investigation begins with a study of the type of individuality that the term *celebrity* defines through a tracing of its usage to its current inherently ambiguous meaning. From this historical establishment of the significance of the use of the term *celebrity* in twentieth-century Western (though predominantly North American) culture to describe a specific form of representative subjectivity, the chapter then moves to a discussion of the merits of various studies of leadership, stardom, and celebrities to determine the limitations of this general approach, which focuses on the public individual as possessing inherent qualities.

Chapter 2 investigates the importance of understanding the development of celebrity power in terms of collective configurations. The historical emergence of the celebrity is linked with the historical movement toward containing the "irrational" mass in Western democratic systems. Public personalities, in general, express a direct connection between the public figure and the populace. In a sense, the celebrity circumvents other structures of power in this direct appeal. The celebrity articulates a tension between the meanings provided by a dominant culture that elevates certain individuals and the readings or rearticulation of those meanings by various collective formations in their selective embracement of these public representations.

Chapter 3 integrates the concepts explored in the first two chapters into a general theory and technique for understanding the function of the celebrity. In this chapter the key analytic concepts are developed. The celebrity's embodiment of "affective power" is discussed in terms of two forms of rationalization: a dominant culture's rationalization of the fragments of the mass into identifiable and categorizable audience groups and the various audience groups' attempts to rationalize or make sense of the incongruities of their social world through celebrating the human agency of particular public personalities. The concept of the "audience-subject" is developed to express the simultaneous construction of celebrity power through its intense development of the individual personality's power and its dependence on collective configurations for the maintenance of its public representation of power. The celebrity is reconceptualized as a sign that negotiates these tensions and contradictions in its formation and disintegration. The technique of conducting a hermeneutics of reception and intention is discussed as a method for comprehending the meaning of individual celebrities as audience subjectivities.

Chapters 4, 5, and 6 analyze the emergence of celebrities in three specific entertainment industries. After a historical investigation of the form of celebrity that has emerged in the film, television, and popular music industries, a hermeneutic of intention and reception of specific contemporary celebrities—Tom Cruise in film, Oprah Winfrey in television, and the New Kids on the Block in popular music—is conducted to reveal the ways in which they embody particular kinds of "audience-subjectivity" and thus house the formation of affective power in contemporary culture. This section concludes with a summary chapter that maps out the interrelations among these types of celebrities, the categories of reception that are privileged in each popular cultural form, and the systemic properties that operate in contemporary culture to construct the discursive parameters of "public subjectivity."

Chapter 8 describes how the system of celebrity informs the operation of political culture. It presents my argument that the disciplinary boundaries between the domains of popular culture and political culture have been eroded through the migration of communicative strategies and public relations from the entertainment industries to the organization of the spectacle of politics. These strategies of defining the public are accentuated in the construction of the political leader. The categories of reception and subjectivity identified in previous chapters in popular culture are charted onto the representations of political leaders. What is revealed is that politics, like the culture industries, attempts to play with and contain affective power through its intense focus on the personal, the intimate, and the individual qualities of leadership in its process of legitimation.

In the final chapter, I identify the principal functions of celebrity that have emerged in conjunction with the development of capitalist democracies. The book concludes with the alignment of the power of celebrity with its capacity to disperse power into the private and individualized sphere of personal affect and affectation.

Acknowledgments

There are many who have helped in this endeavor who are deserving of attention: from Montreal, Marike Finlay, Brian Massumi, and Martin Allor; from Carleton University, Paul Attallah, Chris Dornan, Mark Langer, and Will Straw; and from the University of Queensland, Frances Bonner, Graeme Turner, Keith Hampson, and Angela Tuohy. My family has also supported me throughout the various incarnations of this book. Rea Turner has weathered a great deal and was often my first favorable critic and adviser, and Erin has not known a time in her life when this entity did not exist. My brother Neil provided a lovely office in his practice in the early stages of writing, and my mother and father have contributed in innumerable ways in their support. Those at the University of Minnesota Press have been patient and supportive. I would especially like to thank Janaki Bakhle, Micah Kleit, Lisa Freeman, Jeff Moen, and Judy Selhorst for their efforts at improving my work. I thank all of you for your help and intellectual and emotional sustenance.

Part I

1

Tracing the Meaning of the Public Individual

Most popular studies of celebrity have focused on the elevated individual. A series of questions are asked that continue to be the source of biographical and autobiographical writing on the public personality: What makes the celebrated individual unique? What particular moments in his or her life led to fame? What traits have allowed the individual to rise to public acclaim? These are questions that are looking for the core of the individual and the roots of a causal relationship between the celebrity's actions and the successful consequences of those actions. In contemporary biography, the psychoanalytic tales of how the star's psyche was/is formed predominate as the elixir of truth. Brando is allowed to ruminate in his recent autobiography *Songs My Mother Taught Me* on motivations and undercurrents that helped define his brooding public personality.[1] Michael Jackson, in his 1988 book, *Moonwalk,* explains that "I suppose I got my singing ability from my mother and, of course, God," and that his drive to perform and sing was "as natural to me as drawing a breath and exhaling it." Ultimately, he felt "compelled to do it, not by parents or family, but by *my own inner life* in the world of music."[2] Perhaps Kirk Douglas's viscerally revealing autobiography, *The Ragman's Son,* represents the quintessential revelatory tale of the contemporary celebrity. In it we discover the kinds of repressions, the forms of anger, and the relationships to fathers, mothers, and children that led to the motivated behavior of the screen performances of Kirk Douglas.[3]

The celebrity biography appears in many forms and guises. We receive a weekly diet in various popular magazines. The tabloid press provides a scandalous turn on the meaning of the celebrity and presents us with the possibility that the supposed unique talents of celebrities are vulnerable and subject to dramatic falls as well as equally impressive moments of contrition and resurrection. The British actor Hugh Grant was able to compress a rise, a sexually scandalous fall,

3

and, through talk-show contrition, a return to general acceptance, all in the wonderful synergistic time frame of the publicity buildup for his 1995 Hollywood movie *Nine Months*. In all cases, celebrities are the production locale for an elaborate discourse on the individual and individuality that is organized around the will to uncover a hidden truth, or, as Richard Dyer has developed it, to uncover the "real" person behind the public persona.[4]

This chapter searches the cultural traces for the development of this elaborate discourse on the public individual. This intense focus on the public personality is a peculiarly modern phenomenon that can be discerned from a study of the interpretive writings about the public individuals themselves. The distinctive discursive quality of the celebrity is derived from its emergence from the twinned discourses of modernity: democracy and capitalism. The celebrity as a concept of the individual moves effortlessly in a celebration of democratic capitalism. This chapter addresses the way the celebrity has been represented, critiqued, and celebrated, in order to clarify the articulation of power that the celebrity embodies as an individual.

The specifically modern quality of the celebrity can be identified from a variety of ways of looking at contemporary culture. Through first tracing the etymological roots of *celebrity*, one can establish a genealogy of the use and position of the term that situates the reading of the celebrity by other writers and critics. Much like the concept of individualism, the use of the term *celebrity* in its contemporary (ambiguous) form developed in the nineteenth century.[5] Studying examples of prior usage, one can see the transformation of its sense from an affinity with piety and religion to some modern sense of false value. The two faces of capitalism—that of defaced value and prized commodity value—are contained within these transforming definitions. The term *celebrity* has come to embody the ambiguity of the public forms of subjectivity under capitalism.

In the abridged concise *Oxford English Dictionary*, other than identifying its Latin derivation in *celeber* and *celebritas,* the definition goes no further than to say that the celebrity is one who is "famous" or is a "well-known person." This abbreviated definition could be construed as identifying, in the vaguest way, an expanded stage for public subjectivities; the identification of well-knownness may involve a larger section of the population and may suggest new categories that qualify for popular personal status. Such a transformation of usage becomes evident only when one compares it to prior usages of the term. One sees this transformation by looking in the unabridged versions of the *Oxford English* and *Webster's* dictionaries; there, this current, everyday usage is derived from a certain telos. The sequence of usages listed suggests a historical development of the term that seems to parallel a transforming system of power. In *Webster's Third New International Dictionary*, the obsolete use of the term to denote "a solemn celebration" is listed first. The *Oxford English Dictionary* identifies the first meaning with the more archaic use of the word: "Due observance of rites and ceremonies; pomp, solemnity." The examples given illuminate the precapitalist, seventeenth-century sentiment in the usage: "whose body was remoued with all celebritie and enshrined" (Weever, 1631). In the second usage listed by the *Oxford English Dictionary*, celebrity identifies "a solemn rite or ceremony, a celebration." The third definition comes closest to our modern understanding of the word: "The condition of being much extolled or talked about; famousness, notoriety." Although some examples from the same seventeenth-century epoch are given, the usage seems to have become part of the lexicon of the eighteenth century. Still, the term carried its history's weight of solemnity and religiosity: from Hooker in 1600 — "The dignity and celebrity of mother cities should be respected." An interesting, related example from the mid-nineteenth century gives evidence that the term *celebrity* was no longer a moniker of solemnity but rather a term of some derogation: "They [Spinoza's successors] had celebrity, Spinoza has fame" (1863). In this case, *celebrity* describes a more fleeting, ephemeral connotation of fame. The fourth and final definition identifies the conclusive transformation of the term into the public personality: "A person of celebrity; a celebrated person: a public character." In the examples given under this definition there is a sense of the inauthentic nature of the celebrity: "Did you see any of those 'celebrities' as you call them?" (1849). Even more modern in its assurance of the new status of the term is this: "One of the celebrities of wealth and fashion confessed . . . that . . ." (1856). The air of inauthenticity that rings through these last examples describes the current meaning of celebrity. It has become a term that announces a vulgar sense of notoriety. In English culture, it may have articulated the separation of old wealth and new wealth. The proclamation of one's newfound position and the quest for fame are not forms of distinction that demarcate the landed gentry from the peasants. Rather celebrity can be thought of as a label that works to differentiate layers of the bourgeoisie.

Thus, celebrity status invokes the message of possibility of a democratic age. The restrictions of a former hierarchy are no longer valid in the new order that is determined by merit and/or the acquisition of wealth. This democratic sense of the term is drawn from the original Latin *celebrem,* which had not only the connotation of famous but also that of "thronged." The celebrity, in this sense, is not distant but attainable—touchable by the multitude. The greatness of the celebrity is something that can be shared and, in essence, celebrated loudly and with a touch of vulgar pride. It is the ideal representation of the triumph of the masses. Concomitantly, celebrity is the potential of capitalism, a celebration of new kinds of values and orders, a debunking of the customary divisions of traditional society, for the celebrity him- or herself is dependent entirely on the new order.

Furthermore, celebrity acknowledges a new sense of the public sphere. *Celebrity* is derived from the French *célèbre,* which expresses something "well-known, public." Our modern focus on the new public realm or even the expanded public realm beyond the confines of the church and somewhat redefined by the growth of the state is another feature of seeing new forms of public representations outside of the classic metaphors and symbols of power and influence. From a connotation of religious solemnity to the representation of agnostic fame, the changing definitional focus of the term *celebrity* historically demarcates this transformation of power.

Finally, *Webster's Dictionary* provides one other link with Latin in its definition of the word *celebrate,* offering some salience in our understanding of *celebrity*'s current usage. There, a connection is made to the Latin word *celere,* which means "swift," as in the English word *celerity.* This suggests the fleeting nature of celebrity status, that it is a position without history, without a great deal of cultural import or baggage. Unlike peerage, celebrity draws its power from those elements outside tradition. This power, however, has a certain liquidity, much like the mobility and exchangeability of capital. Its swiftness, like capital's, could also be based on the lack of material basis for the representation of notoriety. The celebrity exists above the real world, in the realm of symbols that gain and lose value like commodities on the stock market.

What I have identified so far is the central position that the term *celebrity* has as a metaphor for value in modern society. More specifically, it describes a type of value that can be articulated through an individual and celebrated publicly as important and significant. The term is linked to past power structures (i.e., the church) and now has connotations that link it to modern power structures (i.e., capitalism).

This definitional landscape of the term *celebrity* also provides evidence that celebrity is implicated in new categorizations of the public sphere. It appears that the modern usage of *celebrity* is connected to the heightened significance of popular culture and democratic culture. The celebrity embodies the empowerment of the people to shape the public sphere symbolically.

Some nineteenth-century writers can be reread into the genealogy of the celebrity as chronicling this transformation of the public sphere and the meaning of the individuals that were part of it. Not all of these authors use the word *celebrity; heroes* and *representative men* seem to be the preferred designations of public figures. Nevertheless, the common thread in these depictions is the attempt to study this new representation of value articulated through a particular subjectivity. *Celebrity* can be thought of as the general and encompassing term, whereas concepts of *hero, star,* and *leader* are more specific categories of the public individual that relate to specific functions in the public sphere.[6]

William Hazlitt, writing in the early 1800s, could be, as Braudy claims, "the first great fame theorist of the modern age."[7] His reading of the nature of the celebrity involved discerning whether or not the individual was pursuing the highest of ends, unfettered by the desire for personal glory. Thus, poetry was written to reach the height of an aesthetic, the height of an individual genius. Hazlitt's concern was the origin of fame and immortality. The nineteenth century marked a period in which the audience, now a wider "democratic" public, determined the nature of fame and celebrity. With the French Revolution and Napoleon's rule, Hazlitt also saw the liberation of the individual to pursue these grand aesthetic moments and achievements, to soar like Byron or Keats. Hazlitt was the first to identify the ambiguity of public fame: " 'The Spirit of the Age,' as Hazlitt defines it, is an individual ostentation that has created good when it has awakened people to the spirit of liberty, but has too often displayed only the gestures of mere ambition."[8]

By the middle of the nineteenth century, two cultural critics, Thomas Carlyle and Ralph Waldo Emerson, saw the need to categorize heroism so that its true characters could be seen through the democratic dilution of virtue and genius into celebrity and fame. The possibility that anyone could be famous was seen by Carlyle and Emerson to necessitate a listing of the ideal types of heroes. For Carlyle, the distinction between a hero and a noted person—a markedly lesser status—was significant. He isolated six ideal types of heroes: heroes of the divine, prophetic, poetic, priestly, literary, and kingly orders.[9] Emerson focused less on heroic qualities and more on the genius of the individual to pull from other individuals of society to create some common and public good. Because of that focus on the individual spirit, Emerson was drawn to identifying each genius individually, from Shakespeare and Napoleon to Plato and Goethe. Interestingly, it seems that both Carlyle and Emerson were acting as protectors of the public good or arbiters of the massive flux of less valuable categories such as celebrity. Like Hazlitt before them, they approached the role of the larger public audience in the construction of the celebrity as an area to consider with some concern and criticism.

Detailing the entire nineteenth-century position of the celebrity in critical and interpretive writing would require a book in itself, and this is somewhat beyond the scope of this project. What can be synthesized from this sketch of three nineteenth-century writers on heroes is their identification of the contentious area that is discursively captured by the antinomic celebrity sign since the nineteenth century: the construction of individuality through the new mass public and audience. The mass audience is central in the definitions of individual value and worth. The celebrity embodies the ideal type of hero that emerges from the mass audience. For Hazlitt, Carlyle, and Emerson, this new power of determining value needs to be connected to (or critically confronted with) historical models of distinctive and important individuals, so that any new form can be truly and authentically validated. The danger of the new celebrity is that it has slipped the yoke of historical validation.[10]

The reading of the public sphere as populated by heroes and great men becomes a declining discourse around public subjectivity in the twentieth century. Celebrity itself generated an entire industry by the second decade of the twentieth century, with the emergence of movie fan magazines (*Moving Picture World,* later followed by *Photoplay,*

Modern Screen, and *Silver Screen*) that openly celebrated movie stars and their lives, subjects far removed from nineteenth-century delineations of heroism and invention. The relationship between the celebrity industry and the kinds of historical validation that Hazlitt or Carlyle looked for in "representative men" had become reworked into a democratic myth of humble beginnings followed by hard work, discovery, and stardom. As Joshua Gamson relates, "The appetite for films, film stars and their movie and private lives had by the 1920s become voracious. By the 1930s, Hollywood was the third largest news source in the country, with some 300 correspondents, including one from the Vatican."[11] Celebrity status became aligned with the potentialities of the wedding of consumer culture with democratic aspirations. The images of possibility provided by films, radio, and popular music represented an accessible form of consumption. The discourse that surrounded these celebrities provided the evidence of access to stardom.

Celebrity status, in its vulgar association with consumer culture, became a central icon for the critique of mass culture/society that was emerging from both cultural conservatives and Marxist critics. Writing in the late 1930s and early 1940s, Horkheimer and Adorno developed a damning critique of what they labeled the "culture industries" that produced celebrities. The thesis of reassuring the individual through the actions of the celebrity/star is elaborated in their classic essay "The Culture Industry: Enlightenment as Mass Deception."[12] As opposed to previous forms of culture, which served to negate the power of existing society, the modern industry, through the star, fosters the celebration of the system. Horkheimer and Adorno emphasize the idea of the malleability of the masses' consciousness. In their discussion of film and radio, Horkheimer and Adorno develop an argument on the modern "cult of the personality" offered by Hollywood. The star is meant to epitomize the potential of everyone in American society. We are psychically drawn to identify with stars as ourselves. This, however, is only appearance. The dialectical reality is that the star is part of a system of false promise in the system of capital, which offers the reward of stardom to a random few in order to perpetuate the myth of potential universal success. The masses are by their very nature psychologically immature and thus are drawn to the magic of these larger-than-life personalities in the same way children identify with and implicitly trust their parents. Mass society has produced a people peculiarly susceptible to these forms of manipulation.

The manipulation thesis pervades the radical critiques of twenti-eth-century mass society. For many members of the so-called Frank-furt school, the success of fascist authoritarianism and leadership in Hitler's Germany served as the backdrop for parallel interpretations of the dangerously false power of the modern celebrity. Herbert Mar-cuse's influential *One Dimensional Man,* written twenty years after Horkheimer and Adorno's famous essay, indicates the sustaining power of the manipulation thesis that celebrity is a site of false value and serves to placate the individual into an acceptance of the modern (un-satisfactory) condition.[13]

Leo Lowenthal, another affiliate of the Frankfurt school, also added to the chorus of criticism of contemporary public personalities. In a chapter devoted to the transformation of the hero in twentieth-cen-tury society, Lowenthal asserts that whereas in previous social systems there had been an emphasis on success being based on hard work, in current society — as he was writing in the 1940s — the key determi-nants are luck and circumstance. Moreover, the celebrity was arising from the arena of leisure and nonfunctional types of endeavors. Low-enthal calls this transformation a progress toward idols of consump-tion as opposed to the former idols of production (i.e., business lead-ers, politicians, captains of industry). The heroes of popular culture simultaneously offer hope for everyone's success and the promise of the entire social system to be open to these moments of luck. Ultimately, the system of modern heroes reinforced the status quo.[14]

The strength of these critiques for this study of celebrity is that they develop a link between theories of the individual and their inte-gration into the meaning of capitalism. Critical theory's combination of Freudian insights with an antimaterialist Marxism derived from the early writings of Georg Lukács on reification provide the first in-depth study of modern popular culture as an entire system. The construction of the mass/individual dichotomy demarcates a temporal assessment of the twentieth century, when the final triumph of a debilitated mass over the potential for true consciousness of the individual is realized. What early critical theorists missed, however, was the complex struc-ture of popular culture and the uses audiences make of popular cul-tural artifacts. Also, their analysis froze the category of the mass into their tableau so that the fragmentation of the mass into other forma-tions and configurations was completely overlooked. This oversight drastically simplified their assessment of stars and celebrities to simple instantiations of a system of manipulation.

From a much more conservative cultural tradition, the development of the celebrity was seen as evidence of the decline in value and standards. Daniel Boorstin's midcentury reading of how fame and its attachments further underlined the way that consumer culture was at the root of a decline in authenticity in public personalities is an emblematic summary. His treatment of celebrity status, rather than emphasizing the power of manipulation, tries to reveal the superficiality of the position: "A star is well-known for his/her wellknownness." He adds that what makes a star is a "definable and publicizable personality."[15] This thesis identifies in outline the postmodern condition of absence of absolute meaning well before it is defined as such. The interchangeability of celebrities means that no celebrity possesses any meaning of consequence. Thus, the system of signification that it offers, the categorization of value, is pure surface. To a degree, this extension of Boorstin's reading of fame explains the rapid succession of famous people and the equally rapid decline of any particular celebrity. Ultimately, the surface meaning system means that the system of veneration, the process of succession of valued human identities, is more important than what any one of the individual celebrities may represent. The convertibility of value, a value that emphasizes inherent "exchange value" over "use value," is the persistent reality.

Considering the celebrity as pure exchange value points to the position of the celebrity in a culture focused on consumption. Boorstin's point concerning the ephemeral quality of the celebrity sign is articulated as an entire system of value in the work of Jean Baudrillard. In several different works, Baudrillard develops a theory around the ultimate freedom of the sign from the trappings of permanent value. The sign can attach to and detach from objects at will. This detachable sign is exemplified by, for example, the fashion industry. The depth of value of any sign of fashion is not to be found. Fashion is a system that celebrates the possibility that an infinite number of signifiers can be attached to an infinite number of signifieds, so that change and transformation of the resultant sign are the constancies of value. In one essay, Baudrillard speaks of this very ecstasy of communication; a certain pleasure and freedom are part of a social system that has moved to the domain of communication and representation.[16] To extend that position, the system of celebrity is the expression of the motility of exchange value in the construction of subjectivity. The interchangeability of celebrities, the nonattachment to the individual, means that we participate in the "ecstasy" of recombining a new representation of celebrity status.

Baudrillard's approach is important to this study because it revivifies the relevant social critique of value of the Frankfurt school. However, there are two areas where the analysis presents a virtual vacuum of insight. First, there is little discussion of people's forms of identification to the transformable signs of the social world. The connection is just not clearly made. What needs to be undertaken is an investigation of the power of the celebrity as a sign with its audience or public, even if that power is temporary and transferable to new signs of celebrity. The actual forms of subjectivity that are presented and accepted as celebrities need in-depth deconstruction. Second, the source of the celebrity sign is not entirely in the manipulative hands of the media or other obvious institutions of power. It is, as Dyer has emphasized, an area of negotiation among the public, the media, and the celebrity. In a form of working hegemony, the celebrity is configured. The more pertinent question may be, Why is the celebrity a very active area of discursive negotiation in contemporary culture? Posing this question helps us come closer to the nature of the celebrity's power.

By far the most developed work on the concept of the celebrity appears in the extensive writings on films, particularly Hollywood films. Here the name *celebrity* is rarely used. *Star* is the usual identification of some persona that has transcended the films that he or she has performed in and created an aura. There are three levels of study of film stars that help further our reading of the modern celebrity: first, the film star has been analyzed as the economic heart of the culture industry; second, the film star, in conjunction with the film experience and generally from within the text, has been studied as a form of spectatorial pleasure and identification; and third, in a way most connected to the meaning of the celebrity, the film star has been studied as a sociological phenomenon that exits the film roles and plays an active symbolic role in the lives of audiences. I will look at each of these levels of analysis separately.

The recognition of the power and influence of the star appears in two related discourses: the popular discourse on movies and the political economic analysis of the cinema. The everyday way to identify movies is through their stars. Indeed, the economic discourse has become an acceptable and popular way of referring to film stars, as box-office draws—a title rarely bestowed on a Hollywood director. The star acts as form of insurance in Hollywood, a kind of guaranteed return on investment for the production company. Production is ultimately dependent now on the star's involvement early on in the pre-production selling of a concept to investors and studios. As in the boxing world, the history of Hollywood can be written as successive generations of box-office kings. From Clark Gable, Cary Grant, and Gary Cooper to Paul Newman, Robert Redford, and Burt Reynolds to Stallone, Cruise, and Schwarzenegger, the mantle of guarantee within the industry is passed.

In the political economic analysis of the cinema, the star also figures centrally in the historical development of the industry. The classic history of the development of the star system relates first to the "invention" of the close-up shot by D. W. Griffith.[17] In opposition to the codes of drama, in which the entire scene and stage are visible, the camera allowed for the framing of actors' faces. Facial expression, with all its subtleties and intimacies, became a sign of the distinctive quality of the film over theater. Simultaneously, the close-up imbricated the actor more fully into the meaning of the drama. The close-up focused on the personal in a way that the stage had never done. This new "intimate" relationship between the characters and the audience altered the normal producer-worker relationship that epitomized dramatic production. The connection to the film audience became more centered on the actor. The new social relations around the production and use of film as an entertainment medium established the potential of the star, who could develop some personal power outside the production with a direct identification with the audience. In this early stage of Hollywood film production, the star as a system of value was still in its embryonic form. The nascent focus on the persona became the economic motor force of film production from 1910 onward, essentially paralleling the maturation of the movie industry.[18] By the 1950s, stars had established themselves as economic entities in the form of corporations; the expansion of the individual star's power was instrumental in breaking the thirty-year-old oligopolistic studio system.

The power of the star has been analyzed from a much different perspective by film scholars who have used psychoanalysis as an analytic tool for the study of the power and pleasure of the cinematic experience. French film writers of the 1960s and 1970s produced an array of texts that analyze the spectatorial forms of identification seen to link the filmic moment to the psychic realm of dream sequences. Christian Metz's influential essay "The Imaginary Signifier" led to a proliferating study of identification through Freudian and Lacanian-inspired psychoanalysis.[19] For Metz, the lead character in a film represents the ego ideal, which resembles the pre-Oedipal experience of Lacan's mirror stage. The character represents a more complete being — much as the mirror represents the more complete being of the child than its everyday uncoordinated baby self — and film's pleasure is partially built on this fundamental misrecognition for identification. The darkened theater, in its resemblance to the dream state, produces an environment consistent with similar psychic transfers and identifications. The images themselves, in a form of infinite repetition, pull us back into the apparatus through the construction of desire and identificatory psychic but temporary satisfaction. The power of the stars, then, in this analysis, is drawn from their positioning of spectators into the desiring apparatus of film. The psychoanalytic approach to the study of film has moved to the intellectual mainstream, with its regeneration in feminist film studies that have reworked Lacan's conception of the cultural construction of identity and desire, as opposed to something innate and immutable, as a site for cultural and political struggle.[20]

The psychoanalytic approach identifies quite a different construction of power from that definitionally embodied by the concept of the celebrity. Whereas psychoanalytic film studies rely predominantly on the text and its ability to engage the spectator in a form of identification, the celebrity is specifically an engagement with an external world that I have called the public sphere. The public subject may be produced by the cinematic experience and may derive its originary power from the fictional film text's construction of ideal self; however, the celebrity element of the star is its transcendence of the text in whatever form. The celebrity derives its power from some combination of experiences that are partially informed by the spectator-film star/character dyad identified eloquently by Jean-Louis Baudry and Metz as elements of a cinematic apparatus and partially from the social and cultural world that expands on this connection between star and spectator. John Ellis's use of Barthes's conception of the photo-effect to describe the presence/absence of the star is the best translation of psychoanalytic approaches to the study of the celebrity. Ellis identifies the very closeness and distance of the film star and the way that the spectator uses film specifically to stabilize the identity of the film star as celebrity, as the fan invests heavily in a variety of images from magazines that add to the image but at the same time make the star less coherent. Ellis is able to identify the contradictions of a publicly organized identity that arises from the fictional film.[21]

The third level of study of film stars engages in a sociological reading of the uses made of film stars by audiences and by a culture at large. The French sociologist Edgar Morin produced the groundbreaking investigation in *Les Stars,* a treatment of the star as a serious object of social study that chronicles the formation of the star system. Morin identifies the star system as the *embourgeoisement* of the medium, a way that film could move out of the carnival setting into a legitimate entertainment medium of the middle class. Thus, the star embodies the "exceptional with the ordinary, the ideal with the fundamentally everyday."[22] The film star actively works on the merging of bourgeois and working-class imaginations. One could surmise that the star is active in placating a proletarian interest that may be separate and therefore threatening to bourgeois cultural hegemony. This is an extension of Morin's thesis.

An Italian sociologist, Fransesco Alberoni, provided one of the first interpretations of celebrities in terms of a concept of power. In an article titled "The Powerless 'Elite': Theory and Sociological Research on the Phenomenon of the Stars," Alberoni makes some distinctions between stars and other public personalities. For Alberoni, stars are a modern phenomenon that has emerged from the developing complexity and social fluidity of modern society. They are an elite "whose institutional power is very limited or non-existent, but whose doings and way of life arouse a considerable and sometimes even maximum degree of interest."[23] What emerges in such a dual system of elites is that each elite is evaluated according to different criteria. Holders of power are evaluated; stars rarely are evaluated in the same way because of their lack of institutional power. Alberoni says that stars are objects of admiration. In contrast, envy often becomes central to the adjudication of political and economic elites. Stars form a second elite community that becomes the center of gossip and discussion in a complex society because of their apparent accessibility and openness to the larger community. Alberoni tentatively concludes that stars are, in part, a transitional phenomenon that identifies the need of the general community for an avenue through which to discuss issues of morality — "family, neighbourhood, of production and consumption etc." — that are insufficiently or ineffectively handled in the rational sphere of evaluating political power elites.[24]

Alberoni's argument centers on the identification of what general needs of a community are overlooked in the organization of a modern, rational, and democratic society and the positioning of stars and the star system to respond to those needs. Although Alberoni addresses the notion of power, his focus on the institutional site of power makes his argument of limited utility for this study. Also, the distinctions he makes between power elites and powerless elites are of questionable validity; our relationship to all public personalities is not clearly divided between some rational assessment and some irrational evaluation. Alberoni sets up a false distinction and thus a false dichotomy.

The film scholar James Monaco, in his edited book *Celebrity*, expands the lexicon for the description of public personalities. First is the hero — a famous person who has actually done something in an active sense. Astronauts, scientists, and inventors fall into the category of heroes because of their active nature. Celebrities, in contrast, are more passive — they are acted upon by the media and constructed into appropriate icons. The second category is the star. Monaco explains that the celebrity as star is not, as popularly conceived, an actor. Whereas the actor assumes roles, the star works on playing him- or herself. Marlon Brando epitomizes the star; we are more interested in seeing Brando than in seeing Brando transform into someone unrecognizable. Monaco states that along with a plethora of stars who fill the television talk shows, American politicians since Teddy Roosevelt have worked toward becoming stars. They attempt to create effective personas of self for the electorate. Finally, the third and lowest category of celebrity is the "quasar"; Monaco finds this the most interesting type, because this individual has virtually no control over his or her image. "It is not what they are or what they do, but what we *think* they are that fascinates us."[25] The media is the linchpin in this construction of the quasar image. The example that Monaco uses is the media construction of the many personas of Patty Hearst in the 1970s.[26] The quasar, who is often an unwilling participant in the celebrity phenomenon, is fabricated into an icon. For example, poster images of Che Guevara have been more vocal than the actions of the revolutionary.[27] The iconic quality of any celebrity is also the zenith of a career. What the icon represents is the possibility that the celebrity has actually entered the language of the culture and can exist whether the celebrity continues to "perform" or dies.

However interesting the categories that Monaco provides, his reading of celebrity is underdeveloped as to how celebrities are connected to the interests of an audience and how their power is ultimately part of a transformed public sphere beyond linking it to the power of the contemporary media—a variation on the Frankfurt school's manipulation of consciousness thesis. Richard Dyer, in a series of articles and books, has been instrumental in developing specifically a study of stars as a subdiscipline of film studies that deals with the connection between audience and constructed star image and thereby provides valuable insights into the meaning of the celebrity. In his most recent book on the subject, *Heavenly Bodies: Film Stars and Society,* Dyer formulates an interesting and useful conception of the star in relationship to the audience:

> Stars represent typical ways of behaving, feeling and thinking in contemporary society, ways that have been socially, culturally, historically constructed.... Stars are also embodiments of the social categories in which people are placed and through which they have to make sense of their lives, and indeed through which we make our lives—categories of class, gender, ethnicity, religion, sexual orientation, and so on.[28]

Dyer explains that the audience is obsessively and incessantly searching the star persona for the real and the authentic. We are aware that stars are appearances, "yet the whole media construction of stars encourages us to think in terms of 'really.' "[29] What is Marilyn Monroe "really" like? Is Paul Newman "really" the same as he appears in his films? These are the types of questions that the magazines and media ask the stars for us. Essentially, these questions point to the social function and position of the star in contemporary society. As Dyer states, the star is universally individualized, for the star is the representation of the potential of the individual. From the time of the Enlightenment, Western thought has concentrated on affirming the concept of the individual. Despite evidence to the contrary—the disintegration of individual power through the establishment of mass society—the individual continues to represent the ideological center of capitalist culture. The freedom of the individual is articulated through the freedom to choose what one consumes, or, alternatively, the freedom to make money. Thus, the star is an ideological shoring up of this triumphant individuality.[30]

Dyer explains that the stars embody cultural contradictions in the realm of identity and, specifically, in the division of public and private realms. As an audience, we are drawn to deconstruct the star, and in that process of reading the elaborate text that goes beyond the screen image, we are compelled to debate the nature of the star's public and private selves. In this intense study of star personalities, the audience fragments somewhat in its identification with individual stars. Some are drawn to the coherent authenticity of stars who appear to represent the same values off-screen as on. Others are drawn to stars who externalize their private torments, in the tradition of Marilyn Monroe. Dyer provides an excellent example of this work of the audience in their reading of John Travolta as the star of *Saturday Night Fever*:

> I haven't done an audience survey, but people seemed to be fairly evenly divided. For those not taken with him, the incredible build-up to the film, the way you knew what his image was before you saw the film, the coy but blatant emphasis on his sex appeal in the film, the gaudy artifice of the disco scene, all merely confirmed him as one great phoney put-on on the mass public. But for those for whom he and the film did work, there were the close-ups revealing the troubled pain behind the macho image, the intriguing off-screen stories about his relationship with an older woman, the spontaneity (=sincerity) of his smile, the setting of the film in a naturalistically portrayed ethnic subculture. A star's image can work either way, and in part we make it work according to how much it speaks to us in terms we can understand about things that are important to us.[31]

Within all this construction of the star by the audience, Dyer also identifies the other dialectic at play in the star's fabrication. The genesis of the star persona is its ability to be expressed in a commodity form. The tensions between these definitions and the star's own attempts at definition, independence, and distinction are the elements Dyer examines in the rest of *Heavenly Bodies,* where he analyzes and "reads" three stars in depth.

Dyer's extensive work on the film star constitutes one of the best discussions available of the various tensions involved in the construction of the modern celebrity. Dyer's work emphasizes three important aspects of the meaning of stars that are relevant to the analysis of the construction of the celebrity presented here:

1. The celebrity is the epitome of the individual for identification and idealization in society.

2. The celebrity is not wholly determined by the culture industries and is therefore somewhat created and constructed by the audience's reading of dominant cultural representations. Gramsci's conception of hegemony best expresses this reworking of the dominant ideological images into social categories of class, gender, age, and so on.

3. The celebrity is a commodity, and therefore expresses a form of valorization of the individual and personality that is coherent with capitalism and the associated consumer culture.[32]

Understanding Celebrity Power through Leadership

As I have indicated, the celebrity is part of the public sphere, essentially an actor or, to use Robert Altman's 1992 film characterization of Hollywood denizens, a "player." In the contemporary public sphere, divisions exist between different types of players: politicians are made to seem distinctly different from entertainment figures; businesspeople are distinguished from sports stars. And yet in the mediated representation of this panoply of players, they begin to blend together. Film stars like Arnold Schwarzenegger share the stage with politicians like George Bush; Gorbachev appears in a film by Wenders; Michael Jackson hangs out on the White House lawn with Ronald Reagan; Nelson Mandela fills an entire issue of *Vogue*. The celebrity is a category that identifies these slippages in identification and differentiation. Leadership, a concept that is often used to provide a definitional distance from the vulgarity of celebrity status, provides the last discursive location for understanding the public individual. The argument I want to advance here is that in contemporary culture there is a convergence in the source of power between the political leader and other forms of celebrity. Both are forms of subjectivity that are sanctioned by the culture and enter the symbolic realm of providing meaning and significance for the culture. The categorical distinction of forms of power is dissolving in favor of a unified system of celebrity status, in which the sanctioning of power is based on similar emotive and irrational, yet culturally deeply embedded, sentiments.

Because of the status and power associated with leadership, it has been an object of study to a much greater extent than has celebrity. In the social sciences, there are two — appropriately labeled — father figures in the study of leadership: Max Weber, from a sociopolitical orientation, and Sigmund Freud, from a sociopsychological perspective. Neither encompasses the entire field of investigation, but the two do figure prominently in most studies of leadership. It should be added that later scholars have not seen Freud's and Weber's discussions of leadership as central to their work. For Weber, leadership outside of the prevailing rationality and bureaucracy is a temporary phenomenon; he integrates leadership into a general theory of rationalization. In Freud's case, his works on the origins of leadership were written after his principal works on psychoanalysis had been published and integrated into a discipline and profession. Because much of his later work contradicts some of his earlier writing on the treatment of individual neuroses, it has been considered to have been written by a man of failing health and intellect, and is often relegated to a status of insignificance.[33]

Weber and Charisma

Weber's contribution to the study of leadership can be summarized through his conceptual development of one word: charisma. Before Weber, this Greek word was rarely used; the same general sentiment was expressed by the term *prestige*.[34] As a result of Weber's reinvestment in the term, *charisma* in its modern usage is roughly synonymous with how Weber describes it. Drawing from the original Greek definition, Weber identifies charisma as a "gift" from the grace of God. This is its vital attachment to the domain of the supernatural. The charismatic leader arises when "extraordinary needs" can be resolved only through a "transcend[ence of] the sphere of everyday economic routines."[35] His power is *ultra vires* of institutional and economic forms of legitimation. According to Weber, charisma is a universal phenomenon. The rational forms of government and power are rejected in favor of a prophet, thus, the power stems from the *individual* and rarely outlives his or her personal reign. In pure charismatic authority, the leader is entirely independent of the status of an office, position, or rank: "The purer charisma is, the less it can be understood organizationally."[36]

Weber's interest in charisma is connected to his general theoretical interest in types of rationality and rationalization. In identifying the development of bureaucratic rationalization so prevalent in modern society, Weber chronicles the domain of the irrational in the legitimation process. Charisma identifies this external force in social transformation. Indeed, Weber considers charisma a motor force of revolutionary change in society. But, because it is a power that relies on instability, ad hoc organizations of devotees and followers, and the will of an individual prophet, it is inherently precarious: "Every charisma is on the road from a turbulently emotional life that knows no economic rationality to a slow death by suffocation under the weight of material interests: every hour of its existence brings it nearer to its end."[37]

All charisma, in the end, goes through a process of "routinization." For example, the formation of a kingship is the institutionalization of an originary charismatic warlord. The vestiges of this charismatic authority can be found in the separation of the king from the routines of the bureaucracy so that the semblance of the monarch's affective power is retained.[38] In a sense, most Christian churches are built on the routinization of the charismatic following of Christ or one of his charismatically inspired followers. The institutions and hierarchy of the Catholic Church exemplify the transformation from charismatic authority to patriarchal/traditional authority. Power is validated through "rational" and normative domains that form the basis of a bureaucracy.[39] Weber also classifies this transformation into the bureaucracy of charismatic authority as the "depersonalization of charisma": the internal gift of charisma is rationalized and made external into qualities that are "transferable, personally acquirable and attachable to the incumbent of an office or an institutional structure regardless of the persons involved."[40]

Weber concludes his analysis of charisma with a further discussion of its demise in the face of bureaucracy so that it resurfaces only when the discipline of rationality is occasionally relaxed:

> As domination congeals into a permanent structure, charisma recedes as a creative force and erupts only in short-lived mass emotions with unpredictable effect, during elections and similar occasions....
>
> Discipline inexorably takes over ever larger areas as the satisfaction of political and economic needs is increasingly rationalized. This universal phenomenon more and more restricts the importance of charisma and of individually differentiated conduct.[41]

The locus of power in the person and personality is absorbed into a structure that represents state power. One senses in Weber's work that he sees the decline in importance of charismatic authority as symptomatic of our society. The tension between charisma's irrational, personal authority and rational, bureaucratic authority is increasingly resolved in favor of the bureaucracy. This is placed by Weber in contradistinction with the former resolution of the irrational with some form of patriarchal and tradition-bound domination.

Weber's arguments concerning the domain of the rational and irrational are central concerns in understanding the contemporary celebrity. Like the charismatic figure, the celebrity demarcates an area of social life and identification that is fundamentally irrational. Weber's hypothesis concerning the resolution of irrationality into bureaucratic rationality offers a useful model for the study of the "resolution" of celebrity status into a rationalized form in contemporary culture. For this model to be useful, some modifications would be necessary in order to explain the contemporary condition of accepted domains of irrational or emotive forms of power (i.e., the celebrity) as part of a larger system of rationality. These modifications may be too radical to fit into the original Weberian model. Nonetheless, Weber's formulations of charisma, rationality, and irrationality are keys to understanding the nature of celebrity power.

Freud and the Leader

Weber's insight develops from a study of the leader himself, and this is its limitation. Freud's work on the leader provides dialectical insight into the understanding of the followers in the formation of the leader. Also, the qualities that seem magical and supernatural in Weber's analysis are based more in psychic prehistory and each individual's unconscious in Freud's.

Freud's principal study on leadership is elaborated in his essay "Group Psychology and the Analysis of the Ego." Other works, including *Totem and Taboo, The Future of an Illusion, Civilization and Its Discontents,* and *Moses and Monotheism,* provide elaborations on his efforts to understand the social world from the position of the individual's formation. As mentioned earlier, these studies of the social world are often looked upon disparagingly by scholars of Freud.

A very good reason for this is that the anthropological "facts" forming the bases of many of these inquiries are suspect or have since been disproved. A very bad reason for this is that they do not fit neatly into the theories that Freud presented in his earlier works.

Freud builds his theory of the advancement of civilization on the repression of libidinal drives, which, on their own, promote chaos and anarchy. It is from this relatively negative position concerning the nature of human beings that Freud writes about the social world. The primitive state of humankind was not the positive and cooperative group, as in the animal herd; rather, it was the horde.[42] The horde, according to Freud, was a loose grouping of humans ruled by one dominant male leader who ensured his power through the total sexual repression of all other males in the group. Indeed, the leader was the only individual in the entire group. From the subjugation of the rest of the males, there existed a crude form of equality among the horde; they all desired the despot's reign to end, they envied his sexual freedom, and they all feared equally the despot's power. This condition is the genesis of the human group that worked cooperatively. In the case of the primitive horde, the result was the murder of the dominant male — an act, Freud relates, that was peculiarly collective and cooperative. All subordinate males were equal accomplices in the murder.[43] Through the combination of collective lament and the new belief that no one could replace the originary father/despot arose an effort to replace him symbolically. Each of the despot's "sons" recreated the condition of dominance in the family, in which the father was preeminent. As Freud relates, it took the genius of the first poet to construct further the myth of the father, in which the despotic horde leader is made into a form of hero who is deified for his strength and power. The myth is further constructed so that this original poet can attempt to assume the role of the original father. Through the power of the ideal and symbol of the hero, the new leader attempts to take on the mantle of power. The rest of the group recognize the reality of their own longing for the same position and so recognize the validity of the poet's construction of the myth of succession.

This is, for Freud, the "primal secret" of society, ritualistically relived in the tribe's annual killing and eating of an animal that has been given sacred, totemic power. It is a solemn invocation of the necessity of some form of imposed order on the multitude so that there is stability. Unleashed libido is the enemy, and the ideal father figure serves as a form of identification that is higher in importance than these individuals' desires, which are divisive to the social whole.

The value of Freud's analysis for this study is twofold: it is an explanation of the origin of collective behavior, and it links the development of leadership to the concept of identification. The leader is central to the formation of both collective behavior and the process of identification. First, the basis of collective behavior is the originary father figure, who, ritualistically, is reborn, revered, and sacrificed as a totem in successive generations. His symbolic power is instrumental in the construction of the superego — the internalization of external authority into the psyche of the individual. The strengthening of the superego is, as Freud recounts, "a most precious cultural asset in the psychological field. Those in whom it has taken place are turned from being opponents of civilization into being its vehicles. The greater their number is in a cultural unit the more secure is its culture and the more it can dispense with external measures of coercion."[44] To use language somewhat different from Freud's, the development of the superego is the naturalization of a certain configuration of power and its associated ideology. When one understands that the strength of the superego is dependent on individuals' degree of identification with authority and, more specifically, leaders, one can see that Freud's political theorizing positions cultural leaders in a central role for social cohesion. There is a transference of identification by each individual from the family power structures to the social power structures.

The model that Freud uses to describe this form of leadership identification is that of Moses and the monotheistic religion of Judaism and Christianity. Without going into great detail concerning Freud's flawed conception of the origin of the Jewish people, the key insight to be derived from his work on leadership is that the current leader embodies something of the past leader. He establishes a psychic connection to these originary figures in order to legitimate his own rule. Thus, any successive leader of the Jewish people after Moses invokes the name of the father and in this way ensures identification with the powerful origin of the superego. This can be called the "return of the repressed"; the original rejection of parental authority resurfaces in its ultimate embrace in a transferred form.[45] The transferred configuration can take many forms. The pope embodies the power of Christ, de Gaulle embodies Napoleon and Louis XIV. The mythic power of identification is taken back to its primal roots for continuous legiti-mation.[46]

The concept of identification with the Other, the common father figure that forms the superego, is useful in identifying the way the celebrity exercises power and influence. It is questionable whether or not the action of leadership chronicled by Freud parallels the relatively passive power of the celebrity. One could say that political leader-ship, in its invocation of the *imago* of the paternal authority, shows in a more visceral way the process of identification and idealization that the celebrity embodies for the population. The leader is the in-stantiation of power; the celebrity is often an example of potential or latent power.

Weber's and Freud's studies of leadership provide some valuable perspectives on the concept and power of the celebrity that extend beyond the literature that has informed star studies. Weber's work on charisma identifies the central relationship between the irrational and the rational in both the processes of legitimation/stability and the elevation of particular individuals. From Freud comes the idea that the role of identification in the power of the leader may be important in describing the latent power of the celebrity. Also, Freud's work un-derlines the importance of the group in the construction of the power of the leader, which concurs, albeit in a different discourse and ter-minology, with Dyer's emphasis on the audience for understanding the significance and meaning of the celebrity.[47]

Conclusion

From the above review of relatively disparate writings on he-roes, stars, and leadership we can conclude that the construction of celebrity power is derived from two domains: the realm of individual identity and the realm of the supporting group or followers. The celeb-rity is centrally involved in the social construction of division between the individual and the collective, and works discursively in this area. Freud mentions that it is often only the leader of the tribe who is completely an individual. The rest of the people must sublimate and repress their desires and thus never achieve the level of ego identity that allows the leader to exercise his or her power in the most arbi-trary ways. Also, the expansion of celebrity status in contemporary culture is dependent on its association with both capitalism, where the celebrity is an effective means for the commodification of the self, and democratic sentiments, where the celebrity is the embodiment of the potential of an accessible culture. In the next two chapters, I investigate further the relationship of the celebrity to collective and individual identities in the context of their discursive work within capitalist and democratic discourses, and propose ways in which we can critically analyze those relationships and the power that they engender.

2

Conceptualizing the Collective: The Mob, the Crowd, the Mass, and the Audience

Up to this point, I have attempted to study the celebrity from the top down: the personality, whether leader or star, is the focus of investigation. In this chapter I will turn the analysis around somewhat and try to understand the celebrity as a construction from the bottom up. Whereas the previous chapter's analysis and review of the meaning of the celebrity is logically an elitist strategy, to study the celebrity in terms of the collective support of the crowd is by contrast a recognition of the importance of the popular, the common, and the base. The perception of the popular collective — often called the crowd or the mob — as powerful coincides with the development of mass democracies in Western culture in the eighteenth, nineteenth, and twentieth centuries. This relationship between the crowd and democracy is critical for an understanding of the divisions in modern society between the rational and the irrational. What I intend to do is map out the perceived power of the crowd or the threat that the crowd symbolizes for the organization of society. Through this review, I hope to elucidate the ways in which the rational and irrational were positioned in the eras leading up to the twentieth century and the connected rise of the celebrity in consumer capitalism.

In the final section of this chapter, I identify a more productive and useful way of understanding the power of the popular than previous crowd theorists or mass culture critics have envisaged, and I begin to explain how that approach is adaptable to an exploration of the position of the celebrity in contemporary culture.

The Transformed Nature of the Crowd: Power after the French Revolution

The French Revolution serves as a dividing line for many historical transformations. For some, Marx included, it signaled the

27

succession of the aristocracy and the breakdown of feudalism by the bourgeoisie and, concomitantly, the further establishment of a capitalist system. For others, the revolution proclaimed the triumph of the rights of man and democracy. For crowd theorists writing in the late nineteenth and early twentieth centuries, it heralded not the birth of the crowd but the birth of the power of the crowd. Up to that point in history, most popular uprisings had been ineffectual in transforming society. Indeed, the goals of the prerevolutionary crowd tended to be issue specific, never possessing the sweeping breadth of the demands for change that were central to the revolutionary crowd.[1] The revolution had politicized the nature of the crowd, thereby making it a political force that could rival other power structures and other symbols of authority and legitimation.[2]

Part of this new power derived from changes in the social structure of European society. The disintegration of rural communities and farm labor and the rapid growth in urban centers created a dislocated group of people who had migrated to the city in search of economic survival in the new manufacturing districts. Without the former connections to family and village, which were powerful technologies of control and discipline, the new city allowed for the development of the anonymous public person. In a type of xenophobic reaction to the dislocated, the elites of French and British culture considered the new urban proletariat and lumpen proletariat to be a threat to order and stability.

Simultaneously, a new economic elite was emerging that had gained its influence and power not through the traditional forms of the primogeniture of the aristocracy, but through the success of new types of mercantilism and manufacturing. Throughout much of the eighteenth century, the economic power of this new elite, often called the bourgeoisie, had not been fully translated into political power. In Britain, the increasing importance of Parliament and, specifically, the more unruly House of Commons marked the transition of power into these new hands. The succession of Oliver Cromwell, a political leader with no hold to the title of monarchy or aristocracy, yet who possessed supreme power in the seventeenth century, identified the genesis of the "evolutionary" transfer of power to the untitled economic elite. In an ideological sense, Cromwell's power symbolically indicated the power of the individual beyond title and tradition, even though his authority maintained the most traditional forms of power and succession to follow. Habermas has used the term "representative pub-lic" to describe the previous display of power by the courts, not so much to garner support for the monarchy or aristocracy, but more to demarcate its existence and its domain. The modern concept of an engaged public or even the conception of the public sphere was de-pendent on the development of new interests and new representa-tions of those interests that have usually been linked to the rise of the bourgeoisie.[3]

In contrast to a longer period of succession in Britain, the French Revolution dramatically delineated the succession of the bourgeoisie to power. The overthrow of the *ancien regime* also identified a his-torical moment when the ideological message *égalité, fraternité, lib-erté* embraced the entire disenfranchised culture, thereby including the new working classes of the city as well as the traditional peas-ants. The heterogeneity of interests and aspirations within the revo-lutionary crowd, in which shopkeepers and merchants were aligned with the urban poor and the new working class — in both a physical "crowd" sense and an ideological sense — is a form of tension that has been negotiated in France, England, and the United States since that era. The power of the crowd for the transformation of society was realized. The inclusion of the mob or the masses in the processes of political change orchestrated by elites necessitated the related need to control the crowd. Certainly the ideologies of equality worked as powerful forces in the construction of American society.[4] The sym-bolic power of an ideology should not be underestimated as a mech-anism of control. Nevertheless, the threat of the seething mob born from the sentiments of equality became a cause of great concern for various elites in the nineteenth century. As the power of the bour-geoisie — the dominant class to emerge from capitalism — solidified, the necessity for social control to preserve economic stability intensified.

In England, several strains of thought developed around the means and methods of controlling the masses. John Stuart Mill's liberalism is probably the most successful at maintaining the ideology of equal-ity within the domain of social control. Mill's liberalism contains the basic belief in the equality of individuals. In an extension of Bentham's position that societal happiness is maximized when each individual pursues his or her own happiness,[5] Mill argues for the freedom of each individual to pursue personal forms of satisfaction. Central to Mill's liberalism is that all should be given this opportunity to reap the fruits of a free society, a communitarian sentiment that transcends the stark individualism of Bentham. Mill wanted the sense of a certain form of community to be part of the conception of all social classes, an idea of community that would ultimately lead to economic and social stability. Thus, education and cultural edification would be essential for the underprivileged, so that they would be aware of and respect central cultural traditions. The extension of the school system in Britain embodies the tension between integrating the masses, and thus alleviating the threat of the mob, and the enfranchisement of the masses as a political force. Within the rubric of liberalist thinking, the extension of equality demanded the safeguards of creating an "educated," thoughtful, and "individualized" working class.[6]

The symbolic language that represented Mill's understanding of the functioning of liberalism is not present in the principal French thinkers on the crowd fifty years later, at the end of nineteenth century. Instead of a philosophical posture, crowd theorists such as Le Bon and Tarde invoke the language of science. Through that discourse, they are able to represent very easily a conservative conception of social structure, one whose true functioning is based on stability and equilibrium. The isolation of a particular problem or symptom of disorder characterizes these works. Le Bon's books are therefore constructed as manuals for social control to be used by leaders in order to maintain stability. Gabriel Tarde, a crowd theorist who predates Le Bon by a decade, writes as the concerned criminologist who attempts to identify, isolate, and, if possible, eradicate the problem of the crowd. In the solidifying of the power and interests of a relatively new capitalist class, there emerged this discourse of social control of the crowd, which now, in its perceived power, represented a continuous threat to bourgeois power.

Le Bon, as McClelland explains, is the Machiavelli of the modern era. Le Bon would have taken the comparison as a compliment, for he considered Machiavelli to be the greatest crowd psychologist, before himself.[7] Machiavelli's genius, as Le Bon perceived it, was his development of a means of legitimacy through the crowd while simultaneously maintaining a method of controlling the crowd. By establishing a charismatic symbol of the state, the leader could maintain a power that had neither divine right nor traditional patterns of succession on its side. The prince's legitimacy rested on his creation of a people who saw themselves and their unity through the symbol of the leader.[8] Le Bon's study of the crowd is, similarly, a method for leaders to adopt in the age of crowd power; the starting point is not the leader, as it was for Machiavelli, but the factual power of the crowd. Most significant about Le Bon's writings is not their accuracy concerning the psychology of the crowd, but their status as both popular and influential texts. According to Moscovici, "Crowd psychology and Le Bon's ideas were one of the dominant intellectual forces of the Third Republic." Moreover, President Theodore Roosevelt, the Chilean president (1924) Arturo Alessandri, and Mussolini, along with a score of other world leaders, sought Le Bon's advice. Horkheimer and Adorno considered Hitler's *Mein Kampf* a cheap paraphrasing of Le Bon's work.[9] This last example makes it clear that Le Bon's influence extended beyond powerful leaders to the intellectual community. Le Bon's *The Crowd* included not only thoughts and practices that leaders considered to have practical application, but also a theoretical position that was deemed by many, including Weber, Park from the Chicago school, many from the Frankfurt school, and Freud, to be critical for understanding the twentieth century.[10] It must be added, however, that Le Bon was often thought of disparagingly; his methods were deemed suspect, his insights said to be overstated or plagiarized, his intellectual rigor derided. But despite these conclusions, Le Bon's thoughts on the crowd had a great deal of salience. At the very least, Le Bon identified a sentiment concerning the modern crowd — a sentiment that ran counter to the conception that human society was progressing and evolving. He suggested that the unleashing of the crowd in democracies also had a dark side that needed to be harnessed and controlled.

Le Bon was the trumpeter of the negative side of democracy. In his interpretation of historical change, he identifies the modern age as the destructive "era of crowds." He also suggests that it is an age of unreason, as "the divine right of the masses is about to replace the divine right of kings."[11] The inevitability of this transformation was the insight that Le Bon gave to twentieth-century leaders and propagandists. The new leaders were the ones who could deal with this new crowd power. What is at the center of this new power is the destruction or substitution of the "conscious individual" for the "unconscious actions of the crowd."[12]

For Le Bon and his followers, the crowd is the site of the unconscious. Civilization, on the other hand, is the result of the few who act as conscious individuals and not as collectives. Characteristically, the crowd is, like the unconscious in hypnosis, open to influence and suggestion. The crowd also contains a more primitive being in its formation, for it operates by instinct and sentiment as opposed to reason and logic. The intellect of any individual in a crowd is reduced to that of the lowest common denominator; the crowd is the great leveler of thought.[13] Le Bon provides a powerful metaphor to encompass these characteristics of the crowd: the crowd is, ultimately, female. He states that in its appeal to and use of emotions and affective power, in its weakness and inferiority of intellect, in its more biologically defined nature, and in its perceived need for a strong leader, the crowd is defined as feminine.[14] What is interesting in this characterization is not its misogyny, but the resonance and influence this description of the crowd has had in the conceptualization and rationalization of mass society in the twentieth century. From the techniques of modern advertising, in which by the 1920s the irrational model of the individual had gained dominance and by the 1930s the entire feminization of the advertising message occurred, to the techniques of propaganda and politics, in which the invocation of a strong leader is critical to the appeal to the mass, mass society has been constructed as irrational, emotional, and thus "female." The fanatical devotion of women to Rudolph Valentino, the 1920s film star, as an idol was also a feminization of how the film industry perceived its own promotional path to success. It is incorrect to attribute these movements and conceptualizations of the mass entirely to Le Bon, for there are other strains of thought that have contributed to the formulations. Nevertheless, Le Bon's thinking provided a genesis for the elements of social psychology that were applied to the new institutions of mass society.

As previously mentioned, Le Bon's negative spirit toward the mass society spawned by democracy was not an isolated phenomenon. In France, the historian Taine, whose writing predated Le Bon's by more than a decade, was the center of a reinterpretation of the value of the French Revolution, which was an assessment of the value of collective action and popular uprisings. For Taine, it was a debate about the nature of man. Like Hobbes's negative assessment of man, Taine argued that the development of mob rule in the French Revolution provided indisputable evidence that the nature of man is neither innocent nor rational; thus the revolution revealed the hollowness of two major tenets — man's rationality and ultimate innocence — of democratic theory. Instead, Taine considered each revolution a return to barbarism and a negation of history in the mob's celebration of the moment and democracy's continuous plebiscite mentality of responding to needs. "Society was to be divided between them and us; they, the sleeping mob, and we, the high-minded keepers of an intellectual and moral culture."[15] Taine's retrospection was also designed to be a warning about the mob's growing power under democracy. The potential for the masses' disruption of society's stability had been solidified throughout the nineteenth century to the point that just the *potential* itself, and not any actual violence, was becoming a powerful force of change.[16]

Gabriel Tarde continued Taine's positivist destruction of the value of the collective from the most normative discipline of criminology. Thus, Tarde's work on the crowd centered on ascertaining culpability and responsibility. In contradistinction to Le Bon, Tarde considered the street crowd as relatively powerless and no real threat. The threat of the crowd was in its form in organizations, sects, and institutions. In this logical segue, Tarde linked crowd theory to a general theory of the social. The crowd, then, was the metaphor for all collective organizations because it articulated the state of nature for man. In fact, Tarde believed that there were two essential states of nature: the family and the mob. The family, if it achieved ascendancy in the society, upheld tradition, order, and veneration of the past. Tarde considered Chinese society to be exemplary of a family-dominant social model. Societies in which the crowd was dominant were inherently unstable, constantly changing, and modeled on "fashion" as opposed to tradition. This articulated the status of the urban society of nineteenth-century France. Neither model emphasized the liberalist centrality of the free individual, which, for Tarde, was a myth in the genesis of social organization. Whether the group was family dominant or crowd dominant, Tarde believed that its cohesiveness depended on imitation and suggestion from a leader. In the case of the family, this leadership came from the father or father figure. In the case of the crowd, it was the leader who fomented emotion in the masses.[17] For Tarde, "the germ of basic order was implanted in the nascent mind by the appearance of the self, the prime germ of social order was implanted in primitive society by the appearance of the leader. The leader is the social self destined to undergo infinite development and transformation."[18]

Another crowd theorist contemporaneous with Le Bon and Tarde was Sighele, who also approached the problem of the crowd from a criminological perspective. Assessing blame required explaining the apparent unconscious actions of the crowd. In contrast to the individual, whose conscious actions could be ascertained and blame adjudicated by the system of justice, for the positivist Sighele there was no empirical evidence to explain and thereby determine responsibility for the contagion and the resultant unity of the crowd's collective consciousness. Here Sighele was drawn to experiments involving hypnotism that had been conducted in French mental clinics. He believed that the model of the hypnotic relation between patient and hypnotist could explain the movement of emotions among the members of a crowd. Believing crime to be the outcome of a more primitive state of being, Sighele considered the crowd's unified soul to be more susceptible than the individual soul to the baser emotions of a primitive man.[19]

In his early writings, Sighele drew from Espinas's work on animal collectivities. In the spirit of a unified scientific approach and social evolutionism, Sighele found little difficulty in linking the natural sciences to the social sciences to explain man's evolutionary path. In this practice, Sighele was no different from many other nineteenth-century thinkers. It is Sighele's continued penetration into the relationship between social evolution and the crowd that is most fascinating for the current project. In a gradual transformation of his position, Sighele identifies the crowd as a "modern phenomenon," meaning that it is an advancement in man's social evolution. His conclusions about this determination are less important for this study than the actual positioning of the crowd's importance in the modern world and the struggle with scientistic reasoning that it posed for this crowd theorist. Sighele continued to believe in the intellectual inferiority of crowds, but he began to credit the crowd with a certain moral superiority. In his native Italy, this moral superiority could bring a nation together and make the social unit much stronger and more integrated. In a sense, Sighele was marking a place for the importance of the domain of the irrational within the social and political realms. By calling his new understanding of the crowd's elevated position "proletarian nationalism," Sighele distanced himself from the normal conservative conventions of the crowd theorist.[20]

As a group, late-nineteenth- and early-twentieth-century crowd theorists allow some insight into how the collective was being reconceptualized in an era of both increased democracy and entrenchment of capitalism. Often the interests of these writers coincided with those of a conservative elite. In this way, their thoughts represented the fears of the elite in dealing with the contradictions of democracy and capitalistic power. Like Moscovici, whose intellectual project has been to recuperate the texts of the crowd theorists, I am not concerned with whether their reasoning is factually or theoretically sound. Neither am I concerned with their theories' predictive power, although Le Bon has often been credited with accurately foretelling the eras of Hitler and Mussolini, which has legitimated or empowered his own writings and opinions. My intent is to identify the connection these theorists have established between the domain and importance of the irrational and its manifestation in modern collectivities and crowds. In a way, I am building a "structure of feeling," to use Raymond Williams's term, around the conceptions of the collective and the irrational at the turn of the century. Through this identification, the ascendancy of the celebrity as a phenomenon of the formation of certain types of collectivities in the twentieth century can be better understood.

There are three principal insights to be drawn from this review of crowd theorists. First, in the attempt to engage the popular and the collective in the formation of the modern celebrity, the crowd theorists of the turn of the century made a complete circle back to the importance of the leader in directing the crowd. As Tarde has explained, members of the crowd are childlike in their allegiance to and blind following of their leader. The leader is seen as central to the collective's formation and incitement. Le Bon admired Napoleon as a leader who came from the crowd and controlled the crowd effectively. Indeed, Napoleon operated as a symbolic representation of what Le Bon thought the modern leader should strive for in his persona.

Second, crowd theorists extended the impact of the crowd to encompass larger parts of the social sphere. Effectively, they universalized the phenomenon of the crowd. Tarde considered all institutions, from sects to bureaucracies, to embody the features of the crowd. Thus, one could see the irrationality of the crowd operating in areas before presumed to be untouched and therefore still operating in a rational way. Le Bon's concentration on the fact that anyone could be a member of a crowd made the phenomenon not just part of the lower classes but part of all segments of society. Even members of the intellectual group could lose their individual insights in their formation of a crowd.

Moreover, Le Bon, along with Sighele, argued that the crowd was not necessarily an evil entity and could produce moments of heroism; it was just that it was intellectually inferior to the individual on any occasion. Sighele's emphasis on the fundamental equality among the crowd members also emphasized the crowd's power to break down barriers of class and distinctions of social rank. All were susceptible to "suggestion" or "imitation." What this conceptualized was an entire society under threat of becoming members of the crowd—not just the rabble, as they were labeled in previous generations, but anyone. Crowd theorists were the first to give credence to the existence of the mass society. Through their works, the concept of the mass gained strength and power as an explanatory category. Concurrently, the explanatory power of other social categories, such as class, was diminishing.

Third, as Sighele emphasized in his later work and as Le Bon also acknowledged, the development of the crowd's power was a modern phenomenon. To label something as modern (or new, in this sense) indicated that it had succeeded former models of the social. All the crowd theorists analyzed above considered the crowd phenomenon to have been born from investment in the institutions of individuality. To use an anachronistic term, the *hyperindividuality* that had developed from the focus on individual power had left the population without the traditional institutions of authority of family, church, and state. In this new condition, the individual was open to suggestion and influence; the irrational forces of the crowd and its leader became the new locus of power for the crowd theorists. Essentially, the crowd had succeeded the individual by the twentieth century. The category that encompassed this rising tide was the mass society.

It is important to understand what I am not doing at this point in the argument in order to realize what I am trying to accomplish. I am not suggesting that crowd theory provided the only model for the social at the turn of the century. This hypothesis is entirely indefensible. What I am arguing is that crowd theory was, first of all, instrumental in the conceptualization of the twentieth-century mass society, and second, that at the very core of this conceptualization of mass society was its irrationality. In the development of certain social sciences in the twentieth century, particularly social psychology, one can see the integration of the conception of the irrationality of the mass from these earlier crowd theorists. What follows is an investigation of the meaning of the mass in twentieth-century thinking to discern these intellectual strains from the nineteenth-century characterization of the crowd as irrational and threatening to civilization. My overall objective in tracing the strains of irrationality is to show that the emergence of the celebrity is connected to both the emergence of the modern mass as a threatening entity and the strategies employed by various institutions to contain the threat and irrationality of the mass.

Diverging Conceptualizations of the Collective as Mass Society: A Comparison between Social Psychology and Cultural Criticism

Twentieth-century writings about the mass can be grouped into work by authors in two traditions: the mass society critics and the "scientifically" inspired social psychologists. As a starting point, writers taking both of these approaches believed in the fundamental baseness and irrationality of the modern mass—a stance they derived from the turn-of-the-century crowd theorists. However, there were some significant differences layered onto this basic starting point of the irrationality of the mass. The principal conceptual difference between the crowd theorists of the turn of the century and the mass society critics of the early and mid-twentieth century is the transformation of the collective from active crowd participants to passive cultural consumers. Mass society critics operated, generally, from the same elitist and conservative position as Le Bon, Tarde, and Taine. However, their concern was the erosion of high culture by the inroads into the collective consciousness of low or mass entertainment. José Ortega y Gasset and T. S. Eliot epitomized this disdain for the popular. For Eliot, the institutions of democracy degraded the culture; he argued for an elite to preserve the transmission of culture from one generation to the next.[21] F. R. Leavis and his followers continued the debate about the loss of appreciation of "good" art and literature. Horkheimer and Adorno, from a slightly different perspective, focused on this same destruction of consciousness through mass culture.[22]

Crowd psychology also developed a somewhat different approach to mass society. Some writers have said that the tradition of Le Bon and Tarde disappeared. Apart from providing the ground on which social psychology developed, the grand theorizing of these original crowd theorists did, indeed, disappear. However, it would be wrong to say that their insights failed to have an impact. Social psychology quickly became a behaviorist science, but its principal area of investigation was the domain of the irrational in human behavior. From F. H. Allport onward, social psychology looked at individual behavior in order to understand the collective. The legacy of Le Bon and the others was the elite's embrace of the discipline of social psychology in trying to understand and conceptualize the mass. Social psychology as an experimental behavioral science was instrumental in the development of propaganda and techniques of political influence, as well as advertising techniques. Social psychology helped to rationalize mass society by providing "scientific" tools to explain and predict the "irrational."

From these two conceptualizations of mass society, an odd dialectic arises. Although both the cultural critics and the social psychologists (or, more accurately, those employing the social psychologists) feel threatened by the mass society, they are at polar opposites as to that threat's resolution. Social psychology's general objective is to maintain the stability of the social sphere through scientific reason. As indicated earlier, social psychological research served the interests of the entertainment industry, the advertising industry, and political institutions. In contrast, the cultural critics worked from the edge of the social world in the arena of cultural and knowledge elites. Their conservatism was not derived from a desire to preserve the conditions of capital, but rather from a desire to maintain and strengthen general cultural aesthetics and tastes. Whereas social psychology acknowledged the irrational nature of the crowd and helped organize it into recognizable markets, cultural critics demanded the pursuit of a higher truth of the individual that could transcend the mundanity of twentieth-century mass culture.

The dismissive attitude that mass culture critics had toward the members of the mass society makes their analysis of the relationship between the masses and the celebrity rather barren. In contrast, the behaviorist approach of the social psychologists applied no standards of taste to their objects of study and therefore provided a much more open analysis of the popular domain and, thus, a richer starting point for understanding the meaning and function of the celebrity in contemporary culture. However, a strong caveat should be added to this endorsement: the scientistic approach limited social psychologists' capacity to see the political import of their research or the ideological sustenance that social psychological research gave to many of the elites. Nonetheless, social psychology in its form as mass communication research recognized the value in studying mass culture to understand its inner logic.

In its behaviorism, social psychology attempted to understand the social from the motives of the individual. F. H. Allport's influential 1924 textbook *Social Psychology* marked the movement of social psychology into the study of the individual. Identifying the collective mind was merely "a convenient designation for certain universal types of reaction."[23] The construction of the social sphere for Allport and succeeding generations of social psychologists was derived from what he enumerated as six "prepotent" reflexes whose modification or "conditioning" creates the socialized individual.[24] Essentially, the individual is habituated into certain social behaviors through the reinforcement of these biological reflexes, such as hunger or sex, or the perceived reaction of struggling or rejecting. According to Graumann, Allport was instrumental in desocializing the individual as well as in reducing the social to individual actions.[25] Allport discounted any notion of the supraindividual minds and proceeded to rationalize the crowd and the public: "The fundamental drives of protection, hunger and sex are the supreme controlling forces [of the crowd]. . . . The public is an imagined crowd of which an individual believes that certain opinions, feelings and overt reactions are universal."[26]

Allport's research, along with much of the experimental work arising from social psychology, is a form of rationalization of collectives for the twentieth century. It asserts the reinforcement of the individual despite the reality of the power of various collectives and masses. It is the function of social psychology to reduce the indecipherability of the mass into its elemental parts. Those parts are housed, ultimately, in the individual. Graumann's conclusion concerning the political position that Allport's research implicitly entails is quite accurate. Allport concludes in his textbook that "progress, which is the achievement of the individual becomes the heritage of the ages,"[27] and Graumann incisively adds to this general theoretical position that it also operates as "a manifesto of liberal ideology."[28]

There are several strains of social psychology in the twentieth century that merit attention because of the way they have aided in the reinvention of the individual's power through universal characteristics of human behavior. It is not within the bounds of this book to investigate the massive amount of experimental literature that has been spawned in this discipline.[29] What I intend is to focus on one subdiscipline of social psychology that developed in American mass communication research in order to understand the approach it offers for understanding twentieth-century mass society. My objective remains to reveal the construction of both the individual and irrationality through this form of research. Because of American mass communications research's relatively close connection to powerful political and cultural institutions, the conclusions of the researchers were often adopted readily in these other spheres and their impact was felt on a societal level. Moreover, in understanding the construction, meaning, and cultural positioning of the celebrity, mass communication research indicates the way the mass was defused into conceptions of individual behavior; the celebrity can be seen as a complementary construction of subjectivity that also individualized the collective sphere.

The development of mass communications as an object of study paralleled the development of the twentieth-century technologies of mass dissemination. Thus, the rapid rise in ownership of radio receivers and the proliferation of radio stations in the 1920s coincided with the establishment of research projects on mass communication. There were a number of hypotheses concerning the incredible influence of radio on the masses. The original models describe this power of the media as being like a hypodermic needle; somehow the nature of radio allows for the opinions and words of the broadcaster to transmit directly into the mind of the listener. As in early crowd theory, the influence of the radio was believed to be similar to mass hypnosis. Thus, much of the early research into mass communication was motivated by its power as a propaganda tool. The dominant figure of this research was Harold Lasswell, who trained originally as an economist. At the basis of Lasswell's work, and therefore at the origins of communication research, was this same fundamental belief in the irrational nature of the masses; the mass was seen as an entity that is essentially out of control but can be easily influenced to follow certain courses of action.[30]

Successive models of mass communications investigated the individual's relationship to the message. In this way they drew from social psychology to understand the emotive and instinctual basis of behavioral changes. As the media industries gained power and influence in the 1930s and 1940s, much of the primary research was funded by such organizations as the National Broadcasting Corporation, the Columbia Broadcasting System, and MacFadden Publications.[31] What these industries wanted to investigate was the nature of the mass as it was defined in terms of audiences. They wanted to know who was listening to what and, to a lesser extent, why. So, the thrust of communication research moved from political studies of propaganda to the study of entertainment technologies. The greatest breakthrough in this research occurred during and after the Second World War, when a new model of the relationship between media message and audience member was developed and quickly gained dominance — at least in academic circles. Elihu Katz and Paul Lazarsfeld's extensive study of the influence of campaign messages in the 1940 and 1944 American presidential elections in a medium-sized city indicated that the hypodermic model of influence was incorrect. Rather, they found that the media's influence was shaped by opinion leaders within the community, who interpreted the media messages and explained their resulting positions to the rest of the people. Hence, Katz and Lazarsfeld developed a two-step flow model that they continued to elaborate into the 1950s: the media influenced opinion leaders (who may already have had predispositions that were not, in actual fact, influenced by the media messages), who in turn influenced small groups of "followers." The general belief in the awesome power of the media to influence people was debunked and derailed. Katz and Lazarsfeld's research proved that the individual still constructed his or her own opinions, even if those opinions were somewhat mediated by local opinion leaders.[32]

The central connection between behavioral social psychological research and mass communication research crystallized following this breakthrough. Many mass communication researchers attempted to ascertain what kinds of satisfaction audiences were deriving from their media use. This was an attempt to invest in individuals basic interests and drives that could be manifested in the programs they watched, the leaders they were attracted to, and any other decisions they happened to make. Individuals' use of the media was seen as entirely "functional" and therefore always connected to the satisfaction of some basic need. Uses and gratifications research, as it soon came to be called, became one of the dominant communication research strategies in the United States from the 1950s to the present. It helped to reposition the identity of the mass in terms of audiences, individuals, and satisfaction. Through that redefinition of the mass, uses and gratifications research developed an implicit conception of rationality and individuality that, like social psychology, defused the fear of the unknown mass:[33]

1. The mass could now be understood as audience groups that were attracted to different forms of consumption of messages for different reasons.

2. The reasons for an audience member to be drawn to a given series of forms of satisfaction rest with the satisfaction of basic emotional and psychological needs. These can be ascertained through either clinical studies of individuals or field investigations of the uses made of media products.

3. By discovering the reasons for the forms of gratification of the audience, researchers were believed to be discovering the elements of human nature that were being expressed in general in the mass society. The apparently irrational choices could be rationalized into natural human tendencies.[34]

The elaboration of crowd psychology in the twentieth century became a study of mass society. From the perspective of aesthetics and literary criticism, the new mass society was considered destructive toward a cultural heritage and a civilization. From the discipline of social psychology, mass society could be thought of as a form of irrationality that could, in the end, be defined in terms of the rationality of the individual. Because of its scientistic methods and its attempts at rationalizing, and thus stabilizing, the nature of the mass, the discursive power of social psychology and the related discipline of mass communication was much greater than any form of negative cultural criticism. The tenets of social psychology, in the discipline's investigation of the individual within the social, indicated that the individual remained intact in modern society. The believed destructive power of the mass society of the individual was proved to be more mythical than factual. From the crowd theorists' fear of the amorphous mass, the social psychologists had developed the tools for understanding and catering to the needs of the individual. What was ignored in this development were the social, cultural, and economic determinants of needs and satisfaction. The innate quality of needs is as mythical as the amorphous mass. Nevertheless, the tools for comprehending the mass in terms of audiences or consumers were critical for the development of a consumer society, in which needs were understood and satisfied in a market setting.

It is social psychology's central role in constructing the modern individual within mass society that is of interest to the current project. The behavioral research was essential for supporting the basic structure of contemporary society. It existed as a scientific support structure for a liberalist ideology of the individual's freedom to make choices, to determine needs, and to satisfy them through the choices offered by a capitalist system. Thus, the development of the so-called mass society had not robbed the individual of his or her basic identity and will; the structures of the capitalist and democratic system, if anything, expanded the choices for the expression of that will. The forms of gratification had expanded with the expansion of consumer goods.

The growth in the celebrity's power is contemporaneous with the rationalization of the crowd and the social sphere through social psychology and other behaviorist disciplines. The relationship could be arbitrary; however, the essential nature of the celebrity is individuality, unique identity. In the rationalization of the social, the celebrity performs the same function as social psychology: it celebrates the potential of the individual and the mass's support of the individual in mass society.

At this point, the conceptualization of the celebrity as an ideological support for consumer capitalism remains more of a hypothesis than a proven statement. To complete our reading of the celebrity we need to engage in a reading of the social that neither negates the irrational nor substantiates the immutability of the individual in mass culture. Also, we need to investigate the ideology behind the construction of popular images in contemporary culture, so the configuration of power can be ascertained in the construction. In the following section, I employ the insights of a cultural studies approach to popular culture to explore the construction of the celebrity from the people. In the final analysis, crowd theorists have presented another elitist conception of the fear of the masses. Also, the social psychologists' research is imbricated in the very fashioning of the dominant conception of the mass by breaking it up into elemental units — individuals. In contrast, many of the popular culture investigations from a cultural studies point of view treat the collective formation of meanings as essential counterideologies to the dominant ideologies of contemporary culture. The social and cultural construction of meaning is not deconstructed into individuals; instead, it is dealt with as a collective formation of representation and meaning.

Cultural Studies' Conception of the Popular: New Notions of Cultural and Collective Sense Making

In some conceptions of popular culture, most entertainment productions are considered to be of minor importance or ultimately harmless. This position is dominant within the culture industries themselves and, by extension, among many people who watch, listen to, or read what is often called light entertainment. In fact, within this thinking, popular culture *is* entertainment and is principally defined by popularity. That is, the greater the number of people who watch a television program, buy a record, or view a film, the more the artifact is an example of popular culture. This is a value-free conception of the popular that dovetails well into the uses and gratifications conception of the audience. The popular audience uses what it finds satisfying and rejects or ignores the rest. The barometers of popular taste are the Nielsen ratings, record sales, and box-office figures. Television programs such as *Entertainment Tonight* and papers such as *Variety* chronicle the ebbs and flows of popular culture as entertainment. Even though the identification of the popular is on the basis of the size of the audience, this approach to the popular tends to be production oriented. The audience is rarely defined much beyond demographic and statistical breakdowns.

A significantly new approach to the definition and conception of popular culture emerged with an increased emphasis on the audiences of popular culture and their practices of making meaning of popular texts. The origins of what has been called a cultural studies approach to popular culture can be seen in the postwar Marxist-inspired scholars of Britain, who began to investigate the productive activities of the British working class, an area virtually neglected in any previous histories. E. P. Thompson, in his seminal *The Making of the English Working Class,* began the process in the discipline of history.[35] Thompson studied how the working class organized itself and emerged as a class. Richard Hoggart, a literary analyst, deepened the meaning and significance of everyday life and habits in his personal (though somewhat condescending in their implicit elitism) accounts of a northern English coal town in *The Uses of Literacy*.[36] Probably the greatest influence on the formation of this new approach to the popular is the work of Raymond Williams, another literary critic, who began to analyze the meanings of popular texts constructed by their readers. Williams developed two very useful terms of analysis to describe the way culture defines itself, in contradiction to the lived culture of a given generation. A "selective tradition," meaning certain cultural artifacts are preserved while others are discarded, helps to reinforce a rather heavily constructed notion of culture and value. In contradistinction, Williams uses the term "structure of feeling" to describe the complex web of interests and understandings that constitute any culture at any given moment. The complexity of the structure of feeling is never captured by the selective tradition, which attempts to provide an official history of a culture. A tension necessarily exists between these two conceptions of cultural experience.[37]

These new ideas concerning culture and meaning were elaborated upon and extrapolated principally by the students and faculty members at the Birmingham Centre for Contemporary Cultural Studies (BCCCS); from their writings, the cultural studies approach to the domain of popular culture emerged. Stuart Hall, the second director of the BCCCS, provides a useful definition of popular culture that speaks of a new counterbalancing weight to be given to the audience's construction of significance. He begins by describing popular culture as a tension between the processes that moralize and educate the working class and the people (and demoralize the poor) and the resistance by those same people to these transformations. He writes: "Popular culture is neither, in a 'pure' sense, the popular traditions of resistance to these processes; nor is it the forms which are superimposed on and over them. It is the ground on which the transformations are worked."[38] The arena of popular culture, for Hall, is a type of cultural battlefield, where, in large measure, the definition and representation of the people are fought over and determined. This is why it is so important to study and understand popular culture: "Popular culture is one of the sites where this struggle for and against a culture of the powerful is engaged: it is also the stake to be won or lost in that struggle. It is the arena of consent and resistance. It is partly where hegemony arises, and where it is secured."[39] This theme is elaborated upon by John Fiske, who uses the same military analogies of struggle in a recent work on popular culture. "Popular culture always is part of power relations; it always bears traces of the constant struggle between domination and subordination, between power and various forms of resistance to it or evasions of it, between military strategy [the power bloc, to use Hall's metaphor] and guerrilla tactics ['guerrilla tactics are the art of the weak']."[40]

There are two distinctions that are developed in cultural studies' analyses of the popular. First, there is the distinction that mass culture does not exist and, in fact, is more of a construction of the powerful to contain the subordinate segments of the culture. The use of the term *popular culture,* therefore, is a strategy to debunk mass culture and its homogeneity with another definition of the people that allows for more heterogeneity. Second, cultural studies underlines the existence of forms of popular cultural resistance. One of the grand traditions within this field is to identify and study subcultural groups to show the reconstruction of dominant cultural forms into different meaning systems that relate to subculture members' particular lived experiences.[41] Although those involved in cultural studies are often drawn to spectacular youth subcultures because of their overt resistance to the dominant culture's symbols, the general tenet of their approaches is that the process of making sense of the social world through the reorientation of given representations is carried on by everyone.

The tension and subsequent reconstruction at the core of popular culture is best articulated by Fiske's aphorism that the "art of popular culture is 'the art of making do.' "[42] What Fiske means is that though the people do not produce the various forms of cultural production, from radio and television to records and films, "they do make their culture from those resources."[43] In other words, the cultural productions operate as raw materials for the representations of everyday experiences. What is accepted or rejected in this domain, what is recombined, rearticulated, or re-presented, is done through the activity of consumption. The audience *works on the cultural product in order for that form to make sense.* The cultural studies approach to popular culture has radicalized the process of consumption. Also, consumption can be an activity, as opposed to the mass cultural definition of entertainment consumption as comprehensively passive. For instance, the punk reconstructs secondhand clothes, which are representations of previous dominant cultural fashion, into a representation of opposition and distinction. He or she acts as a *bricoleur,* constructing new meanings and a new sense out of the given and dominant cultural meaning of objects.[44]

Writers such as Fiske and Iain Chambers have extended popular resistance beyond the bounds of obviously oppositional groups like subcultures. Their approach to popular culture often celebrates the potential and possibility of audience reconstruction or play with dominant symbols and signs of a culture. Fiske explains that the dominant culture consistently attempts to fabricate the "closed" cultural text, that is, a cultural form that permits no reforming of cultural meanings. He adds, however, that there are equally consistent and persistent demands for the "open" text by the popular audience. He describes the realm of the popular as a negotiation between these extremes. His own emphasis is on this general resistance to the closed text. Like Chambers, Fiske chronicles the construction of meanings by the audience, which plays with, parodies, and actively subverts the constructed text.[45]

Cultural studies offers an identification of the collectivities that exist in contemporary culture and their importance in the construction of meaning and representation. Unlike in crowd theory, the collective is not silenced into manipulable automatons. Neither is the collective fabricated into the great harbinger of the irrational. And, finally, within the approach of cultural studies the collective is not dissected and thereby individuated to make possible the identification of the biological and behavioral origins of its actions. Cultural studies offers the current project a useful understanding of the collective and its role in the formation of such cultural images as celebrities. The concept of negotiation and struggle provides a metaphor that can aid in the deconstruction of the ideologies around leaders and celebrities. The celebrity is a negotiated "terrain" of significance. To a great degree, the celebrity is a production of the dominant culture. It is produced by a commodity system of cultural production and is produced with the intentions of leading and/or representing. Nevertheless, the celebrity's meaning is constructed by the audience. An exact "ideological fit" between production of the cultural icon and consumption is rare. Audience members actively work on the presentation of the celebrity in order to make it fit into their everyday experiences.

There are two principal insights to be drawn from cultural studies that are useful for a study of the celebrity's power. Cultural studies is an intellectual project that stresses the subordinate classes' active "making sense" of their situation and environment. The process of "making do," as Fiske expresses it, is in sharp contrast to the irrational conceptions of the mass that are part of both crowd theory and many mass society critiques. There is an explicit notion of rational thought behind the actions of making sense. However, the process of making sense is constrained by the cultural products and forms that are produced by the dominant culture for these subordinate groups. Thus, the process of making meaning and making something cohere with everyday experience is not so much a rational one as a type of rationalization of a very real cultural and political gap in representation and interest. As a political project, cultural studies could be characterized as trying to close the gap between the process of rationalization that occurs in subordinate culture and a new form of rational coherence. This new form of rational coherence of the social would arise in real conditions of equality and democratic culture.

The second insight builds on this first idea of rationalization. Cultural studies recognizes the collective origins of language, meaning, and signs. Again, this is a positive connotation of the activity of the collective, an insight that only Sighele among the crowd theorists even acknowledged. What is of critical importance for the understanding of this collective construction of meaning is that it is constantly forming and re-forming to present and re-present new forms of commonality. The transformative nature of meaning signifies that it is being renegotiated continually. This is an aspect of the working hegemony between different parts of a culture, including the most powerful and the least powerful groups, so that a loose fabrication of a commonality is in place to maintain a consensus among the population. It also means that subordinate parts of the culture are part of this working hegemony and, in some cases, are instrumental in changes in the meanings and sense-making processes that shape the culture.

The significance of these two insights for the study of the celebrity concerns the simultaneous construction that is part of the image of the celebrity. The celebrity is simultaneously a construction of the dominant culture and a construction of the subordinate audiences of the culture. It embodies two forms of rationalization of the culture that are elements of the working hegemony. For members of the dominant culture, the segment of society that controls most of the forms of cultural production, the celebrity rationalizes both their production (by providing a clear embodiment of cultural power) and their conceptions of their audience. For members of the subordinate classes, who constitute the audience of the celebrity, the celebrity rationalizes their comprehension of the general culture by providing a bridge of meaning between the powerless and the powerful. These conceptions of the celebrity, those arising from below (the audience) and those emerging from above (the cultural and political producers), never entirely merge into one coherent form of celebrity identity. They do converge—in a very material sense—on the person who *is* the celebrity. He or she represents therefore a site for processes of hegemony. To use a New Age formulation, the celebrity is a "channeling" device for the negotiation of cultural space and position for the entire culture.

Conclusion

In this chapter I have outlined the way different conceptions of the collective inform the construction and function of the celebrity in modern culture. Through the study of crowd psychology and its successor, social psychology, I have attempted to identify the prevailing sentiments concerning the nature of the crowd and the mass that are critical for understanding the position the celebrity occupies in contemporary society. Crowd psychology delineated the fear of the crowd as it emerged as a powerful symbolic force from the democratic transformations of the eighteenth and nineteenth centuries. Those who tried to comprehend what was believed to be a new phenomenon, or, at the very least, a new threat to power, came to the conclusion that it was derived from irrationality. The techniques of social psychology can be seen as methods of positioning or rationalizing the irrationality and the threat of the masses through the discourse of scientific reason. The breakdown of the mass into its constituent parts—that is, into psychological elements of the individual—can also be seen as a method of social control. The concentration on the individual and the motivation for his or her actions supported the general ideological tenets of liberal capitalism and Western democracies. As I have indicated, the research of social psychology was well integrated into the political, economic, and cultural power structures and was used to comprehend the new mass society.

The contrasting reading of the collective through cultural studies' definition of the popular has provided some of the means for understanding the process of rationalization that audiences go through in making sense of their cultural world. The formulation of the mass not as a threat, but rather as an ideological support for the dominant classes' means of maintaining control and order, identified a dialectic in the construction of the celebrity. The celebrity can be positioned somewhere between the dominant culture's rationalization of what it sees as irrational and the popular audience's use, identification, and expression of the affective power that the celebrity as a system of rationalization has been positioned to reflect.

The following chapter provides a conceptual framework that encompasses these two contentious definitions of the social world and how they are expressed through the celebrity. One of the objectives of the chapter is to explain why the celebrity is central to the construction of rationalization in contemporary society. This discussion involves the importance and the significance of the celebrity in social and individual identity in general. The result is the building of the conceptual framework that will serve as the central tool for the study of individual celebrities that follows in the succeeding chapters.

3

Tools for the Analysis of the Celebrity as a Form of Cultural Power

In the preceding two chapters, I have established the historical position of the celebrity in the conceptions of the individual and the mass in modern consumer culture. I have argued that the development of the celebrity is connected to ways of "making sense" of the social world. The process of making sense through these individuals is simultaneously an activity of the members of dominant culture, who are instrumental in the procreation of the celebrity sign, and of the members of subordinate cultures, who are for the most part the audience that remakes the sign. Because of its embodiment of collective configurations within individual representations, the celebrity is a locus of formative social power in consumer capitalism.

The problem tackled in this chapter is how to unpack the nature of the formative power that is housed in the celebrity. There are a variety of factors in the formation of the celebrity that confuse a simple analysis of the personality. The elements that must be integrated into the instruments of analysis are as follows:

1. the collective/audience conceptualizations of the celebrity;
2. the categorical types of individuality that are expressed through the celebrity;
3. the cultural industries' construction of the celebrity;
4. the relative commodity status of the celebrity;
5. the form of cultural legitimation that the celebrity, singly or as part of an entire system, may represent; and
6. the unstable nature of the meaning of the celebrity—the processual and dynamic changeability of the individual celebrity and the entire system of celebrity.

The complexity of these often competing and contradictory factors makes any discussion of their culturally formative power difficult. The need for larger conceptual tools that address these factors for the study of the celebrity is evident. What follows is a development of three over-arching concepts that aid in this analysis of the celebrity: celebrity as a form of rationalization, celebrity as a sign and a text, and celebrity as an expression of what I call audience-subjectivity.

Celebrity as a Form of Rationalization

The ways different groups in society use celebrities to make sense of their social world can also be seen as a form of rationalization. To consider the celebrity as part of the process of rationalization reimplicates Weber's intellectual project concerning rationality.[1]

Weber's categorization of rationality is connected to what he sees as the progressive disenchantment of the world. The magical, the mystical, and the religious are slowly being eliminated in favor of the rational, the scientific, and the bureaucratic. This form of rationality is typified in the development of the modern bureaucracy. What once possessed affective power is "disenchanted" in its integration into the administration. For Weber, the Protestant ethic was instrumental in the movement of society from the irrational to the rational. In more traditional societies, religion served a rationalizing function of connecting everyday life to that of the deity(ies). Religious priests helped formulate and provide a coherent weltanschauung. The Protestant ethic, as a transitional stage toward modernity, served to internalize through conscience and guilt the values that the priesthood was responsible for legitimating and enforcing. The continuous breakdown of a coherent weltanschauung represented, for Weber, the very problem of the progression to modernity. Instead of unity within the norms and values of the church, a system of competing value systems developed; scientific reason could not possibly present a unified worldview because gaps would emerge persistently in the schema. Ultimately, Weber argued for the existence of different value spheres that were mutually exclusive. Thus, an effective form of rationality could emerge in one field but should not be presumed to inform another. For example, Weber insisted that there was no value-sphere connection between art and politics. Their determinations of value were mutually exclusive.

In all likelihood, Weber would have made these divisions into value spheres more conclusively if he had completed his project of writing a sociology of culture. One could also surmise that a greater investigation of affective or irrational forms of legitimation would have been included in such a study.[2] Instead, Weber left the legacy of contradictory claims about irrationally based forms of legitimation. On the one hand, Weber describes the core of the modern project resulting in greater and greater aspects of our lives being subjected to "formal" rationality, where the individual is objectified and often reduced to a numerical representation for administrative efficiency in state and corporate bureaucracies. On the other hand, he negates the ultimate power of this rationality by qualifying its pervasiveness and by reinstituting a place for irrational forms of legitimation: as I mentioned in chapter 1, Weber explains that revolutionary change in a society is driven by the movement to the institutionally independent realm of charismatic leadership and its associated affective power. Thus, Weber's final position concerning the historical agency of irrational forms of legitimation is not that the irrational is ultimately superseded by the rational, but rather that the two are antinomic. The irrational exists side by side with the rational by fundamentally challenging the type of rationality's value ideal. As well, Weber sees the irrational as innovative, a creative force of history that is rationalized or routinized subsequently in the structures of institutions.[3] Weber provides several other brief discussions of the position of the irrational that are significant to the current study of modern rationalization. First, he explains that, although there is a movement to a greater integration of rationality, there is a countertendency in modernity to reenchant the world.[4] This is driven, Mommsen correctly interprets, by the failure of modern rationality to provide the value ideals that lead to the construction of a coherent worldview. The competing forms of rationalization in the modern world represent a crisis in legitimation. For some writers, such as Habermas, the solution to the crisis rests in a type of Weberian "substantive rationality" in a which a negotiated consensus is reached through "communicative action."[5] For others, the nihilist condition that Weber has identified concerning rationality and its establishment of a variety of value ideals are cause for celebration, because they break down the normative power of the "prison-house of rationality."[6] For Weber, the retreat to the irrational is one way—albeit an unsatisfactory one—to reunify a fragmented worldview. At the very least, researchers must be sympathetic to its reality: "The more we ourselves are susceptible to such emotional reactions as anxiety, anger, ambition, envy, jealousy, love, enthusiasm, pride, vengefulness, loyalty, devotion, and appetites of all sorts and to the 'irrational' conduct which grows out of them, the more readily can we empathize with them."[7] This empathy is as far as Weber goes in working through the legitimate domain of affective or irrational forms of human behavior. Although he acknowledges that rationality is never pure or ideal, he asserts that for scientific analysis, researchers need to maintain that irrationality is ultimately reducible to some form of rationality—they need only do sufficient analysis of interests to determine the nature of these apparently affective forms.[8]

Nevertheless, Weber acknowledges that irrationalism is a force even in the modern, apparently rationalized world. He makes two telling comments that are relevant to the current discussion about the role and place of affective power in contemporary culture. First, he laments that formal rationality is exercising greater and greater control in the modern world. In contradistinction, he also mentions that democratic societies periodically allow for moments of irrationality to be part of the election and the party convention process. These parts of the political culture are partially outside the normal course of rationalization, much as the king's symbolic power is outside the administrative functionings of the state.[9] On its own, Weber's commentary provides a critical insight into the way in which "democratic-capitalism" works. If this is coupled with his comments on the relationship between the irrational power of religion and bureaucracy, one can see the outline of a very useful model concerning the way in which irrationality is positioned in contemporary culture: "A bureaucracy is usually characterized by a profound disesteem of all irrational religion, combined, however, with a recognition of the usefulness of this type of religion for controlling the people."[10]

For Weber, ethnicity and nationalism also come under the same rubric of not possessing a great deal of the type of formal rationality found in a bureaucratic culture.[11] However, as symbolic entities, these affective configurations of power can also be useful for the functioning of the state apparatus.

Can a parallel form of rationalization of the irrational—that is, positioning these undisciplined areas of human life within a prevalent and coherent worldview—explain the role and power of the celebrity? With a certain caveat, I think this is a valid extension of Weber's insight into the cynical and Machiavellian bureaucratic use of the irrational. As Weber acknowledges, some charismatic forms can survive and prosper within institutional settings. The charismatic prophet can be likened to the celebrity. The institutional setting of the church "routinizes" the prophetic statements into a coherent religion, so that some semblance of the prophet's significance will endure. Similarly, the institutions of the culture industry work to routinize the structure of meaning of the celebrity into a form of some durability. The celebrity articulates the transformation of types of cultural value into the rationalizing system of the commodity. The culture industry is re-presenting aspects of the personality, the emotional and affective and hence irrational elements of human action,[12] in the exchangeable commodity form of the celebrity. If the institutional organization of a celebrity system is successful, it has produced a dual form of rationalization:

1. It has effectively integrated the concept of personality differences and individuality into a system of exchange; and
2. it has worked toward the rationalization of the audience to see these representations of personality in the celebrity as legitimate forms of identification and cultural value.

To consider that the celebrity embodies only these types of rationalization creates a lopsided analysis. What has been oversimplified is Weber's identification of the charismatic prophet as being generally outside of institutional boundaries. Pierre Bourdieu has elaborated on the significance of the origin of this power, which is not in the individual but rests in the social. Bourdieu demystifies the concept of charisma and its power:

> Let us then dispose of the idea of the notion of charisma as a property attaching to the nature of a single individual and examine instead, in each particular case, sociologically pertinent characteristics of an individual biography. The aim in this context is to explain why a particular individual finds himself *socially* predisposed to live out and express with particular cogency and coherence, ethical or political dispositions that are already present in a latent state amongst all the members of the class or group of his addressees.[13]

For Bourdieu, in an extension of Weber's position, the prophet's "initial accumulation of the capital of symbolic power arises from his relationship to the laity in contrast to the church."[14] Thus, the charismatic construction of new prophetic symbols "plays an organizing and legitimating role" for the assembling of a group.[15]

The unique power of the charismatic prophet is its direct connection to a particular group of people. If one integrates this insight into the interpretation of celebrity power, one can see a third form of rationalization that the celebrity embodies. Like the prophet's power, the celebrity's formative power rests with the people as an expression of popular culture and social will. The value ideals of the celebrity are not so clearly delineated as are those of the charismatic prophet. Part of this confusion derives from the competing forms of rationalization that the celebrity figure houses. The contradictions of the interests of capital with the types of configurations arising from the populace constitute one reason individual celebrities are inherently unstable. The celebrity works in the culture as a figure who wrests the various forms of affective power into rationalized configurations. For the dominant culture, this usually means working toward an ideological positioning of the subordinate cultures within consumer capitalism. For the subordinate cultures, the celebrity articulates an avenue for the expression of their own notions of freedom, fantasy, and needs. The two forms of rationalization occasionally coincide within the same celebrity construction, but because the interests and values that are part of the two types of rationalization are vastly different, the disintegration of this provisional unity and the subsequent mutation of the celebrity system are two permanent features of the system.

The identification of these types of rationalization within individual celebrities in a system of celebrities will be one of the principal objectives in the case studies presented in the succeeding chapters. Although the concept of rationalization possesses a great deal of explanatory usefulness around the nature of celebrity power, as a tool for analysis it is difficult to operationalize. In order to establish something of a protocol for the analysis of this rationalizing power, the celebrity itself has to be redefined to house the moving and mutating field of its own significance. Analyzing the celebrity as a sign or a text provides some of the necessary conceptual tools for understanding the celebrity's formative power.

Celebrity as a Sign/Text:
Signs, Semiotics, and Significance

Several significant consequences arise from relabeling the celebrity a sign. First, as a sign, the celebrity sheds its own subjectivity and individuality and becomes an organizing structure for conventionalized meaning. Like the sign, the celebrity *represents* something other than itself. The material reality of the celebrity sign—that is, the actual person who is at the core of the representation—disappears into a cultural formation of meaning. Celebrity signs represent personalities—more specifically, personalities that are given heightened cultural significance within the social world.

In terms of a basic semiotic system, the denotative level of meaning of the celebrity is the empty structure of the material reality of the actual person. As in Foucault's interpretation of the author, the celebrity is a way in which meaning can be housed and categorized into something that provides a source and origin for the meaning. The "celebrity-function" is as important as Foucault's "author-function" in its power to organize the legitimate and illegitimate domains of the personal and individual within the social.[16] This power becomes activated only through cultural "investment" in the construction of the celebrity sign. In semiotic terms, the cultural investment is the play of connotation in the sign structure of the celebrity. Connotation, a second-order system of signification that builds on the basic sign of the denotative level, identifies the area of the conventionalization of each celebrity sign. Barthes, in his classic semiological study of contemporary signs, *Mythologies,* attempts to show that the connotative level is the source of the ideological construction of reality.[17] Barthes writes that cultural "myths" are derived from the naturalization of signs: the connotative meanings, meanings that represent specific interests, are generalized to represent the interests of the entire society. Semiotically, the connotative level that expresses specific interests of the ruling classes is conflated with the denotative level, so that social members no longer see the origins of the construction of representation and meaning and consider the given meaning as the real or natural meaning. This ideological work of the sign is the glue that maintains the legitimacy of the ruling classes, the bourgeoisie, in the same way that the cultural sign provides an artificial link between the signified and signifier, the connotative and the denotative.

The construction of cultural signs is never so simply described. The term *connotation* indicates and implicates, in its own meaning, a degree of indeterminacy of meaning in any sign. The celebrity sign or any principal cultural sign is never fully determined or "naturalized." It is subject to a process of negotiation of signification. At any given moment, there may be a governing consensus about what the celebrity represents, but this representation may be from a variety of positions and perspectives. The process of consensus exemplifies Gramsci's concept of a working hegemony within the construction of cultural signs.[18] The stability of a celebrity representation signifies the degree of conventionalization of the sign and the establishment of a stable consensus of its signification. A nearly completely conventionalized celebrity sign enters into the very lexicon of a culture, its personality instantiated and immortalized into caricature in the tradition of celebrity icons such as Marilyn Monroe and James Dean. Even in these instances, these celebrity signs transform and mutate, thereby representing different interests to different audience groups.

The movable field of what celebrities may represent indicates that their signs are part of a system of signs. Meaning comes from a reading of the organization of those signs. Thus, the celebrity needs to be analyzed both immanently, to reveal its internal structures, and relationally, among other cultural signs. Oppositions, distinctions, and differentiations among various celebrities reveal their functions within the culture. To interpret the celebrity as a *text* as opposed to simply as a sign is a fruitful way to extend the insights derived from breaking down the structure of signs. What can be revealed is that the celebrity is composed of a system of signs that includes chains of signification. The chains of signification reveal the layering of connotative meanings that are embedded into each celebrity sign.

Critical to the understanding of the celebrity, therefore, is the *intertextuality* of the construction of the celebrity sign. Although a celebrity may be positioned predominantly in one mediated form, that image is informed by the circulation of significant information about the celebrity in newspapers, magazines, interview programs, fanzines, rumors, and so on. The celebrity, in fact, is by definition a fundamentally intertextual sign. Without the domain of interpretive writing on cultural artifacts, the development of the celebrity personality would be stunted. The descriptions of the connections between celebrities' "real" lives and their working lives as actors, singers, or television news readers are what configure the celebrity status. These secondary sources are primary for deepening the meaning of the celebrity sign and thereby providing the connecting fibers to the culture.

In the investigation of celebrities that follows, I undertake the identification of these connotative chains of signification. Examining the play of connotation can illuminate the ways in which sentiments and emotions are connected to cultural images and objects. Through the study of the celebrity as a sign and text, affective attachments or connotations that are configured around individual celebrities can be revealed. Semiotics allows for the critical investigation of the affective power of celebrity signs, so that an extension of Weber's insights into affective power might be operationalized. As well, it provides a technique for deciphering the links between conceptions of the individual and the celebrity sign. The reading of celebrities is designed to deconstruct these sites of highly mediated individuality. What is investigated is how the celebrity is exemplary of what Lipovetsky calls "la logique de la personnalisation" and what can be identified as hyperindividualism.[19] The intensification of the concerns of the personal and the psychologization of greater areas of life are parallel and related phenomena to the celebrity as hyperindividual. The hyperindividual is the intense representation of what Lipovetsky identifies as the decline of the social into "personalization." Hyperindividuality is concerned specifically with the overcoding of the personal in the domain of media representation.

Two applications of semiotics to the interpretation of contemporary culture also inform the current study. Semiotic studies of advertising have demonstrated successfully the usefulness of the signifier-signified dyad in understanding the way in which capital has inserted itself into the production of signs. Judith Williamson's reading of advertisements points to the ability of advertising to expand the connotations of certain signifiers so that they include the values of the products depicted in some significant social relationship.[20] For example, an advertisement for beer attempts to provide an associational correlation between the product and a certain lifestyle. The product is inserted into successful social relations. Sut Jhally's work on advertisements goes beyond the ideological structuring that is the essential work of advertisements. One of his insights relates to considering the semiotic dyad of signifier and signified as correlative to the dialectic of production and consumption. What advertising—and, by implication, contemporary society—emphasizes through its images is the consumption or exchange value of a product. In the intensification of images and emphasis on the construction of exchange value and consumption, there is a consequential decrease in emphasis on the use value and the process of production. Advertising, for Jhally, provides for the magical and fetishistic transformation of goods, which limits the value of production in the determination of social value of the product. Products are thus involved in enhancing only the social relations of consumption, not production.[21] The current study will investigate, in part, the implications of the commodity status of the celebrity and thereby assess the ideological function of the celebrity in the construction of consumer capitalism through a semiotically derived analysis of the production and consumption components of the celebrity sign.

Finally, some work in cultural studies on the body as text is also relevant to the study of the celebrity sign and its power. Hebdige's integration of Barthes's (from Lévi-Strauss) concept of the *bricoleur* provides a semiotic reading of the way that sense is made by cultural groups in contemporary society.[22] The modern *bricoleur* appropriates objects from his or her environment in order to make that environment make sense and cohere. These objects may have a material reality, but they can just as easily be language-objects, such as a certain argot. Styles of movement, of dress, and of music are all aspects of what Hebdige calls "subcultural style," which may take objects from the dominant culture and remake them to establish oppositional or alternative uses for them. The classic example of this form of appropriation is the safety pin, which moved from everyday object associated with domestic and familial urban life to punk jewelry. The piecing together of an entire style to represent a subcultural identity through an array of signs implicates the audience in the active construction of these semiotic systems. The celebrity system can be likened to the subcultural technique of appropriation of objects to make sense of their urban and subordinate position. Celebrities as signs can be appropriated and integrated into a subcultural system of signs in the same ritual of sense making.

Within generally the same methods, the audience construction of the celebrity can be investigated. Through a semiotic analysis of audience appropriation of the symbols of celebrity, a greater understanding of how the system of celebrity is involved in the making sense or rationalization of the audience's social environment can be achieved. The study will establish the types of distinctions among audience groups that the appropriated celebrity sign represents. Dyer's work on the gay subculture's appropriation of certain Hollywood stars will form the framework for the current investigation of the audience. The investment by the gay subculture in stars' personas and body images as well as the subculture's rearticulation and particularization of the mediated representation of these images offer the current study a conceptual model from which to understand the use and influence of celebrities by audience groups.

The semiotic deconstruction of the celebrity and its audience provides a partial model of the nature of celebrity power. What still needs to be integrated into the technique is a concept that articulates the central role the celebrity plays in the simultaneous construction of collectivities and modern individuality. The celebrity works to unite the socius into identification with particular types, but the celebrity also isolates and divides through the significant representation of his or her individual qualities. This pivotal though apparently contradictory attribute of the celebrity sign can be addressed through the development of a conceptual tool that complements the semiotic investigation. The term I use to describe this contained contradiction is a hyphenated neologism: the *audience-subject*.

The Role of the Audience-Subject

A critical feature of contemporary culture is the power of the audience to divide and differentiate the socius. The audience has emerged in the twentieth century as a social category that rivals and, in some instances, surpasses the power of the categories of class and mass. This categorical and formative power of the audience is at the center of the power of the celebrity. Indeed, the historical emergence of the celebrity sign coincides and correlates with the rise of the audience as social category. It is also significant that both are integrated intimately with the development of consumer capitalist culture. The specific relationship between the celebrity and the emergence of the significance of the audience is the convergence within the celebrity sign of individual expression and personality within a constructed collective (the audience). The celebrity sign, then, contains the audience through positioning the type of identification in terms of individuality. In order to understand this relationship, it is necessary to backtrack somewhat to explore the way in which the audience is a modern representation of social power.[23]

The Audience

As mentioned above, the audience has emerged out of the formation of two other social categories that are powerful in their capacity to position the social world: class and mass. The utilization of class analysis for understanding the social totality arose with great force in the nineteenth century. As a way to differentiate the new industrial class from the mercantile class, and also as a way to distinguish the new capitalist class and the working class from the former landed aristocracy and peasantry, the breakdown of society into classes established a new structure of coherence and legitimation. Fundamentally, class analysis is based on what individuals *do*. Society is organized according to the forms and relations of production, and members of society are positioned into appropriate categories. The categorical legitimacy of class conceptions of the socius is dependent on the general acceptance of defining a person's social identity in terms of his or her work. Although other categories of difference may be pertinent to the establishment of this social identity—for example, religion or leisure activities—the strength of the categories of class that described relations of production were particularly salient and powerful with the emergence and dominance of a capitalist economy. The categorical power of class not only informed and legitimated the dominant sections of capitalist society, it also served as the central subject of its critique. There was general agreement on the empirical reality of the very structure of capitalist society between those like Marx and Engels, who believed capitalist society's contradictions would produce revolutionary transformation, and the "captains of industry" of the nineteenth century, who maintained and profited from the organization of production.

Another type of categorization also expanded in its explanatory power in the nineteenth century. Although bearing several monikers—including mob, horde, and crowd—because of its less discernible identification and origins, the general category of mass was used to describe the growing power of the dominated classes. The power of the category of the mass did not arise from the relations of production; it does not describe social identity through the categories of work. In contradistinction to the categories of class, the mass (or the masses) is a category that emphasizes unorganized political power. As well, the formation of crowds and mobs, as described in chapter 2, also represented a potential threat to the established social structure. The mass as social category is *fundamentally a construction of collective social identity in terms of nonwork or the use of leisure time*. It embodies the dialectical social category in capitalist society to that of class: whereas class articulates a social identity of production, the category of mass can define social identity in terms of consumption. To put it grandly but succinctly, the capitalist project in the twentieth century has been to work intensely to position and differentiate the category of the mass into recognizable and relatively stable categorical configurations of consumption practices.

The audience has become the principal way in which the mass has been positioned in the twentieth century. As a category, it is more intimately connected to the exigencies of consumer capitalism than the indecipherable category of the mass. Through mass-mediated culture, audiences are constructed and defined by the type of programming that is offered. The goal behind the construction of audiences through programs is their "sellability" to advertisers. The defining of each audience in terms of a specific configuration of consumer needs is an objective of both the program and the advertisements; program and advertisement are complementary rhetorical devices in the construction of audiences as consumers. Mass-mediated cultural producers, in their quest to define a recognizable audience, use a variety of social markers of consumption to differentiate the mass. Gender differences modalized around certain products and programs constitute the most obvious form of audience construction that also avoids an explicit reinvestment in the category of class. Extensive demographic and psychographic research is also undertaken to construct recognizable audience groups that can be further constructed around mediated forms and products.[24]

Because of the close affinity the social category of the audience has with the practices of consumption and the construction of consumers, it articulates a form of social power. This is not to say that the categories of class and mass have been completely supplanted or have lost their own forms of social power. However, the category of the audience has been in ascendancy throughout the reconstruction of capitalism into consumer capitalism in the twentieth century. The audience's temporality and fluidity, and its blurring of the lines of class and wealth, are all valuable constitutive elements that work in the maintenance of a continuous consensus concerning the function of capitalism as an effective system of satisfying wants and needs.

Like class and mass categorical constructions, the audience construction also provides categorical power for some type of alternative or oppositional formulation. The audience may be constructed but not completely determined by the exigencies of capital. This fundamental indeterminacy around the interpretation by the audience is what cultural production attempts to recapture in terms of representations to maintain the consensus. The audience in this form of construction thus serves as a kind of cultural innovation for the culture industries.

One feature of the construction of the modern audience is its usual positioning within the construction of the individual personality. Consumer goods, programs, films, magazines, and books are the tools for the construction of the personality through consumer culture. A paradox is central to an understanding of consumer culture's intense focus on the qualities of the individual: working in the rhetorical formats of advertisements, films, and television programs, there is a collective construction of individual difference. Simultaneous to the need for "mass" or collective response to products (in order for producers to sell massive quantities of identical products), the individual power to build difference is highlighted. In order to indicate that this fabrication of difference is an ideological form of individuality, I have chosen the less value-laden terms *subject* and *subjectivity*. Using the term *subject* allows me to consider the way in which discourses of individuality pass through the socius without acknowledging any fundamental reality or integrity of the individual. The current use of the term *subjectivity* is drawn from Louis Althusser's seminal work on identification in his study of various types of ideological state apparatuses.[25] The media, operating as a type of ideological state apparatus, offer images with which the viewer can identify. Althusser calls this process "interpellation" or hailing, where the subject is temporarily positioned or called by the cultural text to see himself or herself as having a relational reality to the text. This process legitimates the various social positions in society. As Fiske explains: "Hailing is the process by which language identifies and constructs a social position for the addressee. Interpellation is the larger process whereby language constructs social relations for both parties in an act of communication and thus locates them in the broader map of social relations in general."[26]

The construction of subjectivities through the various ideological state apparatuses produces an active and dynamic ideology. Interpellation, because of its temporary instantiations, allows for a floating form of subject positioning. It is through ideology that we are constituted as subjects, both in the way that we accept cultural norms and in the way we establish cultural differences and distinctions. Our relation to celebrities, then, is a dynamic system of interpellation in which we see certain kinds individuality as normatively centered and reject others. In some instances we accept the kinds of subjectivity that are represented for us; at other times we actively reject them. The types of subjectivity offered by celebrities, then, are the products of a system specifically designed to construct types of subjectivity that emphasize individuality and personality. It is these qualities of the celebrity sign that make its construction of subjectivity so central to the system of capital.

In the forthcoming analysis of individual celebrities, I have combined the concept of subject with that of the audience to form the neologism *audience-subject*. The audience-subject is in fact what we are attempting to identify within the celebrity sign. The celebrity's power is derived from the collective configuration of its meaning; in other words, the audience is central in sustaining the power of any celebrity sign. The types of messages that the celebrity provides for the audience are modalized around forms of individual identification, social difference and distinction, and the universality of personality types. Celebrities represent subject positions that audiences can adopt or adapt in their formation of social identities. Each celebrity represents a complex form of audience-subjectivity that, when placed within a system of celebrities, provides the ground on which distinctions, differences, and oppositions are played out. The celebrity, then, is an embodiment of a discursive battleground on the norms of individuality and personality within a culture. The celebrity's strength or power as a discourse on the individual is operationalized only in terms of the power and position of the audience that has allowed it to circulate.

My task in the next chapter is to identify the types of audience-subjectivity that are embodied by particular celebrities. This project entails a two-tiered form of analysis. The process of construction of the audience through the celebrity involves a knowledge of the industrial apparatus that is in place. I have chosen three domains of industrial cultural production to focus the study of the celebrity: film, television, and popular music. Other areas, such as sports, business, and religion, are equally valid starting points for an investigation. My reasons for choosing the three culture industries I will examine are fourfold. First, these three identify clear and openly acknowledged industrial strategies around the making of celebrity signs; there is an economic objective behind each of the celebrity designs. Second, I wish to demonstrate how these popular cultural constructions of the celebrity have been appropriated into the construction of the political leader. Other domains, such as religion and business, resemble the political sphere in their appropriation of popular cultural models of the celebrity. The domain of popular culture is not often encumbered with conceptions of other forms of rationality and legitimation that are part of the meaning systems of science, business, politics, and religion. Third, the interrelationships among these three culture industries allow for the development of a systemic conception of celebrities. When celebrities are seen as parts of a system, one can see the ways in which types of audience-subjectivity are situated in opposition or distinction to other types. Film, television, and popular music offer the possibility of identifying the interplay among various forms of audience-subjectivity and how these forms aid in the configuration of the social world under capitalism. Finally, as discussed above, there is a close connection between the development of the celebrity and the development of the audience in the twentieth century as complementary categories of social distinction where both individual and collective constructions of the socius are housed. Because the audience as a social category has emerged primarily in the domain of the culture industries, I have chosen these three segments of popular culture as my starting point for the investigation of celebrity power.

Reception Theory and the Study of the Audience-Subject

It is difficult to identify the audience-subject that is housed in each celebrity sign. What is acknowledged in the construction of the celebrity using this conceptual tool is the central role that the audience possesses. Some of the work that has been conducted in reception theory, particularly that of Hans Robert Jauss, will be helpful in our analysis of the celebrity as audience-subject.

Reception theory offers the current study the integration of textual analysis into an interpretation of the audience. For Jauss, the text— like the celebrity—is not a stable or static phenomenon. Its dynamism results from the way in which the text is interpreted by its audience. Jauss describes this constant reinterpretation of the text by the reader as the changing "horizon of expectations." Jauss's intervention in literary theory is an integration of cultural factors to determine the reading of a text. The changing horizon of expectations articulates the way in which cultural history and literature interact as related systems. The value of any literary work is determined by its relation to prior works read. The reception process, for Jauss, is "the expansion of a semiotic system that is carried out between the development and correction of a system."[27] Thus, any reception is part of a historical chain of reception, constantly being transformed by the current text's relation to the past. Although his early work demonstrates an evolutionary understanding of the development of literature, Jauss plays down this linear telos in his more recent work. Nevertheless, his early work represents a new approach to the text because of his recognition of the investment of the readers or audience in its meaning system. This elevation of the audience leads Jauss to conclusions about reception that correlate with much of the British cultural studies approach to cultural formation. In opposition to the so-called negative aesthetic tradition of Adorno and the Frankfurt school, Jauss explains that literature through reception can not only represent the social world, it can also play a "socially formative" role in the identification of aspirations, needs, and desires within the society. The process of reception and evaluation of the text is produced "against the background of their artforms as well as against the background of the everyday experience of life."[28] Within Jauss's model of reception theory, the activity of the audience is equated with the process of production. In the current study, reception theory offers the possibility of an investigation of the dual and antinomic nature of the celebrity in which audience forms of rationalization are correlated with those of the culture industries to form an unstable but at least temporarily coherent audience-subjectivity. Jauss, although using different objects of study, identifies the battleground for constructing the meaning of the text as the audience.

The work of Wolfgang Iser, who, like Jauss, is associated with the Constanz school of literary studies, offers the current project a needed complement to Jauss's model of reception theory. Where Jauss tends to construct his theory of reception and aesthetic experience on a macro level, Iser locates the construction of meaning not so much between texts as intratextually, and is therefore working, as Holub rightly identifies, at the micro level.[29] Drawing from Ingarden, Iser uses the phrase "the indeterminacy of meaning" to describe the way an individual text is constructed. The reader creates momentary "gestalts" that are altered as he or she continues to read and transforms the impressions of plot and character with the new information. With the celebrity "text," a similar audience relationship to the meaning of the text is produced. The moving signifier of the celebrity is spawned by new configurations of information known about the celebrity's professional life and personal life. New temporary gestalts are formed concerning the celebrity that can be characterized by the pinup photograph. The pinup holds the constructed image of the celebrity in place for the audience, at least until it is superseded by competing pinups of different celebrities who may represent related configurations of individuality.

Both Iser and Jauss have invested some effort in attempting to describe the value of literature, or at least what produces better literature, and it would be unfair of me to use their work here without acknowledging this aspect (even though it has the least "value" for the current project). Jauss and Iser have tried to identify some value in innovation in literature. Jauss, though he later discounted the importance of this argument, has asserted that the literary project is built out of disjunctures. Great works emerge from the break with the horizon of expectation. Iser more explicitly discusses the conception of innovation and its positive value as the presentation of something that breaks the normative convention. He believes in the value of making something appear new or fresh to the reader, and that in that way an aesthetic moment is achieved in reception. It is not my intention to integrate these normative characterizations into the study of the celebrity. Nevertheless, there is at work in the system of celebrity some conception of innovation and the continuous creation of something anew. I consider this to be a cultural trait that has emerged out of concepts of the individual and how to determine hierarchies of individual merit when past forms of social structure no longer apply; I do not consider the innovative moment as some universal value. I thus treat it as a rationalization of the way in which individuality is modalized in contemporary culture.

Finally, reception theory contributes a useful model for working through the way the celebrity sign is constructed into a form of audience-subjectivity. Jauss, in his more recent work in the area of "aesthetic experience," identifies three domains of pleasure of reception: poesis, aisthesis, and catharsis.[30] The third domain, catharsis, considered by Jauss to articulate a form of aesthetic communication, is principally centered on the concept of identification and specifically heroic identification in literary texts. The difference with Jauss's approach to the hero is that he treats the identification as a "modality" of reception, as opposed to the origins within the character itself.[31] Jauss has identified five types of modalities of identification, which will be investigated in the current study of the celebrity. These five types are patterns of identification; all are in existence simultaneously, although particular types of reception predominate in specific eras. The modalities of reception that Jauss has developed to describe an entire system of identification are as follows:

1. *Associative identification:* The barriers between audience and actors are broken, and there is a celebration of active participation.[32]

2. *Admiring identification:* The actions of the hero are exemplary for a particular community — the perfect hero.[33]

3. *Sympathetic identification:* There is a solidarity with the character or suffering personality. We place ourselves in the position of the hero.[34]

4. *Cathartic identification:* Though similar to sympathetic identification, the cathartic form of reception represents an abstraction or an aestheticized relation to the hero. In this way a moral or judgment can be drawn from the aesthetic experience and the reader feels a sense of emancipation through his or her involvement with the character.[35]

5. *Ironic modality:* A consistent denial of any expected form of identification represents this form of reception of the text of the character. There is maintenance of the interaction with the audience without a sense of the closure of character identification. It is the type of modality that is privileged in modernist fiction and postmodern criticism.[36]

In the analysis of celebrities that follows, I will attempt to develop how the technologies of reception are linked to these particular modalities of identification by an audience. In general, I will identify synchronous types of identification as opposed to diachronous construction of reception. I will link these forms of identification to a discussion of social difference modalized around the types of differentiation activated through the modern audience. Reception theory and the modalities of reception and identification listed above will be adapted to the study of celebrity construction in contemporary culture. The analysis itself can be characterized as undertaking a double hermeneutic that correlates with the dual forms of rationalization that construct celebrity identities.[37] The project works through a *hermeneutic of intention* in its development of the industrial organization of public subjectivity in each cultural form. Also, through a reading of the various popular texts written about particular stars, and a reading of the forms of reception of particular products associated with the celebrities, the analysis forges a correlative *hermeneutic of reception.* The negotiated combination of interpretations establishes the meaning and position of the celebrity in the constellation of public personalities in contemporary culture.

The double hermeneutic, employed to reveal the organization of public subjectivity, represents an approach that has not been well developed by other writers on celebrity. Some writers, such as Richard Dyer, detail the forms of reception of stars, but fail to develop adequately the apparatus that is in place that attempts to read and produce stars. Other writers, such as Morin, have provided accounts of the industrial organization of the culture industries as star-making machinery, but fail to recognize that the success of the organization of stars and celebrities is not a fait accompli, but represents a constant effort to reorganize and refit the public presentation of personalities to match audiences and audiences' expectations.[38] Finally, very few writers have successfully linked the developments and shifts in celebrity form that have emerged from these negotiating processes to the organization of contemporary subjectivity. John Hartley's reading of a transformed public sphere where "popular reality" from television sometimes shifts the personal into the political sphere perhaps comes closest to illustrating how celebrities are part of shifted public debate; however, this conceptualization has not so far investigated the formation of public subjectivity.[39] The analysis that follows identifies the forms of subjectivity that are privileged in the public sphere through the celebrity and then correlates those modalities of production and reception into the organization of political representations of self and identity. Emerging from the identification of the audience-subject and the production of personalities by the culture industries and the political culture is a form of identity that permeates contemporary culture and is not arrested by its designation as an entertainment phenomenon or a political phenomenon. The term that captures the special qualities of this identity is *the public subject,* which refers to a representation of individuality and personality that operates in the public sphere. The *public* designation of this form of subjectivity refers to the involve-

ment of the public (through different audience groups in its formation) and the conception of a common and accepted cultural valuation
of fame and significance. The *subject* designation in the term refers
to the individuating construction that is an essential feature of the public personality. Also, subjectivity entails, as noted earlier, a structura-
tion process that includes the audience who identifies the celebrity,
the institutions in place that organize these representations of celebrity
identity, and the celebrity him- or herself. The analyses of celebrities
that follow work to flesh out what contemporary public subjectivity
entails and thereby identify how this form of subjectivity is elemental
in all domains of the public sphere.

Unifying the Approach: Foucault, Discourse, and Power

I have established to this point three kinds of approaches to
the study of the celebrity. My intention in the following chapters is
to analyze particular celebrities by integrating these three approaches
into a unified thematic about the general type of power that is represented by an entire celebrity system. I will illuminate the conceptualization of the celebrity as a form of double rationality through the
general techniques of the analysis of the sign and of the text offered
by semiotics and cultural studies. I intend to use Jauss's characterizations of heroic reception as a way to structure the reading of any celebrity within the constructs of the audience.

Ultimately, what binds the analysis of the celebrity together is the
way in which power is articulated through these cultural texts. There
is a nebulous quality about what the concept of power entails in a
study of celebrity. In the chapter that follows the analysis of celebrities,
where I undertake an analysis of the political discourse that is informed by the system of celebrity, the more classic understanding of
the term surfaces. I intend to link the political nature of power to celebrity power through a Foucauldian conception of the term. Foucault
discusses power not in terms of opposition between those who possess
power and those who do not. Rather, for Foucault power is a much
more pandemic concept; power exists in both the institutional setting and concomitantly in the organization that opposes the institution.
The linkage between these two formations identifies the site of power.
What fundamentally unifies diametrically opposed organizations is
the commonality of a "discourse." Discursive strategies are attempts

to maintain the primacy of certain forms of knowledge concerning the discourse. The play of power is the positioning of the discourse to represent a certain configuration of interests, needs, and institutions.[40]

Foucault provides several examples of the way in which power is expressed through discourse and the discursive strategies contained therein. He calls his tracing of these discursive power matrices "genealogies." For example, he traces the discourse of madness from its classical roots, where the insane were thought to be truth sayers, to the nineteenth century, where madness became an illness that required those afflicted to be cordoned off from the sane. As a discourse, it had been repositioned, for insanity marked the post-Renaissance domain of reason, sanity, and the individual. Madness became a visible threat to a structured system of knowledge.[41] In another work, *Discipline and Punish,* Foucault focuses on the movement of disciplinary strategies from physical punishment to the internalization of discipline into conscience. In terms of prison systems, Foucault notes that Bentham's panopticon articulated, at least metaphorically, the way in which modern discipline achieved its ascendancy through the maintenance of the belief among prisoners that they are under continuous surveillance.[42] The discourse on the internalization of discipline proliferated because it expressed the means and methods of control of each isolated individual in an era that championed the individual.

In his final major work, *The History of Sexuality,* Foucault develops his concept of power more fully. What interests Foucault about sexuality is its discursive power, or what he calls its "bio-power."[43] In volume 1 of this work, Foucault examines the way in which sexuality has been positioned in the nineteenth and twentieth centuries to explain a host of mental ailments as well as a means to freedom and liberation. Instead of identifying a discursive discontinuity between Victorian sexual censorship and mid-twentieth-century sexual liberation, Foucault sees a clear continuity in the use of sexuality as a means of explanation. Discursively, sexuality continues to position and construct the modern subject. Sexuality as discourse thus articulates various configurations of power.

The celebrity, like sexuality, allows for the configuration, positioning, and proliferation of certain discourses about the individual and individuality in contemporary culture. The celebrity offers a discursive focus for the discussion of realms that are considered outside the bounds of public debate in the most public fashion. The celebrity system is a way in which the sphere of the irrational, emotional, personal, and affective is contained and negotiated in contemporary culture.

Affect and Power

I have suggested throughout this chapter that the concept of affect is central for understanding the meaning and power of the celebrity in contemporary culture. It has arisen in the way in which Weber has tried to define the process of rationalization. I have attempted to demonstrate in a previous chapter that the mass has been perceived and positioned as the prime location for volatile affectivity, the center of irrationality. I have also indicated that in the signifying system the realm of connotation can be classified as the site of affective activity. As well, in my integration of Foucault I am privileging the term *affect* to identify the organization of a discourse about individuality through celebrities. To complete the discussion of techniques and tools for the study of celebrity and power, I will conclude by elaborating further on how I use the term *affect* in the forthcoming analysis.

Affect, as a term, has been used principally in psychological research. In behavioral psychology, affect is the middle ground between cognition and behavior: the affective realm is connected to this chain of causality between something experienced and the formulation of a reaction to that experience.[44] Much of the behavioral psychology research has focused on locating how affect leads to abnormal behaviors in people and then working out how to transform the chain of causality.

Freud, in his early writings that focused on establishing the frameworks for the science of psychoanalysis, also developed a reading of affect. Freud's thesis is that people virtually automatically assume rational grounds for their feelings; affective experience therefore leads to the reinterpretation of situations so that the affective experience becomes plausible and integrated into a worldview.[45] What can be drawn from Freud and, to a lesser degree, the behavioral psychologists is that affect is constantly "attributed" to something. Attribution of affect, the process of rationalizing emotional reactions, echoes Weber's reading of the relationship between the charismatic leader and his followers. My use of the term, then, is drawn from this reading of affect and the attribution of affect; the celebrity represents a site for the housing of affect in terms of both the audience and the institutions that have worked to produce the cultural forms that have allowed the celebrity to develop.

Although I use this reading of affect and attribution as a launching point from which to understand the negotiation of meaning that occurs in the organization of the celebrity as cultural text, I extend the meaning of the term to encompass a general cultural condition related specifically to questions of meaning and significance. Different authors have described this breakdown in signification—where meaning itself is in flux—as the postmodern condition. Lyotard, who has written about the breakdown in metanarratives, can be reread faithfully as describing the lack of attribution of affect in contemporary culture.[46] There is a decentering of meaning; affect itself becomes the end point in the causal chain between cognition and rationalization. Similarly, Jameson has taken the clinical diagnostic term *schizophrenia* and reconfigured it as a general cultural condition. He expresses it as the dissolution of hierarchies of value and the living in the perpetual present. In his words, the general culture is experiencing "isolated, disconnected, discontinuous material signifiers which fail to link up into a coherent sequence."[47] Baudrillard's identification of the "ecstasy of communication" is related to the disintegration of a clear-cut relationship between signifier and signified; the ecstasy emerges from the actual play within a long chain of signifiers.[48] Like the experiences of the schizophrenic, the culture's experiences are intense and undifferentiated as past and future disintegrate as points of reference. Further, the contemporary culture experience, although intense, dissipates quickly and re-forms on new sites.

Grossberg has used the term *affect* in several articles specifically to describe this modern cultural condition. In discussing postmodernity, Grossberg focuses on the incapacity of individuals in contemporary culture to "articulate meaning and affect":

> Post-modernity, then, points to a crisis in our ability to locate any meaning as a possible and appropriate source for an impassioned commitment. It is a crisis, not of faith, but of the relationship between faith and commonsense, a dissolution of what we might call the "anchoring effect" that articulates meaning and affect. It is not that nothing matters—for something has to matter—but that we can find no way of choosing, or of finding something to warrant our investment. . . . Meaning and affect—historically so closely intertwined—have broken apart, each going off in its own direction.[49]

Grossberg's conception of articulation between affect and meaning can be reread as a form of attribution, albeit with a decidedly political connotation. With television, there is "an indifference to difference even as it constructs differences out of the very absence of difference."[50] What Grossberg sees is an "affective economy" (as opposed to a representational economy) in operation, where there is a focus on affective investment without the concomitant association of a political investment. Thus, a particular song, such as Bruce Springsteen's "Born in the U.S.A.," can be appropriated as an affective investment by both Ronald Reagan and Walter Mondale in the 1984 presidential campaign: the connection to a clear-cut meaning, which for Grossberg represents an "articulation" of meaning in terms of political action, is elided from the affective moment.[51] In the analysis of celebrities to follow, I interpret the way in which this affective economy is configured in the organization of a celebrity system. The forms of affective power are linked to the power of the celebrity text to move effortlessly between the public and the private spheres.

I use the concept of affect in two complementary ways in the analyses that follow in the next three chapters. First, I identify the ways in which celebrities are positioned by the culture industries for the attribution of affect and how audience groups attribute certain affective meanings to celebrity figures. Second, I describe how the celebrity system constitutes a technique for the organization of cultural investment into the attributes of personality and sentiment, individual subjectivity, and private experience.

Conclusion

The next three chapters operationalize the techniques of analysis proposed in this chapter through a study of celebrities who have emerged in specific institutional sites of the culture industries. I first analyze each institutional site in terms of the way in which the celebrity has been configured historically. This is followed by an analysis of the meanings and various forms of signification that are embodied in specific contemporary celebrities in film, television, and popular music. My objective in this investigation is to work through the nature of the discursive power of the celebrity system—by charting the double form of rationalization and the dual hermeneutic of intention and reception—in order to see how it may inform the general public sphere and political leadership in particular. Following the analysis of the celebrities is a concluding summary chapter in which I examine the linkages between the celebrities in order to identify systemic properties. I then apply these insights to the study of contemporary political culture and political leadership and discuss the celebrity system as a central element of political culture.

Part II

4

The Cinematic Apparatus and the Construction of the Film Celebrity

The emergence of the cinema star, according to Richard De-Cordova, is intimately linked with the decline of the allure of the apparatus of motion picture projection. Until about 1907, the focus of attention was on the technical feat of displaying images and stories on the screen.[1] Most of early cinema was documentary in nature, with aspects of everyday life, circus performances, and sporting events depicted on-screen.[2] This changed somewhat because of the constant need for new and interesting (at least previously unseen) film product. The early connection of film to the craft of illusionism and magic can be seen in the films of Georges Meliès, an illusionist turned filmmaker, and in the position of the exhibition of films as a type of novelty act in vaudeville theaters.[3] In both cases, the enigmatic quality of the production was related not so much to the plot as to how the images were created and juxtaposed. Early films (pre-1907), according to DeCordova, could be characterized by their close connection to "action" and movement. The construction of the film celebrity emerged only after an initial decade of exhibition. It is part of traditional — although now challenged — film history that the large production houses, such as Biograph, impeded the development of the star by not releasing the real names of the actors involved in any film. The impetus behind the development of stardom then was the audience's construction of intertextual continuities. According to Walker, the audience began identifying screen personalities not by their names but by nicknames that attempted to capture the face, body type, or hairstyle of the performer. Designations such as "the fat guy" and "the girl with the curls" became a way for nickelodeon exhibitors to advertise their short features through a recognizable audience interest.[4] Hampton's *History of the American Film Industry from Its Beginnings to 1931* serves as a guide for this reading of early film and its relationship to the construction of personalities.[5] More recent scholarship has disputed the simplicity of this early account in exploring the development of the film star system. Some researchers, such as Staiger, have been able to identify forms of identification that predate previous designations of its development in the early to mid-1910s.[6] The interconnections of filmmaking to other entertainment industries, such as theater and vaudeville, which had well-developed star systems, further complicate the reasons and rationales behind the organization of a film star system. What can be safely concluded is that the reluctance to release the names of performers gradually gave way to an industry that used its performers as one of the primary forms of promotion and marketing of its product.

A more accurate way of describing the emergence of the film star is to see that the film industry was in the process of determining its categorical position in the entertainment industry. In its affiliation with vaudeville, the film industry was part of an already established and successful cultural industry that possessed its own system of fame, prestige, and celebrity.[7] *Variety,* the trade newspaper for most of the vaudevillian performing arts in the early part of the twentieth century, regularly displayed large photos of vaudeville stars on the first page; the featuring of these acts became one of the central means by which the publication attached itself to the glamour of the industry. Moreover, as Allen points out, vaudeville had successfully produced what he calls a mass audience, which included not only the working class but large segments of the middle class.[8] So the film industry had expanded its audience beyond the limited circulation of penny arcades and variations of peep shows to a national audience that encompassed both the working class and the middle class.

Film was also positioned in relationship to traditional theater, which attracted a much wealthier clientele than most vaudeville houses. The way in which the film magazine of the period, *Moving Picture World,* differentiated between the true "acting" of the theater and the idea of performance in movies illustrates that a clear hierarchy of the arts was at work. Prior to 1907, *Moving Picture World* described movie actors usually as "picture performers." *To perform* was understood to connote a display of natural action. *To act* had the connotation of creating the nuances of character, the artifice of becoming the person one was playing. In the development of techniques like the close-up, in the gradual appearance of narrative structure, and in the movement to "feature" length, one can see the attempts to build into the cinematic structure elements that would be emulative of aesthetic value perceived in theatergoing. The increasing focus on individual performers and codes of character, as opposed to the dominant code of action of early-twentieth-century film, moved the film industry into an investment in a star system that at the very least emulated the theater star system. Indeed, Adolph Zukor attempted to inject the aura of the theatrical star into film by contracting with famous stage actors to appear in films. The most famous of these, Sarah Bernhardt, played the lead in the critically successful though less financially successful *Queen Elizabeth* (1912). However, the strategy contained a slightly flawed conception of the movie audience, because the most famous contract players to emerge out of Zukor's Famous Players Company were in fact known only as film stars.[9] The development of the star system thus is most indicative of a cultural industry attempting to capture a certain legitimacy and cultural space. Stars and dramas that emphasized the psychological development of characters articulate an attempt to establish the cinema's affinity with the theater. The actual meanings of the film star of the 1910s or 1920s never achieved this aesthetic connotation because the audience's investment in the star, an audience comprising primarily working-class and middle-class individuals, expressed a distinctively filmic aura for the screen celebrity.

Edgar Morin's discussion of this aura of the film celebrity of the 1920s emphasizes the godlike quality perceived in these select few. One of the first instances of name recognition came with Nick Carter, who was still known only by his screen name. Only after playing a number of different heroic roles did the star become recognizable as a hero himself.[10] By 1919, the star crystallized as an entity distinct from his or her screen personas. As an entity, the star and the industry that by this time surrounded him or her began to protect the image the star conveyed to the public. For example, Rudolph Valentino maintained the image of the romantic and heroic lover throughout his career by actively choosing his film roles to support that construction. Morin notes that Greta Garbo epitomized the separate and aloof quality of the film stars of the 1920s; she "remained mysteriously distant from the mortals" (her audience) both in her screen presence and in her lifestyle in her grand Hollywood mansion.[11]

However, the film star aura was never so simply maintained. It was built on a dialectic of knowledge and mystery. The incomplete nature of the audience's knowledge of any screen actor became the foundation on which the film celebrity was constructed into an economic force. The staging ground from which film actors entered the world of celebrity was publicity. Publicity constitutes the extratextual movement of the screen actor into other forms of popular discourse. The staging of publicity on behalf of individual celebrities became the province of agents and specifically publicity agents. The most famous of these publicity innovators, Carl Laemmle—owner of the Independent Motion Picture Company, known as Imp—was effective in separating the economic power of the individual actor as celebrity from the rest of the film industry. He staged the "death" of the Biograph Girl, Florence Lawrence, through a press release to news outlets throughout North America. Three days later, he staged her reappearance in St. Louis, which included an exclusive feature interview and full-length photo of the star. Within that interview, certain personal details about Florence Lawrence were released that circumvented the Biograph Studios ban on the release of names or information about its film actors. Her audience learned of her love of horseback riding and of the stage, along with other details of her early life.[12] The publicity agent has continued to assume this role of enlarging the meaning of any actor in the public sphere and expanding the audience's knowledge and desire for knowledge of the celebrity's personal life.[13] Walker considers the creation of the film star as public property an industry that was very quickly "10,000" times larger than that found in the theatrical trade: there were more photos, more venues, more fan and movie magazines, and the power of simultaneous releases made the extratextual business of film star publicity central to the entire industry. Between the 1920s and the 1950s, the extratextual discourse concerning movies and their stars in Hollywood was estimated by one writer to involve a hundred thousand words a day. In terms of quantity, this made Hollywood the third-largest source of information, behind Washington, D.C., and New York City. Also between the 1920s and the 1950s, roughly five thousand correspondents were stationed in Hollywood to feed the world the secrets of the stars.[14]

The Independence of the Film Celebrity

At various times in the history of film, the film star has operated as a symbol of the independent individual in modern society. This crucial symbolic value has demonstrated and reinforced the ideology of potential that is housed in all members of capitalist culture to supersede the constraints of institutions for the true expression of personal freedom. As film stars transformed into the clear economic center of film production between 1910 and 1920, they became able to determine the form and content of that production and thus began to act independently.[15] By 1919, a group of film stars that included Charlie Chaplin, Mary Pickford, and Douglas Fairbanks demanded salaries and contracts that could no longer be supported by any studio. Along with director D. W. Griffith, they organized their own production and distribution company, United Artists, in order to control their own films.[16] Although the company had limited success in its early years, the existence of United Artists nevertheless underlined the top film stars' ability to express the independence of their wills and desires. It is interesting to note that the expression of independent will in the form of United Artists eventually adopted the corporate structure of the other major film companies.[17]

The economic independence of the film celebrity has always operated as a symbol of freedom within the industry and for the public. The ability to own a mansion, the opportunity to partake of prohibitively expensive forms of leisure, like yachting or polo, and the time to travel widely are some of the kinds of privileges associated with stardom. They are the rewards of an industry that is connected to a paying public through the perceived "qualities" of its stars.

For the industry, the stars' economic value transcends the nature of their work and thus their wages far outstrip those earned by generally unionized film workers. The celebrity's independent connection to the audience permits the configuration of a separate system of value for his or her contribution to any film. This connection to the audience is on an affective or emotional level that defies clear-cut quantification of its economic import. In recent film history, the star's wage has become one of the principal costs of production. For a star of the first order, such as Arnold Schwarzenegger, Tom Cruise, Meryl Streep, or Dustin Hoffman, contracts of between $2 million and $5 million are not uncommon. Over and above salary, a star may also receive a percentage of the box-office receipts.[18] In such an arrangement, not only is the star guaranteed a very high salary, he or she is also permitted to be involved in the creation of surplus value or profits, like the corporation itself. The star has become an individualized corporate entity, with recognizable brand and hoped-for audience loyalty. Kevin

Costner's involvement in *Waterworld* (1995) best articulates this corporate quality of the star. As production costs soared, Costner renegotiated his fee of $12.5 million by forfeiting his 15 percent share of
the gross receipts over and above his fee in order that the film would
actually be completed as planned. In this instance, through his financial stake in the film's production, the star operated in virtual part-
nership with Universal Studios.[19]

The capacity of the star to conform to the form of a company entails the celebrity's commitment to the organization of capital and
the general operation of the film industry. The independence of the
current top film celebrities is built on a long history of film studio development of their stars. From the 1920s to the 1950s, the studio
system of star-making machinery was in place. By 1930, the consoli-
dation of the industry established five major studios and three minor
studios in Hollywood. The major studios not only produced films but
also distributed them and owned the exhibiting theaters. Their performers, particularly the women, were often signed at young ages to
long binding contracts that stipulated they could appear only in their
own studios' productions. As young performers, their transcendent
power and related connection to the audience, as discussed above,
were virtually nonexistent. They depended on the studios to provide
them with venues and film "vehicles" in order to establish their unique
economic value. Not surprisingly, the studios always had surpluses
of potential stars who could be featured or relegated to the filmic version of a chorus line. The stable of actor/stars affiliated with each studio defined the dependent relationship any new Hollywood actor had
to his or her studio. Once an actor was able to establish an affective
relationship with the movie audience, he or she could enjoy the bene-
fits of being an economic center of the studio system. The film actor
in this process exited the private world of studio politics and entered
the public world of film exhibition.

Agents representing actor/stars since Laemmle have worked at the
interstices of the private and public realms of the movie industry. The
agent's fundamental intention is to construct the star as a clearly separate economic entity, quite distinct from any individual film and any
studio. The agent intervenes in the typical employer-employee relationship that the studio attempts to maintain to articulate the closer
relationship the star has to the audience compared with either the
movie or the studio. The agent actively works to shift the economic

ground so that it is centered on the public construction of the star and away from the studio's original construction and investment in the star. At times, the work of the agent may be in concert with the publicity and promotional work of the film studio. However, when contracts are negotiated, the public nature of the film celebrity's power is the working space of the agent.

The centrality of the Hollywood agent in the separation of the star from the exigencies of the studio is significant. The way in which the film industry now operates with its most famous celebrities demonstrates a general industrywide consciousness of the star's independence and closer connection to an audience. Films often become centered on the star in terms of narrative and financing. For instance, if a star of the stature (i.e., audience allure) of Mel Gibson agrees to be involved in a proposed picture, then the financing of the production becomes all the more realizable. The story may also be adjusted to conform to the public's representation of the star, so that the audience's expectations are met. The film character and the star's public personality may be coordinated so that a continuity is maintained and reinforced.

The building of the public personality of the film celebrity is the work of the agent, whose job it is to forge an independent relationship between the star and the audience. The activity of creating a celebrity from film involves coordinating the reading of the star by the audience outside of the film. The character in the film may set the heroic type that the star embodies, but the relationship to the real person behind the image completes the construction of the celebrity. It is the solving by the audience of the enigma of the star's personality that helps formulate the celebrity: the audience wants to know the authentic nature of the star beyond the screen. Through reading the extratextual reports about a particular film celebrity, the audience knits together a coherent though always incomplete celebrity identity.[20]

Film celebrities' identities, which are made by the audience from the material of interviews, media reports, images, and films, are invested with conceptions of freedom, independence, and individuality. The stars' luxurious lifestyles, many depicted in a syndicated television program devoted entirely to this theme (Robin Leach's *Lifestyles of the Rich and Famous*), would seem to distance the film celebrities from the everyday experiences of their audiences. And, indeed, the stars of the 1920s had an ethereal quality that placed them quite above their audiences. However, with the institutionalization of the Hollywood press corps and the related growth in the extratextual discourse circulated about film stars, film celebrities became a blend of the everyday and the exceptional. The combination of familiarity and extraordinariness gives the celebrity its ideological power. One can see the construction of this unity in the type of acting and performing that has been central to the institution of film.

The Extraordinary and the Ordinary in Film Performance

Once the narrative film came to represent the mainstream of commercial cinema during the second decade of the twentieth century, film performance became principally a form of professional acting. The decline of the documentary, the sports film, and the newsreel as the centers of the filmic experience was furthered by the growth of radio as the preferred new medium for the discourses of news and information. Film acting, however, was perceived to represent the "real" and the "natural" (which are, of course, cultural constructs) to a much greater degree than stage acting. Part of this naturalistic aura surrounding film acting is derived from film's documentarian origins. The theater, with its proscenium, its staging, the clear artifice of the presentation, and the projection of the actors, is not physically present in the film. Instead, we are given an apparently less constructed scene; the camera takes us, for example, into the living room of a house after showing its exterior. In concert with this conception of the naturalness of film and the artifice of the stage, it was generally believed that a good stage actor did not necessarily make a good film actor. The stage actor had to build the believability of his or her character, had to become the character. To stage critics, acting entailed creating a temporary artifice of character, and the artifice had to be discernible. The good film actor, on the other hand, was believed to be someone who did not use the craft and artifice of acting: he or she performed naturally. Film director D. W. Griffith chose his actors more on the basis of their appearance than for their acting ability. Sergei Eisenstein searched the streets to find the faces that would typify the characters in his scenarios. Qualities of beauty, youth, and stereotypical appearance became central to the profession of film acting to a degree they never achieved in stage acting. The ability to "not act" also became a valued commodity in the search for film stars.

Attention to the naturalness of the film performer is also connected somewhat to the historical development of acting in the nineteenth and early twentieth centuries. Richard Sennett has chronicled the transformation of stage performance from the eighteenth to the nineteenth century, and he notes that in the eighteenth century, actors assumed clear-cut social positions and classes on stage, particularly in melodrama. Thus, stereotypes of performance were common; particular actors became expert at portraying particular types of classes or characters. In the nineteenth century, great acting rested on the development of a unique interpretation of the character; in other words, actors, such as Frederic Le Maitre in Paris, achieved renown for their ability to personalize their roles and transcend the text. They were thought to possess some superior quality because they could shock the audience with their ability to act naturally and therefore overcome the limitations of the characters they played.[21] The personalization of the acting profession grew gradually from the late eighteenth century throughout the nineteenth century. As Elizabeth Burns points out, the practice of linking actors' names with those of the characters they played began in the eighteenth century. As a result, audiences would see Garrick's Hamlet or Irving's Shylock; the self and the personality of the self became clear factors in the understanding of the theatrical text.[22]

In the early twentieth century, the acting techniques of Stanislavsky were gaining influence, roughly simultaneous to the narrative development of film. Although it was another three decades before Stanislavsky's techniques were formulated into the Method school of acting in the United States, their investment with the construction of the self through the personalization of the character matched much of the development of Hollywood film acting. The Method technique demands that the actor internalize the psychological makeup of the character in order to achieve a more natural portrayal.[23] This technique was in opposition to the character acting tradition of the British and American stage. The theatrical tradition of the actor's observing behavior and accent from the world around him or her could be seen as developing the character from the outside in; in this technique, meticulous attention is paid to manifest signs of class and habit. Method acting, in contrast, is psychologically deep when it is taken to its extreme of character development.

The salience of Method acting for film stemmed from three factors.[24] The first is linked nominally to technological distinctions. Because film deals with faces and expressions in close-up, it made the grand and sweeping gestures of stage performance look oddly inauthentic. The close-up possibilities of film psychologized and internalized the meanings of filmic texts. With the advent of sound film, the highly developed and resonating stage voice, the very grain of that voice, also appeared unnatural and forced. New ranges and new constructions of character intimacy were possible when voice projection to a theatrical audience was no longer necessary. This relationship between technological change and the personalization of the screen performer is not simply one of cause and effect. The use of film technology is positioned around the articulation of certain kinds of powerful discourses. Film, as a type of mass media, was involved in the expression of forms of individuality that were possible within modern mass society. Film provided a channel for the proliferation of a discourse on individuality and personality. The technology of film is therefore connected to the expression of this discourse on the forms of modern individuality.[25]

The second factor leading to the relative dominance of the Method form of acting in film is that the technique allows for the expression of the personalities of the actors involved in the production. On its own, this may not seem to be a very great consideration, but if one thinks of the various interests involved in the production of a film, one can see the impetus behind constructing characterizations that transcend the individual film. As mentioned above, the film star's agent is actively working to create a unique use value and exchange value for the film actor that can be represented. Barry King has argued quite effectively that the actor as celebrity or star expresses a value that is quite separate from the individual film production.[26] Thus, the film star represents the wresting of control of the production away from the producers and the directors. If a director, like Griffith and Eisenstein, among others, chooses leads on the basis of age, beauty, or other physical features, and not on the ability of the performers to act, then the control of the production rests with the director. His or her ability to edit, to construct the scenario, to juxtapose a series of images into the story diminishes the productivity and use value of the actor to the finished product. However, if the uniqueness of the personality of the star is critical to the success of the film production, then control of the film moves toward the star's perceived interests. Method acting allows for the permutation that the internal expression of a character can also be a playing out of the psychological dimensions of the star him- or herself. According to King, this is imbricated in the control of the economics of production and the division of labor in the film industry: "Under such circumstances, a potential politics of persona emerges insofar as the bargaining power of the actor, or more emphatically, the star, is materially affected by the *degree* of his or her reliance on the apparatus (the image), as opposed to self-located resources (the person) in the construction of persona."[27]

King goes on to conclude that "impersonation," which is the ability to play a particular character, becomes less valued in the economies of film production than the capacity for "personification" — the ability to construct a continuing personal and individual mark in each film role.[28] He explains why:

> The ramifications are complex, but basically personification serves the purposes of containing competition amongst the tele-film cartel companies by representing the star's contribution as resting on his or her private properties as a person.... The centrality of personae (stars) as an index of value provides a form of control — shifting or ever threatening to shift, signifiers from the actor to the apparatus — over the detail of performance in favour of those who have control over the text.[29]

The third factor leading to the interiorization of character and actor in films is connected to the audience construction of the celebrity. Method acting has deepened the significance of the mundane, the everyday lives of relatively ordinary people. In coordination with the conception that film acting does not involve the abstraction and impersonation that stage acting utilizes, the audience is positioned much closer to the enigma of the identity of the film celebrity. Moreover, the psychological identity of the film actor is more central to understanding any of the film's texts. Actors such as Marlon Brando and James Dean were able to build careers on combining the interiorization of Method acting with the search for their true selves. They were able to include the audience in this search for the ur-text of their star personalities.

The Audience's Pleasure and Play and the Construction of Significance with Intimacy and Enigma

The relationship that the audience builds with the film celebrity is configured through a tension between the possibility and impossibility of knowing the authentic individual. The various mediated constructions of the film celebrity ensure that whatever intimacy is permitted between the audience and the star is purely at the discursive level. The desire and pleasure are derived from this clear separation of the material reality of the star as living being from the fragments of identity that are manifested in films, interviews, magazines, pinup posters, autographs, and so on. Depending on the level of commitment of the audience member, certain types of fragments or traces of identity are deemed adequate. For some, the characters of the films themselves, which among them construct their own intertextual framework of the celebrity's identity, are quite sufficient. For others, those called fanatics or fans, the materiality of identity must be reinforced through the acquisition of closer representations of existence and identity. The autograph and the pinup poster epitomize the committed fan of a film celebrity. Belonging to a fan club entails an investment into the maintenance of a coherent identity, as members circulate information about the celebrity that for the members establishes a somewhat separate and distinctive episteme concerning the star's true nature. Recent work on fan culture has articulated the relative affective investment that can be part of the cultural experience of the star for the audience. Fandom can actively transform the meaning of stars well beyond the material presented in magazines and newspapers.[30]

In his book on film stars, Morin lists some of the requests that fans have made of their favorite celebrities. Some ask for locks of hair, others for small possessions that will allow the fan to enter the private sphere of the star through the fetish object. Most ask for photographs. Some are driven to ask their favorite stars' advice on their own personal matters.[31] According to Margaret Thorpe, in the 1930s and 1940s a studio typically received up to fifteen thousand fan letters a week. A first-class star would have received directly three hundred letters a week.[32]

The range of audience participation in the construction of the film celebrity sign is wide and varied. Nevertheless, stars possess a general allure in their combination of the everyday and the extraordinary that is modalized through a discourse on intimacy and enigma. The ordinary elements of the film star are important as a marked entrance point for the audience to play with kinds of identity and identification. Since its inception, the film industry has produced stars who have emerged from apparently "normal" backgrounds. The mythology of stardom that has been circulated in the trade literature since Laemmle's Biograph Girl media event is the possibility that anyone can be a star. Because of the sustained focus on external appearance, as opposed to acting ability, the film star appeared to be chosen quite randomly. Merit was secondary to luck and circumstance. In this way, the Hollywood film industry perpetuated a myth of democratic access. The concept of merit and ability was transposed into the language of character and the personal history of the star. Humble beginnings, hard work, and honesty were the extratextual signs of the film celebrity that supported this myth of the democratic art. The extensive discourse on the stars' personal and private lives often was constructed on how fame and fortune could corrupt the ordinary human being housed in the star personality. This theme became one of the central film story lines of a progressively self-reflexive Hollywood. From *42nd Street* to three versions of *A Star Is Born,* Hollywood reinforced its anyone-can-make-it mythology.

In contradistinction to the democratic nature of access, the image of the film star expressed the inaccessibility and extraordinary quality of the celebrity lifestyle. In double senses of the word, the images of wealth were typically *classless,* and in this way were compatible with the democratic ideology that surrounded Hollywood movies, despite their oligopolistic economic structure. The mansions of the movie stars had all the signs of wealth and prestige but none of the cultural capital to reign in the appearance of excess. The swimming pools, with their unique shapes, the immodest and therefore grandiose architecture pillaged from countless traditions without cultural contextualization, and the elaborate grounds and gates were all signs of the nouveau riche, a class excluded from the dominant culture because of its inability to coordinate the signs of wealth. Movie stars' prestige was built on the signs of consumer capitalism, and their decadence and excess were celebrations of the spoils of an ultimate consumer lifestyle. Their wealth, generated through the expansion of leisure as an industry and the entertainment consumer as a widening domain of subjectivity, was cause for celebration — not cultural responsibility.

To use Bourdieu's typology of taste and distinction, the movie star's ostentatious presentation of wealth exemplified an aesthetic that was obvious and overdone. In opposition, those who possessed not only capital but cultural and intellectual capital constructed their distinctive taste in terms of abstraction and distance from these more obvious and overt expressions of wealth.[33]

The power of the film celebrity's aesthetic of wealth and leisure in the twentieth century can not be seen to be static. With its close connection to the construction of consumer lifestyles, the film celebrity's forays into recreational pursuits helped define the parameters of pleasure through consumption for all segments of society. Perhaps the best example of this expansive and proliferating power to influence the entire socius has been the growing centrality of the Hollywood image of the healthy body. Tanned skin had been seen traditionally as evidence of physical labor, specifically farm labor. Although there may have been a bucolic connotation to the image of the tanned and brawny farmhand, it contained no further signification of an easy, leisurely life. To be tanned was evidence that one had engaged in hard work under the sun. Hollywood film stars helped construct a new body aesthetic as they attempted to look healthier under the intense lighting of their film shoots. The activity of suntanning achieved a glamorous connotation because it now indicated one had the time to do virtually nothing but lie in the sun. The film star worked in this domain of breaking down and reconstructing conceptions of distinctions. Thus, certain expensive or class-based outdoor sports, such as yachting and tennis, provided a conduit between these new body images of health and fitness that demanded time and energy in the sun and the other moneyed classes. Leisure and wealth became in the twentieth century associated with having a tan and a well-toned body; however, these new signs, appropriated from the laboring class, had to have been achieved through sports and hobbies, and not work.[34]

The classlessness of film celebrities despite their clear wealth aligned them as a group with their audience. Their wealth, if thought of as an extrapolation of a consumer subjectivity, also aligned them with an ethos fostered in late capitalism. The construction of identity in the domains of consumption as opposed to production made the film star an image of the way in which a lifestyle/identity could be found in the domain of nonwork. The star, then, to borrow from Ewen's study of the development of a general consumer consciousness in the twentieth century through advertising and general business objectives, performed as a "consumption ideal": a representative of the modern way of life.[35] Anyone has access to the goods of the large department stores, and therefore can play in this democratic myth of identity construction through consumption.

The chasm between the type of lifestyle constructed by the film star and that constructed by the audience is continually filled in by the rumors, gossip, and stories that circulate in newspapers and magazines concerning the complex and tragic lives led in Hollywood. In early Hollywood, the reported excesses of lifestyle and success were treated in a disciplinary manner by the press. If one thinks of a film star as a consumption ideal, then failures and tragedies were the results of a consumer lifestyle that was incongruous with the personal roots of the star. Much of the writing of the personal life stories of the stars, particularly the form of gossip writing that focused on failure, emphasized the traps of success. The discourse on film star tragedy, then, was concerned with the reconciliation of the personal and the psychological with the manner and means of consumption. The root cause for the diversion of lifestyle from the person's true nature was the instant success gained by the film star. The disciplinary morals offered by these scandals of the stars for the audience concerned the need to match one's psychological personality with an appropriate lifestyle and consumption identity. The stars represented extreme constructions of lifestyle. The audience member had to work toward some kind of balance. Finally, the audience also learned about the essential human frailties and personality types of these distant stars. Despite their larger-than-life presence on screen, film stars were essentially human and covered the gamut of personality types.

Summary

The film celebrity as a general discourse occupies a central position in the development of the twentieth-century celebrity, and it is for this reason I have provided a rather lengthy genealogy of its formation. Because of cinema's history, covering the entire twentieth century, and because the cinematic apparatus's development and growth coincided with the growth and extension of consumer capitalism, the film celebrity has provided a way in which the discourses of individualism, freedom, and identity have been articulated in modern society. With the film star's relative nonattachment to material forms of production because of his or her work solely in the manufacture of images, the discourse on and about screen stars was particularly concerned with the manner of consumption and the associated construction of lifestyles. The discourse on film celebrities and their consumption was also integrated into a study of personality, character, and general psychological profile. Through various extratextual sources, the celebrities provided the ground for the debate concerning the way in which new patterns of consumption could be organized to fit the innate patterns of personality.

In the rest of this chapter, I examine a contemporary film celebrity in depth to reveal the way in which these various discourses are modalized through a particular celebrity sign. Within the discussion of the intertextual and extratextual elements in the sign/text construction of the celebrity, I develop a typology of celebrity and audience subjectivity as it relates to film.

Tom Cruise: The Construction of a Contemporary Film Celebrity

The Channels of Knowledge

Tom Cruise is classified by a variety of sources as a movie star. To achieve this status, Cruise articulates through various texts and representations that he possesses certain qualities that are not possessed by others. He exits the realm of the everyday and moves into the representational world of the public sphere. For Cruise, the filmic text, where he performs various roles that are constructed into clearcut narratives, becomes the primary means by which he becomes identifiable as a recognizable public figure. Surrounding the particular moments of each film release are the intersections of several strategic discourses that work to construct the celebrity quality of the film star. On one level, the agency that represents Tom Cruise, along with the corporation and production company that has produced the film, attempts to promote an organized conception of Tom Cruise that is connected with the specific release of the film. Cruise, then, is both contained by the package of the film and is the package that works to draw the attention of the press to consider the film significant or of interest. The film star works in the arena of publicity that predates the exhibition date of the film.

The Origins of Film Stardom: The Physical Performer

The specific constructions that are strategically operated in the release of a film can be likened to Richard DeCordova's historical categories of the development of the star persona.[36] In the early twentieth century, audience knowledge about the performers in cinema was limited. Thus, we see the development of monikers that were connected to their performances on screen rather than their real names. Film actors were identified by the audience and the film industry, as mentioned above, through their physical characteristics. We can call this first category of identification, in line with DeCordova's analysis, the *physical performer:* what is identified by industry and audience are the physical characteristics that make him or her unique in the field of film performers. Thus, this is a discourse that emphasizes beauty or lack thereof, the performer's nose, smile, eyes, entire body type. It is an objectification of the performer that is more often than not metonymic; that is, one element/feature represents the entire performer and connects his or her reality from one film to the next. The metonymic process should not be seen as emerging solely from the industry or the audience. The industry attempts to read the public, based on a variety of polling techniques as well as less scientifically and more culturally defined conceptions of beauty and attraction. The historical organization of this pretesting can be captured by the screen test, where a performer is filmed to determine his or her commodity potential and value to the studio. If the test is successful, then the performer is released in a feature film and marketed as a starlet, a rising star. Audience reaction to the new performer is fully tested after the release of his or her first films. A determination of star quality is determined from this rereading of the film's audience, general public reaction, and the associated press coverage of the individual performer.

Cruise as Physical Performer

In the transformation of DeCordova's categories into an individual celebrity text, one can see that the construction of the physical performer emerges at the beginning of any film celebrity's career. At that point, extratextual knowledge of the actor is limited. Even his or her on-screen presence is often constrained to only moments of screen time—a newcomer is not often the star of his or her early films. Nevertheless, there is a particular quality or group of qualities that become the way in which the actor becomes recognizable as a specific type. When the celebrity is identified in these physical terms, there is the risk that he or she will become typecast, or arrested in the formation of celebrity status and cast in roles based only on some clear-cut stereotypical image/quality.

Tom Cruise's emergence as a film actor and star is first connected to the physicality of his performance. The category with which Cruise was identified, by both industry and audience, was that of youth. In his second film, *Taps* (1981), Cruise, although originally cast for a much smaller part, was able (according to the biographical information made significant when he began to star in films later in his career), because of his apparent innate screen presence, to expand his role into something much larger and more significant. In the film he plays a gung-ho, arms-obsessed cadet at a military academy. His role presents youth as pure action: unthinking instead of contemplative, assured, confident, and narrow-minded in his choice of actions. His character, David Shawn, is willing to murder and quite willing to die. All of this is done with a certain bravado that is expressed in Cruise's use of his smile and grin, something that has become a trademark in his movement to celebrity status. In terms of the film's character, the smile and the grin indicate the reckless insanity of the personality. It was with this role that Cruise's name moved into the popular press.

Cruise's film debut was also in a film designated specifically for a youth audience. In *Endless Love* (1981), a Franco Zeffirelli-directed film about modern obsessive teenage love, Cruise plays a small role that is not mentioned in any of the reviews. What is significant is his position once again in terms of categories of youth. The film industry worked to establish a legion of youthful stars in the 1980s. Connected with their rise were several coming-of-age films as well as the construction of a group of actors who came to be known through the popular press as the Hollywood brat pack.[37] As a market segment, the youth audience was considered to be the very center of the film industry. The development of films that focused on generational themes, and through those narratives established territory for the elevation of certain young actors to stardom, could be seen as a general industrial strategy.[38] Cruise was part of this organization of the film industry around its principal exhibition market.

In these earliest incarnations, Cruise possesses a character type that is closely aligned with his own physical look. He is a physical performer, and our knowledge of his private world is virtually nonexistent. He is characterized by his engendering young male handsomeness. As well, he must be structured and must structure himself into the construction of filmic youthful maleness. The gendering of his physical presence, then, is carried out in reference to past icons who define what makes a male film star. He is thus engendered into a cultural pattern of representation.

What this means is that Cruise, as a new potential star, is mapped onto the types of male stars that predated his appearance. In the postwar period, the intersection of male and youth has been represented by past stars as confused rebellion. The images of Marlon Brando and James Dean, along with Elvis Presley, established this dominant construction of male youth. No doubt the extratextual elements that revealed aspects of their personal lives also enhanced the images of these stars beyond their filmic type. Generally, however the consistency of character type in their films operates as the primary focus for the rearticulation of filmic maleness in future male stars. Cruise's construction of male "physical performer" must reply to the way in which these past stars exhibited strength and presence. Fundamentally, we can see that Dean, Brando, and even, to a degree, Paul Newman represent the interiorization of male power: there is a repressed fury in their performances that is represented by their brooding character portrayals and their bursts of aggression and violence.

These past film stars, then, operate as icons or archetypes that work to define the organization of new types of stars in their originary or emergent forms as physical performers. Cruise's physical performance must also work in response to the antiheroic male film stars of the 1970s: De Niro, Pacino, and Hoffman.[39] Because of their representations of ethnicity and of the working class and underclass, the designation of heroic qualities to these stars seems a misnomer. Nevertheless, they represent film stars: they are instrumental in the organization of film investment capital, they can demand high payment fees as well as a percentage of box-office revenues, and they are easily and readily recognizable in the public sphere. Tom Cruise's emergence as a physical performer, then, must negotiate these filmic identities to establish a certain continuity in the construction of the male film star and the uniqueness or differentiation of his particular example of the lineage. What this entails for the emerging star is that an attachment to the cultural icons of male representation produced by filmdom must be made evident so that subsequent extension of the icon can be made in the growth of the individual star.

What is interesting is that Cruise's first six films are intensely focused on youth and, more or less, on rebellion. In *The Outsiders* (1983), Cruise is involved in midwestern youth gang encounters between the rich and the poor. In the first film that features Cruise in the lead role, *Losin' It* (1983), a generic low-budget male-oriented teenage sex comedy, the emphasis is on loss of virginity, adventure in Tijuana, and a red convertible sports car. His next two movies establish the clear nature of the physical performer Tom Cruise. In *Risky Business* (1983), Cruise plays an upper-class teenager who plays out his fantasies when his parents go out of town and leave him alone for the first time. Finally, in *All the Right Moves* (1983), Cruise plays a very talented quarterback for a working-class town's high school football team. His success on the field is seen as his way out of the dead-end setting of the steel factory community.

As mentioned above, all of these films provide a unified theme concerning Tom Cruise as performer. All of them emphasize his youth. By implication, this emphasis on youth also emphasizes his youthful body and face. Cruise's screen presence, then, is constructed specifically around his embodiment of male beauty. His confidence in movement is part of this construction. His athletic build becomes another marker of his success as engendered representation of filmic male. Iconically, Cruise is connected to stars who represent the very mainstream of American film beauty. In the tradition of Newman and Redford, Cruise embodies Americanness as opposed to some Other of ethnicity. In terms of appearance, he is neither exotic nor enigmatic.

The emergence of the film celebrity is dependent on this original construction of the physical performer, where the actor is celebrated as a "type." The actor remains relatively anonymous except for these screen images. There is no deepening of the meaning of the actor beyond the screen presentations. However, the screen presentations provide a certain redundancy of image, an overcoding that is directed toward a decoding by the audience of the physical performer's reason for being celebrated, the material that can be used to determine the legitimacy of his elevated public stature.

There is a danger that the process of development of the screen star may be arrested in terms of what I have labeled as the actor as pure physical performer. In such a case, the categorization of "type" overcomes the actor's possibility of creating subjective differences in character portrayals. If the type is replicable by other performers, then the inherent value of the emerging screen star is limited. One can see this operation of the economics of film production in relationship to stardom most starkly in the relatively rapid positioning and replacing of female screen presentations. For example, in the James Bond series of films, there has been a consistency in the actors who have played Bond. Sean Connery became synonymous with the Bond persona through the 1960s, as did Roger Moore in the 1970s and 1980s. In contrast, the women in these films have been constructed to be infinitely replaceable, because the nature of their fame is built entirely on their physical performance. The basis of their physical performance is dependent on their ability to present alluring images of the female body. Although the Bond character clearly represents a "type," the patterning of that type engages an elaboration of performance beyond a clear aesthetic of beauty. Built into the type is a construction of masculine allure that permits a greater degree of action, power, and will. The very legitimate characterization of the many female actors who have appeared in the Bond films as the "Bond girls" underlines the film industry's systematic maintenance of a female stardom stalled and often imprisoned within the confines of the category of the physical performer.[40]

The Picture Personality

The progression from physical performer to "picture personality" is the principal subject of DeCordova's in-depth analysis of the early history of screen stardom.[41] It is also analogous to the progression of the individual star from clearly formulated representation of "type" on the screen to the substantiation of the character type through the development of a public profile of the actor that is fundamentally extratextual in the contemporary moment. The key difference between the picture personality and the physical performer in the past was that the actor's name, as opposed to the character's name or type, became recognized by the audience and was used to link films together to provide a consistency around the actor's public persona. As DeCordova reveals in his reading of the popular press of the early twentieth century, the first biographical profiles of the screen stars of the 1910s were focused on this link between their screen presence and their personal lives: a homologous private world was established that would not challenge their filmic characters. It is interesting to see in the genealogy of the construction of current film celebrity that the same substantiation occurs as the physical performer begins to be constructed as a public personality. The example of Tom Cruise's transformation is exemplary.

Tom Cruise as Picture Personality

For Cruise, the line of demarcation between physical performer and recognizable screen personality, which identifies his representation beyond the screen, is drawn with the release of the feature film *Risky Business*.[42] Through this film, Cruise generates a great number of newspaper and magazine articles, not about the film, but about the star. The process of working out the internal nature of Tom Cruise begins. Articles start appearing first in youth-oriented magazines.[43] The film role becomes the basis for determining the real Tom Cruise, as something of a homology is constructed. Cruise, in publicity photos, plays with the image portrayed in the film—his public image becomes conflated with the Ray-Ban sunglasses used extensively by the character. For more mainstream magazines and reviewers, the movie provides the centerpiece for discussion. In these magazines, Cruise is interpreted as representing not only a role, but a generation of youth through his role and his "cool" attitude, best articulated through his use of the Ray-Bans and his relative detachment and distance from indicating the significance of experience. Again there is a conflation of the role with the public world; a connection is made to the resonance of the star's image and deportment in the film and life with the audience segment that has celebrated the film. The image of youth proliferates in other ways, as the look of the star becomes the way in which "Youth" and the interests of youth are represented in various forms of mediated culture.

Critical at this point in the development of the film celebrity is the necessity not to present contradictory evidence concerning the nature of Tom Cruise. His "real" persona is, at this stage, very much connected to that portrayed on the screen. Thus, the elaborate extratextual discourse on Cruise that appears in newspapers and magazines works to bolster the new screen personality. Cruise's own publicists also guard the integrity of the screen persona in an effort to maintain Cruise as a significant and marketable commodity. His commodity status is dependent still on the screen presentation, or what the character on the screen embodies. The production company, the studio, and the star's developing team of publicity agents begin to manage the consistency of the image. In this way, Cruise establishes a new variation on the male film celebrity, one that builds on the previous constructions but provides markers of distinction and differentiation. The form of those distinctions relates to the way in which a new "structure of feeling" envelopes the production of new film celebrities.[44]

This new structure of feeling lends a certain vagueness to the way a new film celebrity emerges. The vagueness relates to the manner in which the audience may interpret this constructed subjectivity embodied in the celebrity as well as the temporality of that construction, where the concrete reality of the celebrity is grounded in the moment. Through his screen image, Cruise has been positioned as part of a new generation of male stardom that has been connected to the way in which youth has rethought their imbrication in the social world. We can see in this formative version of Cruise as a celebrity sign/text that there are certain elements that provide a correlation of Cruise to this new attitude.

Youth — which connoted rebellion in previous film stars — is reconstructed through Cruise: youth is correlated with confidence and savvy. The difference between youth and the adult world in this new configuration is not based principally on challenging the models of success and value in contemporary society, as previous youthful male heroes emphasized; rather, the Cruise persona makes coherent the inherent value of a higher sensitivity to the way in which the system of success works, so that one can use it more effectively to gain personal success. The connection of youth and confidence through Cruise's persona can be characterized as a celebration of personal will, not to transform the system, but to move smoothly through the system to occupy already designated positions of power and influence. Cruise's screen personality has had a certain consistency since 1983. The film texts have worked to reinforce the reconstruction of this new conception of the power of youth, youthful action and agency. It is significant that the character in *Risky Business,* which has been so formative for Cruise's public personality, is depicted as a relatively well-off, probably upper-middle-class teenager. It is the type of image that indicates a clear connection and affinity to forms of cultural and economic capital and the forms of influence they imply. Most of Cruise's subsequent films rarely represent images of the upper classes; but they do present Cruise's characters as embodying the outward features and appearances of wealth as well as clear aspirations to assert their apparent natural right to be part of the wealthy. In most cases the films emphasize the ease with which Cruise can become comfortably successful.

In the filmic texts, this relationship to the ease of success is manifested around either sports/athleticism or the managing of sophisticated technology. In all cases, Cruise is something of a natural, but also a natural risk taker who goes beyond the bounds of the technology or game to demonstrate ultimate human dominance of will. In *All the Right Moves,* Cruise is a high school football hero who, through his sheer talent, can transcend his humble origins. In the enormously successful *Top Gun* (1986), Cruise portrays a character whose nickname is Maverick. He is chosen for an elite fighter squadron because of his capacity to supersede the talents of a technically good pilot. Cruise has not had to work hard to develop this skill; he manifests a natural affinity for handling this technical hardware.

Reinforcements of Cruise's screen personality can be seen in other films. In *The Color of Money* (1986), a more sophisticated film than his earlier vehicles, Cruise plays a naturally gifted pool player who is relatively unaware of the more subtle techniques he could use to win money at the game until he meets an older pool hustler played by Paul Newman. There are a number of layers of meanings in this film, which I will return to later in this chapter. What is significant with reference to the construction of a screen personality is that there is a consistency in the representation of Tom Cruise between *The Color of Money* and his earlier films. The organization of his public persona coheres among these various filmic texts. A particular and idiosyncratic celebrity sign is clearly established that intersects with a given set of values concerning youth, success, and appearance.[45]

Top Gun established the stability of the commodity aspect of Cruise's celebrity sign. It signaled its differentiation from other constructions of stardom that predated Cruise and its clear relationship to a general restructuring of the attitudes of youth and success in the 1980s. It also heralded the power of this particular configuration of screen personality to produce, virtually on its own construction of character, a successful film. Two years following the release of *Top Gun* and *The Color of Money*, Cruise starred in a film that demonstrated his commodity power in the construction of audiences. *Cocktail* (1988), in its opening scenes, seems to provide a narrative continuity for the character, as if this character in this distinct movie has, in fact, emerged like Tom Cruise from *Top Gun*. In the opening sequence, we see Cruise as Brian Flanagan being dropped by his army buddies to catch a bus to "New York": he has completed his army service and is about to go on and achieve fame and fortune in the big city. The Flanagan character in this film never separates from our image of the Cruise star and, in fact, the film — through camera angles, obsessive shots of the Cruise smile and grin, and a celebration of Cruise's body and movement — actively plays and integrates the Cruise screen personality into the meaning of the text. Cruise as Flanagan becomes very quickly a bartending star, which allows him to act within the narrative as the star. The character is thronged by adoring fans in several sequences in the film. These fans, the bar patrons, are predominantly women, and their adulation of Flanagan for his acrobatic bartending skills is connected through the film text to the sexual aura of Cruise as male star. He acknowledges their looks and responds with greater histrionics. His success is further measured in the film by his success in sleeping with women. The women bar patrons in the filmic text represent for the producers of the movie a construction of the form of female adulation perceived to exist in the film audience (the public) for Cruise himself. Through an uncomplicated plot, Cruise's character is constructed as a divided personality, where physical prowess and beauty become separated from the moral integrity of character. The film ends with a reconciliation of the Cruise character, so that his outer beauty is matched by his inner morality and integrity. With this unification, the plot is resolved and Cruise as Flanagan is permitted his version of success: he owns his own bar and possesses his own woman. In terms of a developing screen personality, the meaning of Cruise's celebrity sign is also unified: his physical attractiveness is constructed to be contained by his strength of personality.

Cruise's 1990 film *Days of Thunder* represents the triumph of his "picture personality," or the overcoming of the filmic text with the consistency of his form of public personality/celebrity. The actual filmic text is surrounded with extratextual detail about Cruise and this very personal project. Magazines, in their efforts to anticipate the success of the film at the box office, provide this deepening of the significance of the film before the film's release. These anticipatory stories contain little analysis of the content of the film—the dearth of information ensures that what is discussed coheres with the strategies of the publicity agents and the production company behind the film. In this particular film production, the organization of production is inevitably connected to Tom Cruise's management.

What we find in this reportage is the building of a homology between the film content and the person and personality of Cruise. For instance, we learn that Cruise's interest in auto racing stems from his involvement with actor and professional race car driver Paul Newman during the making of *The Color of Money*.[46] Although this interest is outside any filmic text, it is inside the world of public personalities and celebrities—it is in the realm of public knowledge. *Days of Thunder* works to maintain the coherence of personality on-screen and off-screen. Again, this personality emerges fundamentally in the realm of filmic texts. We also are told that Cruise has indeed become a respectable racer. In several articles, his track time is mentioned as the fastest nonprofessional lap clocked at the track.[47] The truth of the movie text is borne out in the "real" Cruise. Likewise, we are made aware in this extratextual discourse that Cruise is credited with the "story idea." This connection is further substantiated in the film's opening credits.

The extratextual discourse that is coordinated with the release of the film is organized specifically around the star and the star's relationship to the content of the film. Several interviews and features are written on the set. One female writer centers her story on her experiences as a passenger with Cruise in the stock car used in the film. What is being articulated in this story is the proximity of the writer to the "real" Cruise. Although no real interview was conducted, the writer provides evidence for the establishment of the real Cruise personality. Very few words were spoken; instead, there was the evident action and experience of driving at high speed around a track. Cruise, like his filmic characters in most of his previous movies, is a man of action. Words then become extraneous to the experience.[48] This story also provides ample evidence that the film character and Cruise have certain common interests and common characteristics. The separation of the private world of Tom Cruise and the public world of his filmic characters is not constructed. The screen personality predominates in the decoding of the Cruise celebrity sign.

Forms of Transgression: Establishing the Autonomous Nature of the Film Celebrity Sign

In the intense construction of a screen personality, the star builds, in effect, an overcoded representation of him- or herself. This has a certain utility for the recirculation of the screen personality in future films. With Tom Cruise, we can see this most evidently in films like *Cocktail* and *Days of Thunder,* where he reinvents variations of his previous performances. There continues to be the risk, however, that, as in the category of the physical performer, the screen personality will be arrested in his or her construction of a type, even though that type has been particularized and deepened by the actor into a coherent personality.

The maintenance of celebrity status for the film actor involves what I call transgression. DeCordova asserts that the development of stardom is related to the way in which Hollywood actors of the 1920s became the object of intense search for their meaning and coherence beyond the screen into their private lives. There was a proliferation of extratextual discourse concerning stars' lives and lifestyles, a discourse that began to fill the entertainment pages of newspapers and the motion picture magazines of the period.[49] To a degree, these exposés complemented the characterizations the screen actors represented in their films. There were other tendencies as well; for example, as described in the earlier discussion of the screen apparatus and its construction of stardom, the stars were depicted in all their grandeur. Their mansions and their extravagant lifestyles became objects of intense scrutiny. Their lives, though sometimes presented as ordinary in their rituals, were more regularly represented as quite extraordinary. DeCordova notes that stardom was intimately connected to this heightened scrutiny of the actors' private lives. From that close examination, a whole discourse on their transgressions of the norms of behavior became available to the public. Knowledge of their marriages and their divorces, hints of improper liaisons, and scandals that involved sexual indiscretions were commonplace in the press.[50] Film stars, like their theatrical forebears, began to be examples of how the perversions of wealth led to the breakdown of norms. The extratextual discourse that was intensely involved in mapping and charting the private lives of the stars provided a public discourse on intimacy and a constructed narrative or morality tale that implicitly expressed where the normative center of that discourse should be.

Transgressions that emerged from the search of the private lives of stars could lead to several scenarios for the construction of the film celebrity sign. In the instance of Fatty Arbuckle and his trial for manslaughter after one of his "famous" wild parties, the transgression virtually destroyed his power as a celebrity sign. The scandal represented too large a moral transgression.[51] Reporting on Hollywood life rarely reached this level of normative transgression. More typical in style were reports on affairs of the heart and, if those were impossible or implausible, revealing portraits of the everyday lives of the Hollywood stars. In these cases, the levels of revelation would not destroy any actor's sign as a celebrity. Rather, such reporting would function primarily to enhance actors' independence from their screen images. A common form of discussion of stars concerned how they lead normal lives, and in this way, their lives were in contradiction to their screen personalities' extraordinary lives. Another common area was the development of a discourse that served to deepen the text of the star as glamorous. Gossip columnists and Hollywood reporters for magazines and newspapers would chart the public appearances of the stars at restaurants, premieres, galas, and parties. Elizabeth Taylor's elaborate off-screen life, with marriages and divorces, appearances, charity involvement, and spectacular oscillations in weight and substance abuse, eventually made her completely autonomous as a public personality from her screen roles; indeed, her acting is now virtually forgotten in most articles about her. In all these cases, the actors achieve independence from the ways in which their films have painted them. I describe this transformation as a kind of transgression that builds into the star an autonomous subjectivity.

A second form of transgression must also occur in order for the film celebrity to construct a certain autonomy of his or her cultural sign: the celebrity must break the filmic code of his or her personality. The screen personality must be denaturalized into a code of acting. The roles chosen must break the conventional mold of the specific screen personality. This construction of the autonomous film star through acting is analogous to the historical development in the industry of invoking the code of acting to legitimate the cultural form. Producer Adolph Zukor's Famous Players Company, as discussed above, epitomizes this use of theatrical codes of acting to deepen the cultural significance of the filmic text. Zukor brought in stars of the theater to sell film to a "cultured" audience. In a similar fashion, screen stars, in order to demonstrate that they have abilities that go beyond the limited construction of their screen personalities, work to establish their abilities as actors by playing roles that transgress their previous sign constructions. For example, a comedy star like Robin Williams plays a dramatic role, and thereby works to establish his range as an actor. Female stars such as Farrah Fawcett in *The Burning Bed* and Jessica Lange in *Country* play roles that quite deliberately soil their images of beauty with mutilations of their faces and bodies as a way to transgress their "picture personalities," which have given them little room to maneuver and negotiate. The code of acting serves to deepen the celebrity text by demonstrating that skill and talent are elemental in the actor's fame.

Transgressions are also forms of risk in achieving autonomous status. The original connection to the audience is tampered with and the degree to which the star can transform, the limits within which an extratextual life can be tolerated by an audience, is an unknown. As Richard Dyer has emphasized, the trials and tribulations of an actor such as Judy Garland can reconfigure a new core audience that relates directly to the experiences of tragedy: gay culture's embrace of Garland as misunderstood, as maintaining a false exterior, is now the classic case of how extratextual transgressions can form a committed though differently motivated audience for a particular celebrity.[52]

Tom Cruise as Transgressor

The mode of transgression takes on a number of forms and narratives. For Cruise, as for other film celebrities, this implies an extensive study of his personal life. We begin to find out about the development of the Cruise personality outside of the filmic texts, in the images of mass-circulation magazines and newspapers. Biographical details begin appearing that establish the autonomy of the star personality. We learn that Cruise grew up dyslexic and continues to have difficulty reading scripts. We learn that this disability has led him to be a more determined and focused actor on the set. We are also told that, as he grew up with no father present and only sisters, Cruise is very protective of his family, in a very paternal way. Published profiles of Cruise have mentioned these kinds of private details since his appearances in *The Color of Money* and *Top Gun* in 1986.[53] It is also evident that there is a general lack of information about Tom Cruise. There have been very few interviews, and those few that have been granted have invariably been closely connected to the film project being promoted at that time. Both his agent, Mike Ovitz, and more particularly his public relations manager, Pat Kingsley, have protected Cruise; they conduct one of the most elaborate screening processes used by any Hollywood star before granting any interview.[54] There is also very little merchandise made and promoted that celebrates the star Cruise outside his film roles. For example, there are no posters that work to maintain and concretize Cruise's independent value from his films. In this way, Cruise maintains his aura, the enigmatic quality of the star.

It is only with his most recent work that Cruise's maintenance of image control has been broken. Various celebrity-attended functions, the work of the paparazzi, and gossip columnists, among others, are operating in the space between the film image and the supposed "real" person. He is "caught" by these investigators of public personalities as he leaves special events, restaurants, and film premieres, where the defenses of publicity agents are supposedly lacking. Various magazines and television programs compete in conducting elaborate investigations for the truth of a character, for the way in which they can reveal the intimate realm of the star. The interview, a strategy in which the celebrity maintains apparent control, is often used by the more mainstream and entertainment-oriented press. Magazines such as *People* and *Us* tend to ensure the compliance of the stars on whom they produce feature articles. Such a piece may involve a tour of the inner sanctum of the star: we see the inside of the star's home, or perhaps we are taken on a "typical" day with the star. In a 1990 cover story on Cruise in *Us*, the photos of the interior space of his cavernous living room are artfully done. The rest of the photos are publicity stills from his various movies. The text is an interview that attempts to uncover the authentic Tom Cruise. Part of the questioning attempts to determine the validity of rumors and gossip that have circulated about the star, as a function of the more respectable entertainment magazines is to operate as more legitimate sources of knowledge than the supermarket tabloids. We discover that Cruise's nickname is Laserhead, because of the intensity he can muster for any project. As well, there is a discussion about the importance of his dogs:

> *Us:* They also said that your dog was in therapy.
> *Cruise:* (laughing) My dog?! Get the hell outta here! Are you serious?
> *Us:* Dead serious.
> *Cruise:* Oh my God, give me a break! Where do they get this stuff?
> *Us:* So it's not true?
> *Cruise:* Yeah right, like my dog is sneaking out and going to therapy!
> *Us:* Do you have a dog?
> *Cruise:* I have two golden retrievers. They travel with me wherever I go. They're really good. They're just kinda there and they're always happy to see me. I love them.[55]

A *National Enquirer* article typifies the other type of story about Tom Cruise. With the lack of compliance of the celebrity, the story is seen to be more uncensored, less controlled by the star himself. It is in this story that we discover that Cruise's friends consider him a "womanizer" and that he has, after only a few short months, as the headline proclaims, bought a $200,000 diamond ring for his future bride. The scandal, of course, is that his previous marriage has been so quickly supplanted by his relationship with the costar of his last film, *Days of Thunder*. Accompanying the text is a series of snapshots of Cruise embracing his new love, Nicole Kidman, outside a Hollywood restaurant. In contrast to the pictures appearing in the glossy *Us* feature, these are black-and-white photos, clearly unsolicited by either Cruise or his companion. The *Enquirer* photos allow us entry into the private world of Cruise. This visual entry is enhanced by the inside reports on the difficulty Cruise had in convincing Kidman to marry. There are also secondhand quotes from Cruise, from these inside sources, that further the illusion of intimacy for the reader. For example, "I couldn't be happier. Nicole's a one in a million girl and I knew that if I didn't propose to her, I might lose her to somebody who did. Even though marriage didn't work out with Mimi [Rogers], I love being married. And I know in my heart that Nicole and I are made for each other."[56]

For the current argument, the details of Cruise's personal life are not significant; what is significant is that these various constructions of Cruise that appear in the different presses establish the distinction between Tom Cruise on the screen and Tom Cruise the celebrity. In other words, whether the stories and images are controlled by his personal management team or have emerged out of the heightened presence of his image as a cultural commodity in the selling of magazines, newspapers, and advertising, Cruise's public persona begins to be distinct from his screen persona. This form of autonomous subjectivity is very important for establishing the power of the film star as a distinct cultural commodity that is transferable to other domains, other cultural projects, and can be separated from his past films.

As Brownstein has chronicled, film stars have also worked actively to situate themselves in activities generally unrelated to the film industry. Cruise, along with other stars, has aligned himself with a number of what are described as liberal political positions on the environment and nuclear disarmament.[57] In fact, a whole political consultancy business has developed in Hollywood to aid celebrities in choosing issues with which to become involved. Although Cruise is not a prominent member of the politicized community among film stars, movement into the political sphere generally works to establish the relative independence of any film celebrity. The connection with charities or political campaigns deepens the character profile of the celebrity. Instead of being characterized as simply beautiful, handsome, or a mouthpiece for the screenwriter, the celebrity with a connection to these more serious domains adds the possible connotations of depth, intelligence, and commitment to his or her public persona. The public personality then demonstrates a subjectivity that goes beyond the self to the conception of selflessness and public leadership.

The autonomous Cruise is only partially constructed by these extratextual documents that establish his distinctness from his screen presence. Principally, Cruise has focused on establishing his depth of personality through the code of acting. Cruise's transgression into a form of autonomous subjectivity that bestows upon him a certain economic power in the film industry is modalized through his performing in films that work to shatter his picture personality construction. This can be characterized as acting "against type," which means working against how one is constructed in terms of physical presence, and also acting in what are labeled quality films. In terms of the trajectory toward some level of autonomous stardom, this form of acting transgression follows the construction of a clear film personality. In order for a star to transgress, a clear delineation of his or her screen presence must be firmly in place; thus, Cruise's first film that begins to break the boundaries of his film character, *The Color of Money*, is produced and released several years into his career. The difference in this first transgressing film is quite subtle: although Cruise continues to play the talented and naturally successful character, he is surrounded by an actor and director who are both known to be serious and well respected. Paul Newman, Cruise's costar, is an actor who has a very legitimate and lengthy list of film acting credits. As well, Newman is known to be a "serious" individual who has been involved in a number of liberal political campaigns over the past twenty years. In addition, the film builds on the sediments of Newman's own career and film history: Newman re-creates the character of "Fast Eddie" Felson from the 1961 film *The Hustler*, twenty-five years later. Finally, the director, Martin Scorsese, is the preeminent "quality" American director of the past twenty years. The various layers of meaning that surround Cruise's performance construct the atmosphere for the invocation of the acting code.[58]

With *Rain Man*, a 1988 film, Cruise further constructs a tension between his overcoded screen personality type and the transgression of the type through the discourse of acting. Once again, Cruise is surrounded by quality. Dustin Hoffman, his costar, is an Academy Award winner; he will win a second Oscar for his role in *Rain Man*. Barry Levinson, the director, has produced a series of "thoughtful" and artful comedies. The code of acting is central to the construction of the entire film. Cruise continues to play within the general range of his previously constructed screen personality; however, it is the content of the film that ensures a different reading of Cruise. Hoffman's portrayal of Raymond Babbitt, the autistic brother of Cruise's character, Charlie Babbitt, has been described as "acting non-stop," with Hoffman immersed in the mannerisms of his character.[59] This is the textual detail that becomes the central theme of most reviews of the film in the critical and noncritical movie press. From *People* we are given to understand that Hoffman stayed in character in everyday life in his complete employment of the psychological aspects of the Method form of acting. The *New York Times* labels the film a star vehicle for Hoffman in his continuous quest for the accolades of the Academy. Cruise is carried in this tour de force of the film acting profession. However, Vincent Canby asserts in his *New York Times* review that although Hoffman upstages everyone in the film, Cruise is "the real

Figure 1. The principal publicity and promotional still for *Rain Man* (1988). Brilliantly embodied in this shot (and the film) are Cruise's acknowledged picture personality and a form of transgression and transcendence of his typical film persona. The sunglasses echo back to his *Risky Business* (1983) days, whereas his connection to Method actor and Oscar winner Dustin Hoffman moves Cruise into the orbit of credibility and autonomous stardom.

center. . . . It may be no accident that Charlie (and Mr. Cruise) survived *Rain Man* as well as they do."[60] Cruise, through this film, is working to transform his public image from malleable and predictable male film star to serious actor who chooses very carefully the productions with which he is involved. A new series of connotations become associated with a Cruise film. Because of his newfound capacity as an actor as well as his proven ability to attract other quality actors and directors to any given project, Cruise now becomes a moniker that has a certain guarantee of quality. Within the cultural production of films, the name Cruise develops a brand-name status that not only includes his promise of alluring filmic masculinity, but also is symbolic of serious and quality films. It is in this brand-name status that the star's subjectivity becomes melded with his commodity status. The establishment of brand-name status that represents quality also is a sign of star autonomy. It indicates that the actor has in fact moved to the center of the production and that his or her status may be equivalent to that of the auteur or the producer or both.[61]

Cruise ensures this construction of his autonomous power through his involvement in *Born on the Fourth of July* (1989). It is in this film that Cruise employs the acting code to transgress fully his "naturalized" film persona. Indeed, the very plot of the film is organized around the transformation of an athletic young man into a paraplegic Vietnam veteran. Cruise, in portraying this changed man, also indicates his ability to provide a sense of his own commitment to the code of acting that in its intensity rivals the work of Dustin Hoffman in *Rain Man*.[62] Much of the textual material written about *Born on the Fourth of July* is concerned with Cruise's complete transformation of self in the role: this transformation indicates how deeply he has committed to the character. Often pointed out in background articles is the fact that Cruise, like Hoffman in *Rain Man*, stayed in character to test his believability in everyday life. For Cruise, the success of the test was determined by his unrecognizability as the star "Cruise," to the point that he was treated "like any other wheelchair confined person": he wanted to feel the frustration and anger that would arise from the disability and the inaccessibility of the world to physically handicapped people.[63] To be able to dismantle the star's image in the "real" world is the clear mark of a star able to transgress his or her categorization as star and integrate the professional dimension of serious actor into his or her celebrity and concurrent commodity status.

In the latest stages of Cruise's construction of public subjectivity, one sees the capacity for an indulgent integration of public and private life to be played out in his new films. *Far and Away* (1992), a sweeping gesture by Cruise and director Ron Howard to construct a dramatic Irish/American period piece in the tradition of *Doctor Zhivago*, unites as costars Cruise and his "real" wife, Nicole Kidman. Cruise's autonomous economic power permits the development of such a project; his perceived-to-be-stable audience operates as the risk capital insurance that leads to the film's production and distribution. Cruise is also building a unity between his filmic presence and his "real" life. The romantic dyad so crucial to the Hollywood film is doubly celebrated through this film.[64] Cruise maintains his clear relationship to his constructed picture personality, which, through his new autonomy as star producer, can envelop a version of his private life.

His 1993 releases provide further evidence of his centrality in the organization of Hollywood productions. Both films rely on best-selling novels for their advance publicity and their cultural significance. Cruise manages to merge in these films the integrity of acting performance with the recognizable personality he developed in his 1980s films. As in *The Color of Money*, Cruise costars in *A Few Good Men* (1992) with a major and therefore legitimate screen star in Jack Nicholson. In *The Firm* (1993), Cruise reestablishes his persona as the successful young man destined for further success. In both of these "serious" films, Cruise operates as the connecting fiber from an older generation of audience to a younger generation that happens to be more central to the industrial organization of the film industry.

By far the most interesting of Cruise's transgressions, both within the film text and extratextually, is his 1994 film *Interview with the Vampire*. Cruise's being cast as the star of the film version of Anne Rice's 1976 novel became a source of hysterical controversy. The author herself was outraged that Cruise was to play the Lestat character, but having sold the film rights to the book — and considering Cruise's contractual involvement with the film — there was little Rice could do to remove Cruise. Rice saw the image of Cruise — his essential picture personality as an all-American, wholesome, and youthful star — as antithetical to her character Lestat, a being motivated by homoerotic companionship and baroque bacchanalia in his insistent bloodsucking killing as a vampire. In effect, before it went into production Rice disowned the film publicly, along with countless fans of her books who were equally vocal about the casting of Tom Cruise. Further controversy stirred as Cruise was believed to have eliminated from his character the possibility of explicit homoeroticism in the film (later attributed to Rice's original screenplay and subsequently supplanted and reinserted into the movie by the director, Neil Jordan).[65] With the release of the film, Rice recanted equally publicly, dramatically endorsing the film and its star through an advertisement in *Daily Variety* that was subsequently reprinted by Geffen Pictures in the *New York Times*. In the ad, she said, in part: "I loved the film. I simply loved it.... I never dreamed it would turn out this way.... The charm and humor, and invincible innocence which I cherish in my beloved hero Lestat are all alive in Tom Cruise's performance."[66] She then went on

Figure 2. Crossed audiences: Cruise as Lestat in the video version of *Interview with the Vampire* (1994). A public revolt spurred on by author Anne Rice and proliferated by her fans intensified around the casting of Cruise in this film version of Rice's novel. The controversy served as advance publicity for the film and underlined the creative "risks" Cruise was taking with his core audience in playing a dark character.

to thank her readers for their concern about the cast and the production of the film, and attempted to allay their fears and pumped-up desires to boycott the film.

Cruise's star construction in *Interview with the Vampire* provides a wonderful blend of transgression and maintenance. The novel's homoeroticism, though muted, is still found in the film. Also, Cruise as Lestat is not a pleasant character. Cruise thus evokes once again a form of transgression through the code of acting. Yet both he and his costar Brad Pitt are depicted for the most part as beautiful and handsome representations of masculinity, which ultimately facilitates their success at procuring a succession of victims. It is the conflict between Cruise's dominant picture personality and the transgressive nature of the text that produces a massively proliferating discourse about Cruise and his suitability in the press. Cruise's star construction becomes the site upon which a number of fears about norms and sexual morality are activated.

Figure 3. Cruise as Lestat seducing Louis, Brad Pitt's character, into eternal vampiredom. The camp sensibility and homoeroticism provided an intriguing enigmatic shift in Cruise's star persona. His public appearances reinforced an embrace with a rougher and far from clean-cut image that emphasized aura and distance.

Subsequent to the film's release, Cruise was involved in a number of interviews. The most noteworthy of these took place on Oprah Winfrey's television show, where Cruise, with a goatee and long hair, answered questions from an audience that had just seen the film. The separation from his overcoded image of a clean-cut American star perplexed Oprah's audience. Indeed, the dominant theme was "How could you produce such a dark character and such a dark film? We don't need any more of that." Cruise's response became his defensive mantra throughout the program: while smiling (an appeal to his dominant picture personality), Cruise responded, "It was a vampire movie, and vampires act that way." The homoeroticism was also mentioned by a gay audience member, who thanked Cruise for the film and how it related to his experiences. Cruise, looking appropriately embarrassed, explained that it was acting and that the male companionship made sense for the Lestat character. The postrelease interviews and new image of Cruise produced a deepening of the Cruise persona; that very deepening through both acting and controversy continues to produce the autonomy of Cruise in the public sphere. His face and his actions continue to produce interest and become the nodal point for a wider range of discourses on individuality, sexuality, morality, and, self-reflexively, the celebrity himself.

Conclusion

What must be remembered about these various constructions of a film celebrity is that they are modalized or operationalized in the audience. The film industry, the coterie of personal agents surrounding the star, and the star him- or herself are involved in this active building of a public personality. Integrated into that structure is some measure of the response of a public and then the reformulation of that response (in whatever form) into the further cultural production of the celebrity. The audience, then, for Tom Cruise is not necessarily very involved in the meanings of his public personality. For some in the possible audience, there is an absolute abhorrence of his physical presence. For others, there is mild acceptance of his various constructions of self. The audience then moves in and out of using the film celebrity to represent idealizations of self or alternatively dystopian visions of self and others, or even of allowing the celebrity's public personality to mean nothing at all. The full complexity of the interaction of the audience with the celebrity apparatus is beyond the bounds of this analysis; what can be seen are the outlines of celebrity construction that are actively used by the audience.

The film celebrity emerges from a particular cultural apparatus. In its diverse incarnations, the film celebrity represents the building and dissipation of the aura of personality. The filmic text establishes a distance from the audience. The extratextual domains of magazine interviews, critical readings of the films, television appearances, and so on are attempts at discerning the authentic nature of the film celebrity by offering the audience/public avenues for seeing the individual in a less constructed way. It is important to realize that these other discourses that try to present the "real" film star are in themselves actively playing in the tension between the film celebrity's aura and the existence of the star's private life. The will to knowledge about the star's private and personal domains is coexistent with and dependent on the constructed aura or controlled domain of knowledge provided by the narratives of his or her film texts.

Finally, the film star has been constructed to represent the ultimate independence of the individual in contemporary culture. In the most obvious way, the film star is granted economic power to fabricate a lifestyle of wealth and leisure through the income earned from film releases. In a less obvious way, the film star's private life is chronicled to demonstrate the star's relationship to the normative center of the society. Film stars, collectively and historically, have been granted this normative leeway in the organization of their personal lives. Their lives become the idiosyncratic markers that demonstrate the expansive limits of individual independence in the culture. However, the normative leeway is granted only to those who can actively construct their individual autonomy from other constraining apparatuses. The ultimate film star or celebrity, then, has *individually* transgressed the constructions of public personality that have been placed by the film apparatus and the public. With this status, the film star is constructed to possess a great deal of power to determine his or her own future, film projects, and public image.

5

Television's Construction of the Celebrity

Compared with the film industry, the institution of television has positioned its celebrities in a much different way. Whereas the film celebrity plays with aura through the construction of distance, the television celebrity is configured around conceptions of familiarity. The familial feel of television and its celebrities is partially related to the domestication of entertainment technologies from the 1920s to the 1950s. Like radio, its precursor, television brought entertainment into the home. And in terms of the common space of the family, the television occupied a privileged location in the living rooms of most homes in North America. The uses made of television were also modalized around its position as a family entertainment technology.[1] The work of television production in its first two decades (from the late 1940s to the late 1960s) was the maintenance of a large mass audience, so that the same programs would be acceptable to all members of the family. Although different time periods were targeted by producers and advertisers for different audiences (e.g., daytime for women with the correlative program, the soap opera; Saturday morning for children; Saturday afternoon for men and sports), there was a relative lack of audience differentiation beyond this level.

The television celebrity embodies the characteristics of familiarity and mass acceptability. Part of the expression of the celebrity in the televisual world has emerged from the way in which radio personalities were constructed in the period prior to and including the Second World War. Radio, like television, had become a form of home entertainment and a source of information. In the 1920s and 1930s, radio established the domestic quality of broadcast technology, and it was this quality of the home mass audience of radio that was inherited by television.

The way television disseminated its message — that is, through broadcast — also established a similarity of its celebrities to former radio stars, and also made both groups qualitatively different from

119

film stars. On one level, the difference in exhibition between film and broadcasting led to different organizations of capital in these entertainment industries. Box-office receipts from film exhibitions established the requisite exchange relationship with the film audience. Film stars' box-office value could be at the very least partially determined by these direct payments by the audience. In contrast, the broadcasting audience made no clear designation of allegiance to stars and personalities. More critically for the broadcasting industry, there were no receipts derived from the audience when a program was broadcast. As long as a person owned a receiver and was within the signal range, he or she could be a member of a broadcasting audience. Originally, the selling of receivers generated enough capital to sustain programming. However, once the market was saturated with radio receivers, broadcasting as an industry for the generation of profits was no longer lucrative.[2] In the United Kingdom, the servicing of broadcast programming came from annual licensing fees and the establishment of a national public corporation, the BBC.[3] In the United States, broadcasting became modalized around the selling not of receivers but of audiences—more specifically, the selling of audiences' time to advertisers.

The development of the CBS network in the late 1920s is indicative of the way in which broadcasting, both radio and television, became an industry. CBS, without ownership of stations, guaranteed sponsors that their particular programs would be broadcast over a wide geographic area at the same time through a network of affiliate stations that had agreed to set aside airtime in return for the specific program content. Thus, an advertiser, through a weekly program, could reach a massive audience. The personalities of radio and then television were intimately connected to this form of generation of capital. Bob Hope's 1930s program, for instance, was connected with its sponsor, Pepsodent. Other corporate- or product-named programs included *A&P Gypsies, The Everready Hour, General Motors Family Party, The Cliquot Club Eskimos,* and *The Palmolive Hour.*[4] Somewhere in the middle of any program, there would be an endorsement of the sponsor's product by the show's host or star. In some cases, the product would be integrated into the show's content. In terms of early American radio, the radio personality could seldom divorce him- or herself from the organization of broadcasting around advertising. Although

with the advent of television the full sponsorship of individual programs was drastically reduced, as networks attempted to gain control of
programming and the construction of audiences, advertisers and
sponsors have always been central in the shaping of American broadcasting.

It is difficult to discern all the implications for the construction of
the television celebrity of this historical association of broadcasting
with the generation and selling of audiences to advertisers. What
can be said is that, because of the obvious and omnipresent advertising
function of television, the celebrity who arises from television programming is associated more directly than the film celebrity with the industrial nature of entertainment. In contrast to the film star, the television
personality is surrounded by other messages that are unconnected to
the narrative focus of his or her program. These disjunctures are nor-
malized into the flow of television. The film star's filmic text is relatively integral, uninterrupted by other messages, other images. The film
star maintains an integrity of being; the television star is pulled out
of an aesthetic into the bare economics of production and consumption. Whereas the film celebrity maintains an aura of distinction, the
television celebrity's aura of distinction is continually broken by the
myriad messages and products that surround any television text.

It would be unfair to say that film production companies are not
in the business of constructing audiences, or that they do not use certain stars to give human and cultural shape to their products so that
they resonate with their audiences. Clearly this is part of the manner in
which scripts and films are chosen for funding and production. However, in the television industry, this task of constructing audiences is the
essential work. The packaging of audiences for advertisers may produce a television program that is somehow not contradictory to consumer culture and, ideally, connected to the products advertised. Once
again, the sponsored nature of American television tends to construct
celebrities who are inoffensive to the way in which television is involved in the perpetuation of consumer capitalism. The aura of the
television celebrity is reduced therefore because of three factors: the
domestic nature of television viewing, the close affinity of the celebrity
with the organization and perpetuation of consumer capitalism, and
the shattering of continuity and integrity of character that takes place
through the interspersal of commercials in any program.

The Unique Nature of the Television Celebrity

There is an active construction of a different relationship to the audience by television personalities that in effect creates an aura more of familiarity than one modalized around distance. John Langer, in an article titled "Television's Personality System," argues that this construction of what he calls "intimacy" is the reason television does not produce stars but rather personalities. He elaborates on this point by explaining how television is positioned "to personalize wherever it can, rarely using a concept or idea without attaching it or transforming it through the 'category of the individual.' "[5] Borrowing from Stuart Hall, Langer calls this elaborate development of a personality system one of the "preferred codes" of television. The personality system, he concludes, works as a form of symbolic product of television that provides totems of personality types for the audience.[6] In this way, the personality system is configured around its ideological work to draw the viewer into an acceptance of a capitalist culture and political structure. In the argument that follows, I focus very specifically on the intense emphasis on the familiar in television, and in this way build on Langer's discussion of the function of the television celebrity. A large part of this familiarity emerges from the modes of address that are possible on television. One can see this in operation in the types of personalities found in broadcasting in general and television in particular.

One of the problems in any attempt to analyze television in some unified way is that it is a technology of transmission that distributes a wide variety of content and programming material. Making claims about the types of personalities that are produced by such a medium presents the danger of making an essentialist argument about the technology. In the following analysis, I attempt to focus on clear patterns of production/reception that are connected to television's construction of familiarity, a form of construction that has led to generic sites for the production of celebrity. Each generic site has a particular history, but it is also defined by a particular form of address of the audience. What follows is a discussion of those types of address that are common to television and the forms of subjectivity clearly emphasized by those types.

The Presenters of News and Live or Simulated Live Television

A dominant feature of the televisual universe is the host, the familiar face and personality who guides the viewer through the discontinuities of any television program. Here the mode of address is direct: the viewer is spoken to and looked at quite directly. There is no pretense that the audience is not there, as in most dramas. In this way, the host serves as the means by which the audience is included in the program. The host speaks to the audience, but within the program he or she represents the audience's point of view.

Complementing the direct form of address is the implication that a great deal of television programming is live. This construction of time operates at several levels. Television news programs, like their radio precursors, actively work to produce the simultaneity of their news and reality. In contrast to newsreels shown in movie theaters or morning newspapers, news broadcasts are changeable up to the last moment before airtime.[7] Their distinctiveness is derived from this characteristic of immediacy and thus constructed sense that what is reported is very close to the real events. The news anchor serves to validate this close relationship to the real by working in real time, even though many of the news reports he or she introduces have been taped well in advance and have been drastically edited for broadcast. The news anchor knits the fabric of reports into a connotation of currency. This verisimilitude in recent years has been enhanced by the use of satellite and telecommunications technology to allow anchors to talk directly with reporters on the scenes of events after their taped reports have been broadcast. CBC's *The Journal* and PBS's *MacNeil/Lehrer Report* rely primarily on the use of interviews that, though often taped hours before broadcast, are edited to seem as if the entire event is occurring at the time of the newscast.

The news anchor is also principally involved in the live broadcasting of news about crises and special events that preempt the regular television schedule. He or she (anchors are predominantly male) becomes directly associated with the significance of the events and, in a mutually complementary signifying system, both substantiate the significance of the event and the significance of the news anchor. As opposed to other actors in events, the anchor is inserted into the construction of all these significant moments. Thus, memories of the explosion of the space shuttle are associated with the news anchor who provided a frame for the experience. Similarly, the live reporting of the Los Angeles earthquake becomes framed by the way in which, say, Dan Rather appeared to construct the crisis. The Canadian Liberal leadership convention, where Jean Chrétien was elected, as a televisual event is constructed through the apparent interpretation of objectivity provided by, for example, CBC's Peter Mansbridge. It is in these moments of live television, the times when a crisis is covered, that television moves to the very center of cultural experience. Not only do the images of the spectacular explosion of the space shuttle, the bombing of Baghdad, and the "chase" of O.J. Simpson in that white Ford Bronco become burned into our cultural retina, but the anchor is legitimated as cultural interpreter. Indeed, the anchor represents stability and continuity despite the apparent chaos of a crisis or the incomprehensibility of an event. The presence of the anchor provides security, particularly when he or she has built up a history of covering a succession of special events and crises.[8] When the rest of the universe is in flux, the anchor remains in control as a monitor of any threat to the audience.[9]

Because television network news anchors cover these live "historical" events as well as appear nightly on national news programs, they begin to be perceived as representing the networks themselves. Their institutional identities become blurred with their news personalities. In American television, Walter Cronkite embodied the spirit of CBS for two decades, while Huntley and Brinkley represented NBC. In Canadian television, Peter Mansbridge has become the generalized spokesperson for the CBC network; he, like other network anchors, represents the ultimate integrity of the network.

The host role is not specific to television news. It arises in a variety of other programs as well, from talk shows and variety shows to game shows, sports programming and commercials, as a way of indicating some reference to the real time of the program—to show that, in fact, the program corresponds to everyday life and responds to everyday events. In the talk-show format, the contiguous address of the host to the audience through his or her looking and talking directly into the camera is a technique of inclusion. The studio audience further buttresses the construction of the currency of the event of the talk show. The audience also works as a representation of the television viewing audience. The questions of the studio audience to the guests are meant to represent our own queries. The host organizes the entire event so that his or her own position is seen as sensible and rational. Talk shows are formatted around what is perceived as topical, and topicality is related to the show's construction of the currency and significance of the show. More significantly, topicality is one way in which talk shows compete for an audience. In recent years, topicality in American daytime talk shows has centered on a kind of voyeurism by the mainstream culture for the margins of personal and collective behavior. The host in this configuration of the audience as voyeur is both the privileged viewer and the moralizer about these rather marginal micropractices. He or she rationalizes and makes coherent the cultural center's interpretation, first by labeling the marginal and then by constructing the ethical field in which the marginal/ized cultural activity can be positioned. Thus, the host legitimates a mainstream construction of self through a systematic delegitimation of the margins. The nebulous quality of what the mainstream of the culture actually is, is grounded in the very physicality of the host.

In more entertainment-centered, primarily late-night, talk shows, the construction of the live nature of the program is organized around its resonance with other media events. The guests are primarily performers, writers, and actors who are promoting recently released films, books, theatrical or concert productions, or recordings. Again, there is a live studio audience, which constructs an atmosphere of an event that is particularized in time and place. The host's role is to produce a setting in which the guests will reveal something about themselves that goes beyond their intent of either personal promotion or cultural product promotion. This is the promise of the program and the allure for the audience. The entrée into this more hidden world of the stars is through humor, which persistently hints at the breakdown of the barrier between the personal realm of the guest and the public persona.

The format and style of late-night live television talk shows, with their combination of humor and news of the unseen world of entertainment, emerged during the "golden years" of television. The role of host has been predominantly taken by a recognized comic. From Steve Allen and Jack Paar in the 1950s and early 1960s to Johnny Carson and current hosts Jay Leno and David Letterman, the use of humor for transgression of public discourse into the personal has been established. Talk shows reenact one of the central functions of television: to familiarize. Film stars, in their live appearances on the programs, break the narrative closure of their filmic texts. Instead of the displaced time of the filmic text, they enter into the current time of live television. The dialogue between host and celebrity guest plays with the open address of the conversation. The studio audience and the home viewing audience are acknowledged and looked at directly.

This acknowledgment of presence serves to reduce the aura constructed by the narrative of film, where the film actor lives in a world quite separate from the film viewer. The late-night talk show decontextualizes the aura of the star and re-creates the possibility of the star's establishing a more personal and familial public personality. The celebrity guest enters into the daily circulation of images and meanings of the audience. Indeed, his or her new non-narrative-centered discourse is that of conversation with the program's host; the style of discourse is itself heavily invested with the ordinary, the everyday, the familial.

The host in the various formats of live and simulated live television is also a celebrity figure, but a type that is specifically created by the institution of television. A central part of this unique type of celebrity is its ultimate dependence on the system of celebrity that exists in other political and cultural domains. The television host's status as a celebrity is built on proximity to other celebrities and celebrity systems. The proximity is created by television's active work in the familiarization of the public sphere and the personalities of the public sphere. What this entails for most television hosts is a deepening of the private textual quality of celebrities, so that their images possess some sort of "characterized" depth of personality. Their own status as celebrities is also modalized around familiarity. Their daily presence on television punctuates the televisual world for the audience with recognizable faces and personalities with recognizable characteristics. The hosts provide the consistent frame for television, a frame that builds audience familiarity.

The Stars of Soap Opera

Other formats that are unique to television also produce recognizable personalities for the viewing public. One of the dominant forms of daytime television in particular is the soap opera. In this form, one can see the prevailing televisual discourse of familiarity clearly in operation. There are several components of soap operas that underline the discourse of familiarity. It is in the origins of the genre that one can see the way in which an intimacy and familiarity with an audience was constructed.

The genre of soap opera emerged originally on radio in the 1930s. Indeed, some of radio's programs were transferred to television in the 1940s and 1950s; one of these, *The Guiding Light,* is still in production and on network television. Prior to the appearance of soap operas, there was very little daytime programming on radio. Most of the sponsors' budgets, and thus the work of the networks, was focused on evening programming. The soap opera represented an attempt by radio producers to sell the idea of daytime programming to sponsors of household products. The key attraction for the sponsors was that the audience in the daytime would be made up predominantly of women who were involved in daily household chores, the kinds of activities that were connected to the soaps and cleaners that these manufacturers offered. Women were also the principal buyers of household cleaning aids. The soap opera was a form of drama that conformed to the exigencies of the sponsor to insert the utility of these household products into a compatible setting. Thus, the action of the soap opera in these early productions invariably occurred in a domestic setting—more often than not, around a kitchen table. Promotions for the sponsors' products were inserted into the dramas in the form of helpful hints. Often the matriarch of the soap opera, the central, older, sagelike figure, was also the spokeswoman for the product. Ma Perkins would incorporate the values of Procter & Gamble's Oxydol into her general comments on the importance of family values in times of tragedy.

By the mid-1930s, Procter & Gamble was the largest sponsor of radio programming in the world, sponsoring more than 664 daytime hours of programming.[10] Other manufacturers followed suit, including General Foods and Pillsbury. In the organization of broadcasting, the structuring of programs to recognizable markets was critical. Equally significant was connecting the content of a program with the products being advertised. Generically, soap opera was about the home, the family, and the neighborhood. It dealt with intimate though often tragic details of particular families.

The soap opera was also a never-ending saga. As an open-ended text with no complete resolutions, the soap opera attempted to parallel the domestic life of its audience. For the first thirty-five years of their existence on radio and television, soap operas were broadcast live each weekday. This established the currency and uniqueness of each program and the requisite audience loyalty to its continuous development. In combination with this currency and its intense focus on the domestic setting, soap operas attempted to insert drama, and by implication their sponsors' products, into the everyday lives of their audience members, as a kind of ritual catharsis.

Most of these components of the soap opera continue to be central to its current form on television. Although the programs are now taped and some scenes and sequences are videotaped in exterior settings, the soap opera maintains a concentration on domestic, textually open-ended drama that is broadcast daily. Thematically, soap operas are concerned with intimacy. The level of intimacy in what the audience learns about characters today clearly goes beyond the familial level of the early soap operas. The audience is invited into the bedrooms of the characters, into the details of their relationships through private conversations, and into dream sequences that identify characters' desires and aspirations. The invitation of the soap opera to the audience is to comprehend fully the motivations of each character. This entails an incredible investment on the part of both writers and audience in the character's psychological profile. In fact, this intense investment in the psychological makeup of characters has been the principal transformation of the soap opera form. Full familiarity with a given soap opera now implies an understanding of each character as an individual that goes beyond exterior appearances into the hidden world of dreams.

Soap opera's themes of the intimate and the familiar have led a number of writers to think of soap opera as producing fundamentally feminine texts that differ in their character construction from the masculine narrative of film. Tania Modleski asserts that soap opera's unending text, its very lack of closure, defines a feminine identification with characters and story.[11] Martha Nochimson has further expanded this thesis to explain that soap opera is quite explicitly a feminine discourse that enacts female desire in a resistent way.[12] Mary Ellen Brown's work focuses on the remaking of soap opera into other forms of talk and gossip; in other words, soap opera allows for the reworking of the text into women's everyday lives as fans.[13] These studies emphasize the particularly intensive affective investment in television soap opera that articulates its ready-made movement from text to the intimate and the familiar.[14]

Because of the full and intimate sense of knowledge of the individual soap opera character, the regular audience impedes the possibility of an actor in a soap opera becoming known beyond his or her role. Although there are several magazines that feature stories about the stars of soap opera as real people outside of their work, the actors continue to be identified, even in these magazines, principally by the characters they portray on television. In a sense, the characters' inner lives are what interest and intrigue the reading audience. As Jeremy Butler explains, the actors are in a "prison-house of narrative" that resembles the powerless status of film actors prior to the First World War.[15] Unlike other celebrities, soap opera stars experience relatively little interest in their personal lives as real people. As the genre gains legitimacy, however, even this boundary begins to slip. The proliferation of soap opera magazines suggests an entire industry of deepening the meaning of the familiar TV soap stars.

Situation Comedy Stars

Television is populated with a parade of celebrities in its process of familiarization of the audience with significant individuals. In a general sense, television provides a cultural space for the deepening of the cultural texts of the celebrities that emerge in other domains of the culture. Television does construct its own specific types of celebrities and works to enter some individual celebrities in the system of celebrity. As I have discussed above, the host is one example of this self-generation of public personality. Prime-time television drama is the other active center in the creation and construction of celebrity figures. Another unique form of celebrity in prime-time television emerges from a genre of television that is more or less idiosyncratic to television: the situation comedy.

The family has been central to the situation comedy genre throughout its history. Answering the question of why this is so once again substantiates the claim that television is involved intensively in making the world familiar. From the earliest examples of the situation comedy on television, specifically, *I Love Lucy* and *The Honeymooners,* to more recent incarnations such as *The Cosby Show* and *Family Ties,* the dramatic tension and resolution in these programs have been organized around the family. Even in shows that on the surface appear not to be based on the family are structured so that the work environment resembles a family environment. These include programs from the 1970s such as *The Mary Tyler Moore Show* and more current shows such as *Designing Women* and *Murphy Brown.* Because of this family orientation, there is an implicit assumption that any conflict contains within it a resolution that will not substantially alter the relations among the characters. The family, in all its various forms of televisual presentation, is ultimately immutable. The characters must return to their mapped-out roles within the family each week. It is the seriality of the situation comedy that helps reinforce this ideal of the constancy of the family. Moreover, seriality also aids in the construction of television as a visual landscape that is populated with familiar images.

The situation comedy also represents the way in which television is constructed to attract audiences for sponsors. The seriality of the programs not only creates familiarity for the audience, it helps establish a recognizable and repeatable construction of the audience for advertisers. Once network television achieves a certain standard of popular success with a given program, it freezes the general structure into a serial form. In this way, some of the indeterminacy and risk surrounding the way in which mass broadcasting audiences are formed for the generation of capital and profit are limited.

The stars produced through the television situation comedy have several clear-cut tendencies. The familiar characteristics of the star, because of the seriality of the form, determine the way in which his or her public personality is decoded by the audience. The character's name often dominates over the actor's name in public memory. Thus, we remember Archie Bunker and less the actor Carroll O'Connor.[16] In more recent situation comedies there has been some active conflation of characters with some actors' public personas. Roseanne plays a variation of her public self within the family comedy setting. Bill Cosby's character Cliff Huxtable is not a character clearly separable from the way in which Bill Cosby is conceived in other spheres. What situation comedy develops is a concentration on the star's features as they are expressed in the weekly appearances of his or her character. Over time, there is a convergence of the star's personality with the character portrayed. The resource for new developments within the serial draws on the psychological deepening of the lead character through the personality of the star.

Conclusion

With reference to the system of celebrity, television is generally an ancillary system. It is less active in the generation of new celebrities than in the process of substantiating the significance of public personalities that have emerged in other domains. I have called this the familiarization function of the medium. I have used the term *familiarization* in a number of senses to demonstrate the manner in which television is involved in such a process. Briefly, these include its domestic use and the related family structure under which it is viewed by its audience; its predominantly live or simulated live format style, where recognizable hosts provide the anchor that helps to determine the significance of the wide array of representations and meanings channeled through the medium; the primary function of selling audiences to advertisers, which makes the institution of television construct generally an inclusive as opposed to an exclusive audience; the serialization of content; and the intense focus on the personal, the psychological, and, in some cases, the intimate in the actual content of programs. The celebrities who do emerge from television either service the process of familiarization (i.e., the hosts) or work in the domain of the familiar and the intimate (i.e., situation comedies and soap operas).

In the following section, I present a study of Oprah Winfrey to particularize the phenomenon of the emergence of celebrity within the institution of television.

Oprah Winfrey: Familiarizing the Unfamiliar

Oprah Winfrey is a star of television. Her status as celebrity is connected to her continual presence on her eponymous daily nationally syndicated talk show. Television, as discussed above, tries to develop familiarity with the individuals who are presented. Winfrey, similarly, works to establish herself as a familiar face and personality within the format of an "issue-oriented" daytime talk show. In contrast to the film star, the television star who emerges as host and interpreter of the culture for the audience is treated as someone everyone has a right to know fully. His or her television life is subjected to daily scrutiny through his or her show. The talk-show host's opinions are obvious and forthright; his or her level of knowledge, humor, and idiosyncrasies are his or her own, even though they are presented for public consumption. Where the film celebrity projects a number of public images through performances as an actor, the television talk-show host, though constructing a public persona, is also constructed as clearly presenting him- or herself. The gap between the fictional or mythical and the real life of the celebrity is narrowed through the relationship of the program to real time and the relationship to a live audience. The construction of sincerity and conviction is supposed to be part of the authentic host. There is little mystery. Television works at constructing the familiar, and the talk-show host is an example par excellence of the form of familiarized subjectivity that television constructs for its audience. Oprah Winfrey is a particularly rich example of how the discourse of the familiar is modalized through the stars of television. The capacity of the television host to play in this construction of the familiar usually determines his or her success. Oprah Winfrey is not only seen every weekday by 15 million American viewers and 113 million worldwide,[17] she is also the perpetual subject of the ancillary press, which further constructs her as the familiar figure — indeed, someone whose behavior the public can actively influence.

I divide this analysis of Oprah Winfrey into a number of specific sections in order to reveal the institutional factors at play in the structuring of this specific television star. The first of these is concerned with the ritualization of personality; it details the way in which Oprah is structured into a specific and recognizable personality through her programs. The second section, concerning the discourse of the Other, attempts to map the terrain that Oprah negotiates between audience and self-identity. The third section builds from the discourse of the Other to attempt to discern how Oprah's constructed public personality is a blend of the ordinary and the extraordinary. The final section details the way Oprah is reviewed and talked about in magazines, on other talk shows, and in newspapers, and how she engages in responses to that coverage directly and personally. The personal and familiar details of Oprah Winfrey are public knowledge as she continues to represent televisual familiarity.

The Ritualization of Personality

Much like most of North American television programming, *The Oprah Winfrey Show* is slotted into a regular time period. Moreover, also in keeping with the structure of daytime programming, the show is produced twice daily. It is presented as though it were a live program. In this way, in its study of issues and problems, it constructs the conception of currency; the issues being discussed are of vital concern for that particular moment. Very quickly, the format of the program begins to determine the varied content of the program, as the ritual of viewing by an audience must be maintained.

There are several forms of ritual that are part of the program and serve to shape what Oprah Winfrey represents as a personality. The format of the program, although it has variations from show to show, establishes certain conventions and thereby positions Oprah's role in the ritual. We can think of the format as a narrative that is subject to repetition and some type of closure. In the simulated live talk show, the narrative appears to be totally changeable; however, the repetition of codes indicates that roles and positions are clearly defined.

The program is constructed with a series of characters who have clearly defined roles and scenarios in each program. Oprah is the central and continuing personnage. The audience, the guests with "problems," and the professional expert operate as infinitely replaceable characters and yet fulfill roughly the same function in each of the show's narratives. What follows is a discussion of the ritualization of personality through a critical review of the principal characters who are part of the talk-show narrative, which has become ritualized into a format.

Oprah as Narrative Character

From the opening still images, which depict Oprah in various fashion magazine-type poses as well as stills from previous programs, the talk-show narrative establishes the central character. The images imply that Oprah has an alluring, exciting personality. The program then is organized not only around the issue or problem of the day, but also around Oprah's own interests, her own ranking of concerns. Oprah's personality is structured to envelop the treatment of any issue. The preferred or dominant reading of the program's content, then, involves looking for the codes of transformation of Oprah herself as she works toward some resolution in her own mind. In a program on children bullying their parents (March 10, 1991), Oprah, in a very typical way, resolves the apparent impasse of attempting to assess blame by concluding that it is a family problem as opposed to a problem contained within any individual family member. It is a temporary solution, nevertheless Oprah's form of resolution is pivotal to the narrative construction of the show. Although the program's content is organized generally around crises and conflicts, the narrative does tend to progress toward the resolution of the disequilibrium that is repeatedly affirmed by Oprah. Oprah then directs the program to follow her transforming embodiment of concern, from the introduction of the problem to the discussion of the problem, to the organized confusion reflected by the audience's various questions, to the resolution of the problem through Oprah's interpretation of the expert's advice. Each new episode follows the same patterned format, which is articulated through the Oprah character.

The Role of the Studio Audience

The construction of the Oprah character is dependent on her relationship to other principal characters in the narrative. The studio audience serves a number of functions. In the construction of the celebrity sign of Oprah Winfrey, the audience is centrally engaged in the expression of support for her popular sentiment. Oprah establishes intimacy with her studio audience. She moves among audience members with her microphone, servicing their questions for the guests. Often she holds their hands as they prepare to become the center of attention, not only of the studio audience but of the home viewing audience as well. Their questions may contain a degree of anger or hostility, but generally that hostility is directed at the guests. Oprah remains their ally. She also represents their channel and avenue to public discourse. In a reciprocal relationship, Oprah Winfrey symbolically represents empowerment. Much as on the radio phone-in shows or other talk shows, the audience members become key participants in the program's content. Their involvement, however, also operates at an ideological level of representing the way in which the general public opinion is sought in political discourse. Their active participation, their keen interest, and their level of investment in the program's content are symbolic presentations of democratic action and will. Joshua Gamson, who has conducted research through participant observation of TV studio audiences, has described how television producers pump up studio audiences as additional props for their programs: "The producers attempt to control audience behavior, to elicit particular behaviors that are in line with the production needs of the program."[18] Although the involvement of the studio audience is active and concerned, it remains ideological because of its function as representing the concern of society in general. Studio audience members, in their activity, are representative of the massive home audience, and it is this connection that endows them with a particular form of representation of society. In a sense, the unseen and unheard large home audience also empowers the studio audience; the studio audience members' voices enter directly into public opinion because they are being heard. For a moment, the studio audience members are part of the array of public personalities who are granted voices and personal opinions in the public sphere. Gloria-Jean Masciarotte describes this formation as a new social subject as the "making of the self" within the program's non-resolution "in terms of mass subjectivity."[19] Instead of a mass version of the talking cure, where there is an "I and You" relation of power, the program produces an "aggressive serial spectacle of I's," "a resistant relationship of I to I, [and] an irritated architecture of subject to subject."[20] The program thus moves the individual speaker from the audience to a kind of social subject engaging in a newly defined public sphere.[21]

Permission to enter this restricted territory of the public sphere is granted through the celebrity sign of Oprah. In turn, Oprah's power as a celebrity is dependent on this intimate connection to a loyal studio and home audience. Her connection to her audience is embedded in her celebrity sign. This power is reconfigured within the institution of television into the language of guaranteed audience ratings, which in their turn can be used to sell Oprah as a commodity for the selling of other advertised commodities. Within the institution of television, the maintenance of a close connection of a celebrity to a large, stable audience works to secure the commodity status of the celebrity. Oprah Winfrey has made the audience itself, as expressed through the live studio audience, part of her identity as a celebrity.

In the show's structure, the solidarity between the studio audience and Oprah Winfrey is ritualistically established through the applause that punctuates commercial messages, through the close proximity of Oprah to her audience, through Oprah's periodic displays of emotional empathy with individuals, and through audience members' periodic provision of anthemic statements of support for Oprah and her point of view.

The Expert

There is a dialectic that occurs in most episodes of *The Oprah Winfrey Show*. After hearing from the "problem guests" and after the guests are asked a series of questions by the studio audience and

Figure 4. Oprah Winfrey on *The Oprah Winfrey Show* (August 1995). Oprah classically speaks with her audience as the (predominantly female) studio audience and Oprah face the guests. This capacity of familiarity is instrumental in the development of the television celebrity. As host, Oprah plays with the roles of public advocate and channeling device for others.

Oprah herself, an expert is positioned in the mediating role center stage, among the guests. The expert's role is to provide the solution to whatever the dilemma happens to be that day. It is clear that he or she is operating as the voice of authority. In this capacity, the expert brings a certain knowledge and power to his or her reinterpretation of the problem. Often the expert has a doctoral degree, and often he or she has written books on subjects related to the specific topic. The authority's expertise and identification of a social problem no doubt has been the organizing impetus behind many episodes of the program.

The authority, however, does not provide the necessary closure and resolution of the problem raised in the program. Rather, he or she serves as an essential instrument for the way in which Oprah works the program to a resolution. The experts provide the raw material for Oprah's reinterpretation. Oprah positions herself as, once again, the representative of the audience and, by implication, of the ordinary people. She rewords the professional's advice into language of practicality and usability for the audience. The expert's advice then is transformed into the everyday language of Oprah and her loyal audience. The expert's advice works to legitimate the transformed advice of Oprah. Oprah once again becomes the channel for the organization of the program's narrative.

Problem Guests

Although it is not always the case, the program's guests often push the narrative to a temporary state of disequilibrium. They represent what has to be resolved in some fashion during the program to provide a closure. They become the personalization of an issue or concern. The core issues of the program revolve around interpersonal issues that are given a social dimension because of their pervasiveness in the United States. As Oprah has said, if one person has a personal concern or problem, then the likelihood is that millions of audience members may have had similar experiences and problems. In a sense, Oprah's program operates as a public confessional, where, in its public presentation and generally secularized form, the various participants invest themselves in a variation of the talking cure. The voicing of problems and the articulation of conflicts are seen as ways in which problems and conflicts can be resolved. The program, through its guests, primarily, and then by invocation some audience members are drawn into involvement, is often designed to break open secrets and taboos of discussion so that they become the subject of public debate. The guests then are coaxed into confessionals of their private worlds; the objective of the program is that there will be a resonance of similar concern once those private worlds are exposed for public consumption. The guests then operate as the entrée into a discourse of intimacy and privacy on a public stage. Oprah is once again the channel for such disclosures.[22]

Summary

Through the various principal characters described above, the television personality of Oprah is constructed. She is built on two principal elements that relate to the personal and the personality. First, Oprah's subject matter, her relationship to her studio audience, her empathy, and her relaxed manner indicate that her celebrity is dealing with the institution's construction of personality around familiarity. For Oprah this is often extended to a level of intimacy. Second, Oprah's close proximity to her audience is constructed so that she is represented as a populist, someone who has emerged from the people to articulate their concerns. From the assemblage of character types, a ritual of performance is organized for Oprah. In its daily serialization, the personality Oprah becomes the linchpin for the temporary resolutions of the narrative.

A Discourse of the Other

The emergence of Oprah Winfrey as a television celebrity is built on a series of binarisms that work to differentiate her presented subjectivity. The function of this construction of differentiation is to establish a reconfiguration of a committed television audience. Changes and transformations in the construction of television audiences are difficult to chart, but I think they can be represented through an analysis of the forms of new celebrities that are allowed to develop in new programming. Programs attempt to carve up the possible audience into large and recognizable units. Television programming is designed to construct a connected series of programs that resonate in some way with the social context of a section of the population who may have similar patterns of consumption and lifestyle. I am condensing here the elaborate lengths to which programmers go as they attempt to construct and maintain audiences for television — it is not my intention to detail those techniques. However, an essential part of this work — determining the connection of a potential program to a potential audience — is to ensure that the central characters are compelling enough to the viewer that the viewer will continue to watch. The television celebrity's primary task, in terms of the programmer, is somehow to embody this affective attachment to the audience. With each new program, the celebrity must somehow embody a difference that is connected to some new way to configure the mass audience.

The Oprah Winfrey Show was designed through its star to reconfigure daytime audiences through its construction of difference. The show is an attempt to recast the social world and the categorization of groupings in the social world in terms of slightly different definitions and distinctions. To use terminology not normally associated with the apparatus of television, the positioning of a new television program is a construction of a discourse of the Other. I want to try to explain how Oprah is constructed as a different daytime television talk-show host. The Other as it is inscribed in mass-mediated culture establishes an inclusionary discourse for normally excluded peoples from positions of power. The construction of Oprah's subjectivity is therefore a new televisual construction of an inclusionary hegemony. The marginal figure embodied by Oprah's blackness and womanhood can be modalized as a representation of populist sentiment in the televisual universe.

Women, Television, and Social Issues

Oprah's celebrity sign is built on differentiations from those of her predecessors. Television targeted specifically at a predominantly female market is not a new phenomenon. As discussed above, the genre of soap opera, which was intimately connected to the advertising of household consumer goods that were believed to be purchased by housewives, emerged as a broadcasting form in the 1920s. Various phone-in talk shows, entertainment interview programs, and current affairs interview programs have become a relatively cheap staple of broadcasting, primarily in non-prime-time hours. *The Oprah Winfrey Show* is in this lineage of daytime talk shows sandwiched between daytime serials, game shows, and commercials for household products.

The direct predecessors of *The Oprah Winfrey Show* were the various female-hosted talk shows of 1950s, 1960s, and 1970s daytime television. *Dinah!* hosted by Dinah Shore and *The Virginia Graham Show* were two of the more widely syndicated programs of that era. Local programmers also often produced female-hosted programs that bore a resemblance to these nationally syndicated shows. The format was organized around the social ritual of the morning coffee klatch. Guests, who were treated with familiarity, deference, and a high degree of sycophancy, talked about their latest trials and tribulations. It was a format that comfortably encompassed actors, authors, and singers on publicity tours. There were male-hosted daytime talk shows that also emulated this structure, such as *The Merv Griffin Show, The Mike Douglas Show,* and, later, *The John Davidson Show.* Most of the male hosts of these programs were crooners or romantic balladeers, singers of the kind of popular music directly associated with and targeted at a female audience, and thus perceived by television programmers as "natural" celebrity hosts for daytime "women's" television.

Oprah Winfrey's program has been placed in opposition to this generally quiet and unobtrusive form of daytime programming. As opposed to the many programs on daytime television that are organized around the possibility that viewers will miss portions, *The Oprah Winfrey Show* is obtrusive in its insistent demand for listening and watching. Whereas much of daytime television can be thought of as an ambient medium that accompanies household chores, *The Oprah Winfrey Show* is designed to be watched intently. This form of programming for daytime television emerged with the popularity of *Donahue* during the mid-1970s. Unlike the myriad talk shows filled with the noncontroversial—mildly revealing discussions of stars, cooking segments, and possibly some form of entertainment—Phil Donahue's program was constructed specifically around controversial social issues. *The Oprah Winfrey Show* is built on the same foundations of entertainment programming that *Donahue* established as viable commercial television a decade earlier.

Both programs rose from local success to national syndication and thereby worked independently of network television contracts.[23] This gradual building of an audience from a regional base has become an essential component of both Oprah's and Phil's construction of their celebrity status. It established their celebrity signs as something more authentic, more grounded in the day-to-day conditions of everyday people. And in the programs' style, as discussed above, the audience is included in the content. The microphone is thrust by the host into the audience, so that its members can participate in a discussion. The host guides an often chaotic and raucous, though ostensibly democratic, discussion. The traditional host's proximity to the guests and relative distance from the studio audience are transgressed. The audience speaks and questions. The mythic construction of a form of populism is the dominant sign of the new program and the populist persona of the host.

In the domain of public personalities, Oprah Winfrey and Phil Donahue share the same status as representatives of those members of society who are generally excluded from positions of power. They are constructed as indefatigable champions of nonelites. Like the radio open-line show, they symbolically represent the people and their interests as they attempt to raise public awareness about particular social issues. Because of their positions as outsiders, they try to present the various discourses of the excluded and marginal in the social world to determine how they can be reintegrated into the social mainstream. Oprah and Phil represent a cast of American liberals whose main approach to social problems is articulated through the slogan "Something should be done about this." Their concern, their seeming commitment, and their intensity during each program work to reinforce their positions as crusaders for political and social rights and responsibilities for the underrepresented. In this way, they resemble the investigative journalist who is also committed to particular political positions. Oprah, like Phil, begins from a point of involvement and commitment to social responsibility; this commitment serves as the launching board for the drama in each program.

The question that arises from this development of a type of television celebrity very much attached to at least the publicization of social issues is, How did it emerge within the traditionally conservative institution of television? Fundamentally, this becomes a question of how this form of debate is connected to the construction of sizable audiences that can be sold to advertisers. The answer lies in the way the programs attempt to rearticulate the daytime television audience into new patterns. *The Oprah Winfrey Show*, specifically, is built on the success of *Donahue*, with several significant differences and oppositions. Phil Donahue's program developed in response to the growing political awareness of women in the 1970s. Television's rearticulation of this discourse of empowerment came in several forms. In prime-time television, series such as *The Mary Tyler Moore Show*, and *Rhoda* depicted single, career-oriented women surviving in the modern world. In daytime television, the plots of soap operas were transformed to include female leads with professional positions. *Donahue*, in this social context, can be seen as television as an institution recasting the female audience as a politically and socially sensitive population. This new form of talk show, then, was an expression of the empowering sentiment concerning women's rights within the structure of television programming. Donahue, the liberal Catholic father, epitomized the type of American male most sympathetic to the rights and interests of women. The program translated these new issues and concerns into a conflictual, emotionally charged relationship that worked to provide solidarity among women in the audience in support of Donahue on particular issues.

The Oprah Winfrey Show, which began in the mid-1980s, is constructed as an outlet for general outrage, primarily for women. As a program, however, it had to differentiate itself from its predecessor and now competitor, *Donahue*. Like its predecessor, *The Oprah Winfrey Show* was first a local program that, in head-to-head competition, produced better ratings than *Donahue* in the Chicago regional market and, prior to its move to Chicago, in the Baltimore market. When it was nationally syndicated in 1986, it was also enormously successful at attracting large audiences. Most critics attributed this to the frankness and "sassiness" of Oprah's personality. In comparison with the hosts of other programs this characterization of Oprah may be quite true, but what is more significant about this presentation of a television celebrity is that the celebrity more closely represented the audience itself. Oprah was a woman — not a man — sensitive to women's issues; Oprah also was a black woman. With her rounded, heavy figure, she also did not possess the physique of a beautiful actress or model. In all these ways, the celebrity sign of Oprah was constructed to represent that she had herself in her own lifetime become empowered. She, at the very least, represented symbolically the potential of empowerment of women, of marginalized groups within the American system. She represented, above all, a personality that emerged from the more common people and maintained a sensitivity to their needs. *The Oprah Winfrey Show* was organized around a presentation of Oprah as an accessible figure who was passionately interested in a host of issues. She then became the channeling device for providing the form of dramatic tensions and resolutions between persons and issues that have become the entertaining element of the program. Once Oprah's integrity was established within this format, which essentially could be translated that her celebrity sign had a certain stability, the topics themselves became less significant. Thus, we find innocuous themes discussed or Hollywood celebrities being the object of scrutiny on certain episodes.

Oprah's slide into prime-time television in 1993 was fabricated on her accessibility and sensitivity to marginalized cultures within American culture, particularly when individuals from those margins have become contemporary cultural icons. Her February 1993 prime-time interview with Michael Jackson at his bizarre Neverland Ranch provides the material for the forms of cultural power that Oprah now possesses: she is unthreatening to the most reclusive of black celebrities and therefore can gain access to their private and, in Michael Jackson's case, idiosyncratically indulgent, intimate worlds. Jackson's familiarity with Oprah, his constructed "candidness," is evidence of her equality with the star. Her sensitivity and sycophancy, her exclusive and unique attributes employed to make the unfamiliar familiar for a moment, allow us to see the mystery of the celebrity Jackson personality. On her afternoon show, Oprah is the populist channel to empowerment no matter what the object of discussion might be. In her special prime-time interviews, Oprah embodies the hegemonic power of television to include and encompass through private revelation.[24] Both are forms of a public talking cure that television has embraced and that Oprah has occupied as therapist.

The Uses of Oprah

Because of this construction of the celebrity sign that maintains its distinction through a form of familiarity and populism with an audience, Oprah as celebrity is seen to be approachable by that same audience. There is a tension in the construction of any celebrity whose fame is built on approachability and proximity to his or her audience. The familiar cast of the Oprah celebrity sign also emphasizes its ultimate vulnerability: because she is constructed as "from the people," the rationale for her position among public personalities cannot be based on her unique merits or gifts to any great degree. Her reason for possessing an exalted status, then, is never secure and is always the subject of debate and inquiry. Because of the nature of Oprah's celebrity sign, there is no real distinction in textuality between the textual and the extratextual, as in the case of film stars. Her continuous presence on television and her ubiquitous presence in various news sources means that her ability to construct a distance and aura is limited.[25] Oprah is constantly being accused of something in the tabloid press. In 1991, her status as a single but long-engaged woman was the object of a certain frenzy of concern. In the tabloid *Globe*, Stedman Graham, Oprah's fiancé, was exposed as someone hiding his family and its inbreeding past.[26] At the same time, Oprah also either is defending herself or being defended by others in various more legitimate press accounts.[27] Indeed, the debates that circulate about Oprah indicate that, as opposed to film celebrities, Oprah is much more familiar and also susceptible to the advice of her audience and the press.

The Use of the Name

In terms of the ancillary press and in relation to her own program and her own fans, Oprah Winfrey is known simply as Oprah. This may seem of minor significance, but under closer comparative inspection, it may shed some light on the construction of celebrity intimacy. With film actor Tom Cruise, his last name, Cruise, becomes his signature. The use of the first name connotes familiarity and lack of distance, whereas the use of the last name emphasizes formality. On one level, the use of the names is clearly an effort to provide differentiation: Oprah and Cruise *are* uncommon names. On another level, however, it indicates a gendered difference in the construction of celebrities and also a difference in institutional construction of celebrities. One can identify through this subtle difference that familiarity and intimacy are much more central to the construction of a female celebrity than to the construction of a male celebrity, and more common for a television celebrity than for a film celebrity. Where Cruise is an object of some mystery, and his power is related partly to the control of information, Oprah is constructed to be an open book — the intimate details of her life are not only well publicized, but also subject to debate. Indeed, we are invited into a debate about what is proper for Oprah in her life. Cruise, in contrast, builds respect by establishing a private and autonomous life — we are offered only illicit glimpses into his private affairs; our knowledge is restricted. With Oprah our knowledge of her behavior is much less restricted, and debates rage among her attackers, her defenders, and her own defenses of her well-publicized actions.[28] We are given information about Oprah *as if* we could give advice directly to her. With Cruise, personal information constitutes a type of voyeurism into the exclusive domains of the celebrity.

The Use of the Body

The celebrity sign of Oprah, like that of other female celebrities, is very much focused on the corporeal. Her body is the object of intense scrutiny and, among the audience, debate about her beauty, attractiveness, and transformation. The camera itself is blamed for the transformation of the natural body; according to popular wisdom, one looks ten pounds heavier on camera. Images of the bodies of female stars provide some of the raw materials for the construction of norms and normative positions about what the body should represent and what the ideal body should be. As I mentioned in a previous chapter, the body is seen as something to be altered to fit into the structures of the normative range of what is considered beautiful. It is now de rigueur for professional models to have breast enlargement surgery. Plastic surgery — to improve the shape of the nose, to make the lips fuller, or to remove a rib to improve the look of the torso — is a regular occurrence in the reconstruction of predominantly, though not exclusively, female celebrities.

As a female public personality, Oprah is implicated in this discourse of representation of the body. In the context of Oprah's position as a television host, her body has become the way in which a discourse of the body has been debated and discussed. Her body image has in itself formed the foci of a number of issues and topics; the distinctions between program and personality are blurred and blended. Oprah is constructed as an issue in the extratextual realm of newspapers and magazines and as an object of concern on her daily program.

Oprah has gone through several transformations of the body that have been used to substantiate her celebrity sign in some way. When she emerged as a national celebrity with her syndicated program in 1986, Oprah was heavyset and did not conform to the exigencies of the positive public presentation of the female form; she was outside of the normative construction of beauty because of her weight. What her figure did emphasize was that women who do not conform to the current body aesthetic can achieve success. Her body represented and subsequently organized a discourse of defiance and independence. Along with being black in a mediascape dominated by white culture, Oprah's body image represented a challenge from the margins. It was perceived as not particularly acceptable as a public presentation of women, but, within the context of a program that deals with human issues, it was seen as complementary to the show's content. Oprah's body image built her authenticity and reinforced perceptions of her sincerity.

In 1988, Oprah went on a severe diet. In the course of the season, she unveiled herself in a pair of tight designer jeans. She demonstrated her capacity to transform, to construct a new body image through apparent willpower. Unlike cosmetic surgery, weight loss is a form of body transformation that is conceptually within the realm of possibility of a large sector of the American population. Oprah engaged in a type of body transformation that could be understood and appreciated by a vast audience. She announced triumphantly in both the tabloids

Figure 5. Oprah's blending of the public and private worlds. The everydayness of Oprah allows her persona to move seamlessly from the public to the private and personal realm. Gender and body control provide for the proliferation of debates and discourses through Oprah, as the private world is personalized by Oprah. In a publicity vector, Oprah's transforming body becomes a form of promotion for countless other media sources that are at least partially organized around a related female audience. (Courtesy of the National Enquirer)

and mainstream entertainment magazines, "I'll never be fat again." In an article in *Essence,* a magazine aimed at black women, Oprah writes about how the weight loss has given her freedom and how now she is truly happy: "When I was overweight, I was living a lie. I could say 'I feel great about myself,' but I really didn't. There were times when I could get dressed and think that I looked okay, but there was always that feeling of being blocked. It was like having a brick wall in front of you that keeps you from moving forward."[29] She also solemnly swears that a weight problem is "not going to control my life ever again."[30] Oprah engages in public discourse about herself and her problems. There is very little attempt to separate her personal transformation from her public persona — we are aware of both the public and personal sides of Oprah. We appreciate the transformation.

Within a year after these interviews and articles appeared, Oprah had started to gain the weight back. In a February 1991 issue of the *National Enquirer,* a headline announced, "She's fat and happy at last."[31] In a cover story in *People* she was quoted as saying, with the same resolve that was in evidence about losing weight, "I'll never diet again."[32] In November 1990, she integrated her new body transformation into her show, titling the episode "The Pain of Regain." And she explained to her audience that "if you lose weight on a diet, sooner or later you'll gain it back."[33] The text is surrounded with images of Oprah when she was slim, juxtaposed with images of Oprah's fatness before and after the diet. Questions concerning her possible marriage to her boyfriend are framed in terms of her weight in several publications.

The saga has continued into the mid-1990s. Oprah's incarnation in 1994 and 1995 is concerned with diet and exercise that can be maintained. A cookbook by Oprah's personal chef, Rosie, through Oprah's production company and a special program devoted to her low-fat recipes, has become an international best-seller. The saga of her preparation to run a marathon allowed the supportive press to develop myriad profiles on the new Oprah.[34] The debate on her body as a kind of public forum has transformed somewhat; according to some, her loss of audience in the 1994–95 season is attributable to her new, less accessible, less vulnerable, slim image. Her body has become a representation of how familiar she can actually make herself with her audience.

Conclusion

The slide from public to private realm, which is expressed in
the public debate concerning Oprah's weight loss and weight gain,
leads to two overall conclusions about television celebrities as well
as celebrities and forms of celebrity construction in general. The first
is related to the way in which gender determines the interpretation of
legitimacy in the realm of the public personality. Oprah's body transformations functioned as a way in which discourses about the body
and body image could be openly discussed. A woman's body is seen to
be problematic and therefore necessitating transformations. Oprah positioned her own body as the physical embodiment of the debate. The
level of debate, though apparently conflictual, also ended up conform-
ing to the structure of her construction of human and social issues in
her television program: the personal struggle that is the core of the
content of the program is the domain of the public struggle. This leads
to the second conclusion: the debate about Oprah's body is also a
function of the way television constructs familiarity. The television
host is a celebrity whose separation from the audience and audience
concerns is never clearly made. The real life of the host, if the host is
constructed, like Oprah, as authentic and sincere, is never elided from
the stage performance. This unity of being goes beyond a homology
between the person and the celebrity; it is actively developed each
day by Oprah and other hosts in their programs. The private person
and the issues of the private person are the subject of the talk show.
The public person who guides this discussion is reconstructed to be
familiar and accessible; in other words, his or her public persona is
intensely invested with issues and concerns of the private sphere and
the associated subjectivity of that sphere.

Oprah Winfrey presents the full complexity of the television celebrity, which is often a form of public personality that depends upon
proximity to and powers of explaining other celebrities. Oprah articulates the way in which the apparatus of television works to recast
the audience through its identification with new faces of familiarity
and new constructions of social concern. She is a constructed television celebrity who is built on a reconfiguration of the women's television audience. Although not obvious, this reconfiguration of the television audience is very much connected to the organization of the
industry around the sustainability of audiences, which are retrans-

lated as markets and consumers. The greatest evidence of this recon-figuration of audiences is represented by the massive income Oprah Winfrey makes each year for her work at audience formation: $50–$60 million. It is also generally conceded that Oprah is the most powerful person in contemporary television. Her ability to manage the movement of the private into the public has allowed her to develop autonomy through her ownership of a successful production company, a large studio, and six television stations.[35]

The Meanings of the Popular Music Celebrity: The Construction of Distinctive Authenticity

The transformations that have taken place in popular music in the twentieth century can be attributed to a number of factors, including the use of new technologies, changes in the size of performance venues, the growth of the recording industry, and the segmentation of the mass market. Discursively, all of these factors have been modalized around concepts of authenticity. At the center of these debates concerning the authentic nature of the music is the popular music performer; how he or she expresses the emotionality of the music and his or her own inner emotions, feelings, and personality and how faithful the performer is to the intentions of the musical score are all part of how the individual performer is determined to be authentic. What follows is an examination of the genealogy of the popular music celebrity and how the focus on the star has shaped debates concerning the authentic quality of popular music. Like the movie industry, the popular music industry has become located primarily in the United States. Aside from a few deviations, the following discussion of the industry-celebrity relationship in popular music is concerned with American popular music.

The Industrial Construction of the Popular Music Star

The development of celebrity status in the production of popular music is closely connected with the mass reproduction of songs. In the nineteenth and early twentieth centuries, sheet music production and distribution were the economic heart of the music industry. Performers in music halls and vaudeville theaters became the principal means of expanding the market for particular compositions beyond regional boundaries and interests. As vehicles for the promotion of songs, song performers were very important for the music publishing companies. At the same time, poor material—that is, unpopular songs—could hurt singers' performance careers. In the construc-

150

tion of the sheet music commodity, the singing star was simultaneously developed. Above the illustration on the cover page of most sheet music productions, the name of the performer would vie in size with the name of the song. In this way, the buying public was able to link song with singing star. Million-selling song sheets were not uncommon in the late nineteenth and early twentieth centuries. In fact, between 1900 and 1910, one hundred song sheets sold a million copies each and therefore occupied the very center of the music industry.[1] The audience for popular songs was composed primarily of the middle class, among whom a popular pastime was to sing the pieces with piano accompaniment in their own living rooms. The arrangements were quite simple, so that the singing and playing could be handled by a large amateur population.

Essentially, there were two overlapping markets for song production: the stage performance and the song publication. The performer, working with elaborate orchestration and arrangement, created the professional version of the song—the official text. At the turn of the century, the nascent recording industry built on the reproduction of these official texts of music and song. To establish a recording's authenticity, the most famous performer associated with the song would be enlisted to sing it. Thus, the recording industry used the system of stars established by the music publishing business for its foundation.

The industry, centered in New York City, rapidly developed a division of labor in order to maintain a level of production that could satisfy the primary market of song sheets and the secondary market of records. This entailed the employment of what were called "tunesmiths" to manufacture new songs for performers and publication. It was critical to the organization of the industry that these composers were employees, because the principal means of revenue/profit accumulation for the industry was the copyright, which was held by the music publishing company. This gave the company, not the individual, the recording and publishing rights to any song produced by its employees for fifty years. The tunesmiths themselves were usually paid a flat rate per song. For example, Charles Graham, the writer of a popular song of 1891, "The Picture That Is Turned Towards the Wall," received about fifteen dollars for that work.[2] The writers of Tin Pan Alley remained relatively anonymous for the first two decades of the twentieth century. Songs were identified either by their titles or by the names of the star performers associated with them—also employees of the recording industry.

The other critical transformation of musical culture that the music industry fostered was the active generalization of regional differences. The tunesmiths were often involved in the appropriation of regional folk music—which was intimately connected to particular communities' systems of meaning—and the homogenization of its appeal. David Buxton connects this transformation to the industrialization and urbanization of American culture and the new social needs that emerged as people were divorced from these regional contexts. The songs produced maintained an abstract stylistic connection to regional folk music, but were new in their appeal to persons living and working in the cities. The types of songs produced could be said to contain traces of social memories of regions; these traces, from an array of sources, were now used to construct differences and variety in popular song production.[3] The repetition of an uncopyrighted folk song generated no capital; variations in the composition and lyrics of folk songs allowed for the application of copyright and the generation of capital. As many authors have attested, one of the key sources for appropriation (because it was free) was antebellum black American music.[4] This appropriation of black musical style into the mass production of popular music established one of the dominant strains of contemporary popular music.

Singers of the late nineteenth and early twentieth centuries were part of this process of generalization for the mass market of regional styles. Buxton describes most vaudeville and music hall singers as local celebrities.[5] They left their home areas to perform in other communities and presented musical styles that were not of the regions in which they performed. Thus, their market reach was somewhat limited. Buxton uses the example of the transformation of country music to detail the changes many performers underwent to appeal to the developing mass market. The original country musicians who recorded in the 1920s were older part-time musicians who had achieved a certain celebrity status within their region playing a particular style of music. Performers like Fiddlin' John Carson and Charlie Oaks were well into their fifties when they first recorded. According to Buxton, record sales and radio play fostered the attribution of distinctive regional style to the personal style of the recording artist. The recording artist, because of the consumption demands of an audience whose use of the music was less connected to the cultural significance of a particular regional musical style and more connected to a general capitalist culture and leisure, quickly depleted his or her traditional repertoire of songs. Because of this different relationship to the music, which had been abstracted from its regional source, the recording artist became the center for production of new songs in a similar style. By the 1940s, a performer's musical style became a resource upon which he or she would draw to construct new melodies and thus new "personalizations." The incorporation of regional style had been completed through the development of the versatile country music artist.[6]

The Technology of the Popular Music Celebrity

Through the use of the technologies of reproduction and distribution, the possibility of a fundamentally different relationship of the audience to the pleasures of popular music and their stars became manifest. The breakdown of difference on the basis of region became reconstituted in the urban setting in terms of tastes, likes, and dislikes. New conceptions of authenticity had to be developed in popular music that integrated this new relationship to musical style.

The technology of reproduction problematizes the concept of authenticity. In the development of the popular music celebrity, the recording technology has worked to authenticate the particular and individual performance, partly through the progressive perfection of sound recording and sound reproduction technology. However, the construction of the technological reproduction of songs has also changed the meaning of the live and in-person performance of concerts. The music industry, through its stars, has constructed two sometimes contradictory levels of the "real" and authentic. The recording has become the true representation of the music; the concert has become the faithful reproduction of the "authentic" recorded music.[7] It has become a common experience of concert audiences to sense the inadequacies of the live performance in comparison with the recorded music they associate with the performer. Studio technology and studio sound, with its twenty-four-track editing capability, cannot be matched by the indeterminate acoustics of the concert hall/stadium, the fallibility of performers, and the inability to produce all of the same recorded sounds within less controlled environments. In some instances, the stars of the concert no longer actually sing or perform; instead they lip-synch and dance to the reproduced sounds of their records in front of the audience.[8] I shall return to the new meanings of the live concert in a subsequent part of this chapter. What I want to deal with specifically here are the different meanings and experiences that are offered by the technology in the production and consumption of records, and how these have constructed the types of celebrity figures that have emerged in popular music in the twentieth century.

First of all, as I have mentioned above, recordings tend to sanctify particular performers' renditions of particular songs. A song, in essence, becomes a sign of the performer. It has been quite common, therefore, for popular music celebrities to "possess" signature tunes. Roy Rogers's "Happy Trails," Sinatra's comeback "My Way," Judy Garland's "Over the Rainbow," and Paul Robeson's "Old Man River" are all examples of songs and performers that are inseparable.

The same focus on the correct or original version of a song by a particular star changes the uses made of music by the audience. With song sheets, the audience was involved in their own reproduction of the work. With records, the use of music became oriented toward an audience of listeners, not amateur performers. The record professionalized the means of musical production through its coding of orchestration and the performer's singing, codes that far surpassed the capacity of the amateur piano player and singer. To hear a particular song in the home increasingly meant listening to it, either on a record or on the radio.

The domestic nature of the technology of reception worked in the reorientation of the perception of the popular music performance and performer. Within their own living rooms, listeners could enjoy the very best and most popular singers and performances. The record player privatized the technology of exhibition. Moreover, the activity of listening permitted the investment of personal experiences into the meaning of the music to a greater degree than did concert performances. In the privatized world of consumption, the listener, by purchasing a record, could sense his or her personal possession of the song and performer. Though distanced through technological apparatuses, performer and audience were brought closer together by the audience's listening to recorded music, thus domesticating entertainment and the performance of the popular music star.

In successive technological inventions, the private and personal activity of listening has been privileged. The development of the 45 rpm record and record player in the 1950s was a way to increase the sales of smaller format, more portable machines for the rapidly expanding youth market. Middle-class teenagers could potentially have their own record players and singles record collections in their own rooms. Similarly, transistor radios could be produced cheaply in compact, lightweight sizes for personalized uses.[9] Popular music, through the portable transistor radio, became an integral part of a variety of leisure pursuits. Transistor technology was embraced particularly by youth in their attempts to construct distinctive social spaces. Finally, consumer acceptance in the early 1980s of the Sony Walkman, the entirely personalized stereo radio and tape player, articulated the ultimate privileging of private listening practices. With headphones, the Walkman listener isolated his or her pleasure in a manner that the radio speaker never achieved. The tape player also allowed for the personal programming of taste; the listener, with complete portability, was also independent of radio stations' programming styles. All of these technological innovations have served to personalize the relationship between the musical artist and the listening public.

Technology and Performance

In terms of the technology of musical production, one can identify a trend that has also been configured around the privileging of the personal and the individual. This movement can be seen in the changes in popular music performing styles that resulted from the integration of electronic recording and the use of the microphone.

The first performer to sell in excess of a million records was the opera star Enrico Caruso, in 1901.[10] Caruso possessed the technical perfection of the voice—at least as it was understood in the aesthetics of classical music. In contrast, popular music singers of the past thirty-five years have eschewed the classical perfection of the voice in favor of expressing the emotionality and personality of the voice. The other model of the professional vocalist from the early recording era of popular music—equally rejected by most contemporary performers—was the music hall and vaudeville star. Like the opera singer, the popular singer was able to project his or her voice to the very back of the concert hall. Al Jolson epitomized this early-twentieth-century style of singing, where the power of the voice—its depth and range—qualified the singer for star status. However, the invention of the microphone made the need for such large, full voices less central in popular music. Al Jolson, with his half-singing/half-talking, minstrel/vaudeville style, never adapted to the microphone. Rudy Vallee, the megaphone star, was the first to work comfortably with the microphone in expressing the new possibilities of intimacy that it allowed. Bing Crosby, along with a host of other singers known as crooners, managed to use the microphone as if he were singing quietly to one other person.[11] The relaxed nature of the crooning style became dominant on 1930s radio shows hosted by the leaders of various big bands of the swing era. This movement to intimacy and personal style complemented the development of the receiving technology of popular music. Since the crooners, vocalists have continued to experiment with the "grain of the voice," the texture of vocal style that can express intimacy, individuality, and a range of emotions.[12]

Popular Music's Performance Codes

Performance also emerged from the structure of the popular music industry. With specific people employed as composers—the tunesmiths of Tin Pan Alley—there was a complementary network of stars to interpret those songs. The division of labor between stars and the relatively anonymous songwriters was further accentuated by the major Hollywood studios' purchase of the principal music publishing houses of New York during the 1930s. The movie musical, which served as a promotional vehicle for the introduction of film sound, also aided in the construction of identifiable images and personalities connected to the popular songs that were heard on the radio. The emphasis on the vocalist was in sharp contrast to the big band/swing era's emphasis on the band leader. In retrospect, it is surprising to learn that Crosby, the most famous of the crooners, was relegated to the back row of Paul Whiteman's orchestra and, like other vocalists of the early swing era, was treated like any other musician with an instrument to play.[13] Film and radio exposure gradually changed the orientation of the music industry toward the star vocalist.

In sharp contrast to the construction of the star vocalist in mainstream popular music, the black popular music tradition of the twentieth century presented the model of the singer-songwriter. But within black blues and jazz, there was a gender division in place from the 1920s to the 1940s that articulated the acceptability of black female performers singing for white audiences and the inacceptability, in most clubs, of black male performers singing for white audiences. Bessie Smith, the renowned female blues singer of the 1920s, was a veritable star. In contrast, black male blues performers such as Blind Lemon Jefferson and Robert Johnson performed and played in relative obscurity, even though their music formed the basis of much of the blues repertoire of singers like Bessie Smith. It was impossible for these musicians to become included in the culture industry's star-making machinery.

The integration of this other contrasting tradition in the production of popular music into the mainstream of the industry is connected to two labor and copyright disputes that took place in the early 1940s. First of all, the American Society of Composers, Authors and Publishers (ASCAP), an organization that represented composers and publishers and collected royalties for the use of songs on radio and by performers, demanded a 200 percent increase in royalty rates in 1941.[14] The radio networks refused to pay the increase and subsequently organized Broadcast Music Incorporated (BMI), their own copyright organization, and started to play records that were not under ASCAP's jurisdiction. This led to the use of non-Tin Pan Alley songs, which generally meant country and western and blues music. In 1942, a musicians' union strike meant that once again radio was without the records it had relied upon for its shows for the previous decade. The radio networks turned to the only nonunionized musical worker — the vocalist. According to Buxton, this led to further reliance on vocal stars in popular music and a decline in the influence of the big bands.[15] The temporary dependence on marginal musical sources by radio, combined with the fostered maturation of the solo singing star, permitted the development and acceptance of the performance style of the rock and roll of the 1950s.

Several writers consider the singer Johnnie Ray to be the transitional figure in the development of the contemporary popular music performance style.[16] Ray freely acknowledged that he was not a very good singer; rather, he could be characterized as an expressionist. He integrated the body and sexuality in his often tearful pleas to his audience; his movement was described by one music critic as "writhing" in torment. He gesticulated wildly with his arms, unlike the controlled, virtually unmoving professionalism of Sinatra, whose only bodily gesture of individuality was the snapping of his fingers. Ray often punctuated the finish of a song by falling dramatically to his knees as he caressed the microphone. Elvis Presley's characteristic roll of the hips and snarl carried on the tradition of expressing individuality in performance through the public codes of sexual gesture. The stance of the male rocker, the guitar as phallic symbol, and the energy and vitality of stage movement and acrobatics have all become codes of rock performance. The rock performance style emerged out of the confluence of black performance style with the need to express the sincerity of personality and individuality of the performer/star.

The Rhetoric of Performance

Although the integration of sexuality and expressivity into the performer's style identifies a break with some of the past traditions of twentieth-century musical representation, there is also a continuity of form in performance. The mode of address, unlike in the play or the film, is constructed to be direct. Whether on record or in concert, the vocalist includes the audience in this address. In the love song, the address is quite direct; the audience replaces the lost or newfound love. In the blues song, the address is often one of lament; it remains a story directed at the audience, as if it were another individual in the conversation. Indeed, structured into the blues song is the call and response between guitar and vocals. It is quite common for blues audiences to "respond" in simple affirmations, as if engaged in conversation. The directness of the address of the musical performer has always constructed the relationship between performer and audience at a very personal level. Classical and professional performance codes attempt to distance the singer from the content of the music. In the attempt to express the emotions of the musical and lyrical content of the song, the contemporary popular music performer has worked to authenticate his or her performance through acknowledgment of the direct nature of the address. The personal sentiments expressed in the song's lyrics are freely exposed in action and voice. Audience participation and response are encouraged in the concert setting during the performance of most songs. In this way, a ritualized dialogue is maintained between performer and audience.

There also exists a rhetorical dialogic relationship between the concert performance and the recording. Audience members' use of the concert is mediated by their prior use of the records. In the production of popular music, most of the music performed in concert has appeared in recordings prior to the concert appearance. The concert is used by the band or performer and the recording company as a method of promoting the record commodity; it sustains interest in the product beyond its release date in the popular press, in trade papers, and with fans.[17] The concert is therefore not an introduction to the music for the fans, but a form of ritualized authentication of pleasure and meaning of the records through a "lived" experience; it heightens the significance of the records and the pop star. The fan is demonstrating his or her solidarity with the artist's message and with the rest of the audience. The concert, then, becomes much more a display and expression by the audience member of a personal commitment to and a celebration of the performer than an appreciation of the performer's skill and technique in performing live.

Youth and the Construction of the Contemporary Popular Music Star

Central to the construction of the popular music star of the past forty years is the capacity for its sign to express the difference and significance of youth. It has been argued, by Simon Frith and others, that in the postwar years the teenager became a kind of categorization that broke with the usual form of differentiation on the basis of class.[18] Youth was one of the ways in which categories of consumption could redefine the social world, and therefore it became a useful passageway for the elaboration of a new consumer subjectivity. The potential youth market in most Western societies grew enormously after World War II. In England, teenage disposable income grew by 100 percent between 1938 and 1958; similarly, in the United States, teenagers' average weekly revenue grew from $2.50 to $10 a week.[19] Without the weight of family obligation, teens could devote their income completely to the construction of a style of leisure consumption. The cues for the construction of a distinctive style were drawn from the movies and popular music, which began servicing the social needs of this new market.

Several authors have interpreted the new divisions in society created by the development of a separate and distinct youth culture in terms of the way the dominant culture viewed the transformation as a threat.[20] The 1950s have been construed as a period of moral panic, when the dominant culture considered the new ethics, the new focus on sexuality, and the emphasis on leisure, entertainment, and pleasure as assaults on the traditional values of hard work and just reward. Teenage films of the period oscillated between depicting the pleasures of the new morality and the dangers of excess. Popular music—specifically rock and roll—stars represented the incarnation of excess, decadence, and pleasure without connection to morality. For parental culture, according to this interpretation, rock and roll stars presented the emulatory material for the corruption of their teenagers. A clear-cut generational opposition is at the center of the moral panics hypothesis, which asserts that the progressive forces of change aligned squarely with youth and its representatives in popular music, and the disciplining nature of the dominant culture was articulated through the category of parents. Popular music, then, became a kind of battle-ground of ideal representations to include youth. On one side, black performers like Little Richard and—more dangerously, because their turf was the racial and economic center of American culture—white performers like Elvis Presley and Jerry Lee Lewis, who had integrated black performance styles, represented the out-of-control nature of teenage lifestyle. On the other side, the disciplined singing and performing style of performers like Pat Boone, who reinterpreted rock and roll with larger orchestrations and less sexually suggestive lyrics, represented the acceptable form of youth culture for parents and the dominant morality.

What needs to be integrated into the moral panics hypothesis, which continues in various forms to be at the center of the study of contemporary popular music, is the fact that the oppositional structure between parents and youth has been fostered by elements of the dominant culture itself. The 1950s, therefore, represent not only the clear distinctiveness of a youth culture, but a clear-cut emergence of a market segment for the circulation of goods and services. The new threat of youth is the integration of a consumption ethic into the general culture. The clash between a production and consumption ethos, openly displayed in the 1950s and 1960s, is configured through a generational conflict. Implicit in the structuring of a conflict in generational terms is its ultimate resolution through the succession of one generation by the next. Thus, consumption in the succeeding generation can be seen as a positive form of constructing one's social identity. The division of the social world into patterns of consumption generally configured around the concepts of style and lifestyle has become naturalized and is no longer in opposition to a morality of work and production. The oppositional structure of the 1950s and 1960s was reconfigured by the 1970s and 1980s into stylistic differentiation. In terms of the market, the differentiation is labeled market fragmentation or segmentation.

Popular music and its celebrities have operated at the nucleus of the production of stylistic differentiation through consumption and leisure. The presentation of the star, his or her musical roots, style of dress, manner of speech, and public display of sexuality are all signifi-cant markers for the structuring and differentiating of youth culture. In the 1960s, differentiations of style were modalized around the dis-play of authenticity as a rupture from the performing styles of past generations. The largest and most enduring transformation took the form of a move toward performers' writing their own material and the related celebration of the singer-songwriter. In this way, new artists appeared to the audience to control their own destinies and thereby directly shaped the entire recording industry to reflect specific aspira-tions and desires. Top stars demanded and received "artistic free-dom" partly through the opportunity to produce their own records and partly through the financial rewards of large royalties and record sales that allowed them to experiment. The star's cultural power de-pended on a very close affinity with a specific and loyal audience. The star, then, was actively engaged in the construction and differentia-tion of audience groups, in terms of style and taste, and in authenti-cating their elevated position. The popular music star, more than other forms of celebrity, had to be a virtual member of his or her own au-dience in order to sustain his or her influence and authenticity, and the commitment of the fan.

In the 1960s, some performers constructed their authenticity around naturalness and the rejection of performance codes. Folk performers such as Joan Baez eschewed the concept of spectacle in dress and ap-pearance to be more closely affiliated with the audience. Barefoot, without makeup, and wearing simple clothes, Baez would sing with only the accompaniment of an acoustic guitar. The stylistic configu-ration she portrayed was emulated by a generation of women. Rock performers like the Rolling Stones built their authenticity on their musical and lyrical roots. Their musical and performance style of overt sexuality was built on black rhythm and blues. Bob Dylan's authenticity depended on a literary aesthetic code of the genius creator.

Innovation and Transformation in the Popular Music Celebrity

A recurring technique for establishing authenticity in popular music performance is the breaking of codes and the creation of new or transformed codes of style. *Style* may indicate, for example, a different musical code, a new form of dance, or an altered way of dress. The new style is invariably drawn from a particular audience group or subculture and is then rearticulated by the popular music performer. Style represents a statement of difference as well as a statement of solidarity with the particular audience. A change in style indicates a reassertion by the performer of his or her own authenticity. Any style eventually loses its power to represent difference, as the marketplace continuously appropriates the idiosyncrasies of codes of style for commodity innovation. Thus, the popular music performer is also continuously appropriating new representations of individuality through style.

There are two implications connected to the instability of the codes of style of popular music. First, popular musical style is defined through collectivities. The subcultural and marginal origins for the appropriation of style demand an affinity with the meaning and significance of the subcultural style on the part of the popular performer. It is also relevant that popular music is collective in nature; the dominant structure in rock music is not the individual performer, but the band. A band may have a leader or key figure who comes to represent the band publicly, but the band's name usually is more widely known than are the names of any of the individual players. Collective forms of identity, then, are central to contemporary popular music. The individual star may emerge from this emphasis on collective identity, but in distancing him- or herself from the band, the individual draws on codes of performance that are more connected to the conceptions of the singing star of the 1930s and 1940s.

Second, popular music's attempts to break and remake codes bring the form into closer alignment with movements in modern art than with other culture industries. The popular musician's play with style can also be thought of in aesthetic terms. Moreover, many of the British popular music groups of the 1960s and 1970s were formed in the art schools opened in the 1950s.[21] Artistic movements such as avant-gardism, dadaism, impressionism, abstract art, surrealism, and, most significant, pop art have entered into popular music partly in the form of album covers and partly in terms of the claims and pretensions of practice that musicians have maintained in their pose as popular artists. A number of romantic connotations of the nineteenth- and twentieth-century artist have been integrated into the posturings and styles of the contemporary popular music celebrity. The pallor of the rock star recalls the consumptive starving artist or the genius whose body has been ravaged by excess and drugs. The litheness and thin frame recall the youthfulness of the romantic poets, who, like the near mythic Thomas Chatterton, died before they were thirty.[22] The experiential lifestyle refers to a number of artistic movements that have emerged out of the twentieth century. The anarchy and nihilism graphically depicted, for example, by the Who's ritualistic destruction of their instruments, hearkens back to the dadaists. The bohemian lifestyle that surfaced in many European cities in the nineteenth century has served as fecund ground on which to construct the pop star's public presence.[23] Finally, the ultimate play with the pretensions of artistic posture are articulated in the music videos produced to embellish the image of the popular group. Videos are often filled with surrealism; they represent avant-garde filmmaking that serves to associate the popular star with the style and romantic connotations of the innovative artist.

Summary

The celebrity of popular music is constructed from elements quite different from those that make up the film celebrity. These elements are related to the technology of production and reception, the form of address that is peculiar to the singing of a song, the industrial and commodity configuration of the musical product, and the audience's collective and individual relationship to the music and performer. Fundamental to the construction of the popular music celebrity is the conveyance of both commitment and difference. *Commitment* in this context refers to the audience's close and intimate relationship to the pop star as well as the way in which the artist conveys his or her authenticity in representing the audience. In some cases, authenticity is displayed through emotional sincerity: the performer's direct and personal address in the song is further individualized through the private forms of reception. This kind of personal relationship between performer and audience describes the more classical construction of the popular music star to emerge in the twentieth century. In other cases, authenticity is expressed through the performer's communication of solidarity with an audience. The focus in these instances is on the creation and maintenance of codes of difference and particularity by both audience and performer.

The development of this second discourse on authenticity in popular music coincides roughly with the emergence of rock music. Within rock music, the appeal to authenticity has been developed by industry, artist, and audience into the formation of taste cultures, where the expression of a particular consumption style becomes more central to the public presentation of identity. As discussed above, popular music has been at the interstices of the formation of a new consumer subjectivity. Its active work in construction of new collectivities and new social categories on the basis of lifestyle and taste has bestowed on its representatives — its celebrities — social power. Occasionally, the social power that has congealed in popular music has facilitated the organization of social movements opposed to the general organization of the social structure. In a sense, the configuration of power in popular music identifies an elemental risk in the organization of new social identities in consumer capitalism. Differentiation and innovation to create distinction are fundamental parts of commodity production; however, they necessitate an active play with the meanings and social needs that are embodied in the commodity for the consumer. The popular music celebrity represents the continuous reorganization of consumer subjectivities into collective forms of identity.

In the following section, I present an analysis of the group New Kids on the Block in terms of the way the celebrity signs of the group and its members have emerged in the public sphere from the organization of the popular music industry. The discourses of authenticity, commitment, and difference operate in the formation of any popular music group, and the following hermeneutic reveals the particular manner in which these discourses operate in the formation and success of New Kids on the Block.

The Construction of a "Phenomenon": New Kids on the Block

An integral part of the lexicon of the popular music industry and its forms of self-promotion is the concept of the "phenomenon." Because of the 90 percent failure rate of recordings manufactured to generate profit, the industry is organized toward "hitting."[24] The 10 percent of records that actually generate earnings not only subsidize the failures but also account for the substantial profits of the entire industry. Thus, in actual fact, very few of the recordings made generate most of the revenues. As a result, the industry appears to be disorganized; it seems to be incapable of determining with any consistency which records and acts are going to sell well and which acts are going to be financial losses. The industry attempts to solve this problem in three principal ways: by issuing compilations of recordings that have previously sold well ("greatest hits" records); by concentrating on production, distribution, and promotion of established acts (e.g., the Rolling Stones are what is often called a "bankable" act); and by intensely promoting specific new acts with costly videos, tour support, and advertisements.

The popular music industry is often described as volatile and unpredictable. The product the industry deals with is, possibly more than other cultural products, in the domain of affect and outside of the realm of reason and the rational. Music and the uses of music are very much connected to the emotive side of human existence. The recording industry is constantly trying to tap this emotive side through the production of music. In a sense, it is attempting to contain feelings so that, at least temporarily, they can be defined by singers or songs.

The "phenomenon" in popular music is the recording act that has somehow captured a massive audience. In the language of the industry, these phenomena are out of the industry's control. The term *phenomenon*, which was used to describe the Beatles in a previous era and New Kids on the Block in the late 1980s and early 1990s, borrows from the manner in which nature is described: much like a hurricane or a tornado, the popular music phenomenon is a naturally occurring event that appears to be unpredictable in time, place, or force. It "hits" with incredible power and, if strong enough, may "hit" more than once. A rash of sales statistics chart the power of the phenomenon: in 1989, New Kids on the Block sold more than fourteen million records in North America, composed of ten charted albums and singles; their album *Hangin' Tough* was the second best-selling album of that year; in terms of concerts, the group made $73.8 million in ticket sales in 1990, which places them second in all-time concert tour revenues.[25] *People's* cover story on New Kids revels in the language of powerful nature: "The Kids are riding the crest of the most frenzied pop-music phenomenon since Beatlemania."[26] Integrated with this force-of-nature conception of popular music's construction of the relationship between the audience and the cultural product is the language of warfare. New musical groups "explode onto the scene," and a recent surge in the popularity of dance music was called an "explosion." In the 1960s, the plethora of successful British bands in North America was described as an "invasion." Following the punk "invasion" of the 1970s, there was the "new wave," which in its terminology successfully blends militaristic language with another metaphor from the forces of nature.

This use of natural phenomenon/battlefield terminology by the popular music press and the industry itself has developed over time into a shorthand method of trying to describe the irrationality that is central to the way the industry operates. As well, descriptions of popular music changes and transformations, often referred to in previous decades as "crazes," have functioned as central metaphors in the discourse of cultural change itself, of a culture in constant transformation and upheaval. It is a discourse that, through its emphasis on unpredictability coupled with the inevitability of change, reshapes people's actions into reactions to these various phenomena. The invasive discourse that surrounds popular music is constructed to encourage us to be caught up in the wave of sentiment that affirms the significance of the latest phenomenon. In that affirmation and acceptance of the new musical sound and group, we collectively are encouraged to let the sentiment of the last phenomenon dissipate into history. With New Kids on the Block, the mainstream press explains that the "fever" they have created has "reached delirium status."[27]

The framing of popular music discourse in the language of spontaneous and explosive phenomenal change is also constructed to emphasize the cultural products' close relationship to the audience. What is being underlined is that the audience is determining the style of music, the types of personalities elevated to superstar status, and the timing of change and transformation. The industry becomes in this construction merely a way of channeling the popular will. As it is explained in one of myriad biographies that have accompanied New Kids' emergence, the group's popularity may be accounted for by the fact that "they care about their fans so much."[28] Popular music phenomena such as the New Kids on the Block are pure expressions of popular will, which is represented as pure sentiment.

To describe the nature of these phenomena of popular music, which are organized around personalities and groups, is thus a very difficult process. They are packaged in a discourse of change and are intimately tied to the way in which cultural change is articulated in postwar American society in particular and Western society in general. This discourse of change is elemental in their formation in the culture and elemental in their construction of power. As well, they house formations of collective sentiment and feeling; in other words, they are defined to a degree by the audience that, through a specific array of cultural products, feels connected to the phenomenon. In embodying a form of collectivity, the popular music phenomenon represents the modern crowd in all its irrationality and emotionality. To extend logically from this, the popular music industry, in its perpetual construction of new phenomena, is an apparatus that tries to organize and focus the crowd's intensity into recognizable forms and products of consumption. The industry is an apparatus for the congealing of emotions and sentiments into recognizable sounds, images, and personalities that work to maintain the intensity of emotion. When the emotional intensity dissipates, the industry works to construct new forms of intense sentiments around new images, sounds, and personalities. In many senses, the popular music industry works to manage the contemporary crowd and, in fact, to organize its irrationality.

The Established Structure

The industry, in its massaging of public tastes, has developed certain patterns or structures in how new popular music celebrities are presented. What appears to be new and is presented as new and different to a large degree is organized around these structures of representation. Thus, New Kids on the Block, in terms of marketing positioning, style of promotion, and industry support, had certain precursors. The group was also positioned by the industry in clear opposition to and distinction from other forms of music and celebrity images. This form of distinction and opposition is also a well-trodden path; apart from differences that emerge from musical style and the contingency and lived experience of the group's core audience, New Kids on the Block followed this structure.

First of all, central to the identity and position of New Kids on the Block was the youth of the group's members. Within popular music, minor differences in age can be constructed as crucially significant. The emergence of any new star is often organized to present his or her youthfulness in contradistinction to established acts. New stars represent the vitality of their music. They also are constructed as a form of initiation for new music buyers. The bulk of the record-buying public is roughly between the ages of sixteen and thirty-two, and is overwhelmingly male.[29] As discussed above, the music industry is involved in the servicing of a youth market that first arose with the growth in disposable income among youth in North America following the Second World War. Since the 1950s, popular music stars have represented the same age (and generally the same sex) as the central record-buying demographic. However, there have always been some pop stars who have been marketed to appeal to a demographic much younger and more female than the central record-buying public. New Kids on the Block was a group that was positioned to appeal to the neophyte consumer of popular music.

If one looks at the history of pop stars who have been marketed and positioned in the role of "teen idol," it becomes readily apparent that though all are musical performers, music has often been less central to these individuals' profitability as celebrities than have other products. Marketing of the teen idol generally focuses on the image, which is circulated in a number of formats that go beyond the musical product: posters, animated television series, Barbie-sized look-alike dolls, comic and photobiographical books, fanzines, clothing, and lunch pail designs, to name a few of the more visible and successful examples. The intense focus on the image has often been the line of demarcation between male and female audiences, preteen and young adult audiences, and, in terms of musical categories, pop and rock.[30] The teen idol is structured to appeal to the preteen and young teen female pop audience member and children in general. Teen idols are generally scorned by older music buyers as inauthentic and fabricated. For the younger record-buying market, the teen idol is the conduit for the move from the toy market of childhood into the market of youth. Teen idols are positioned as transitional icons for the youthful audience that will ultimately form the future mainstay of recording industry sales. It is because of this transitional quality that teen idols are commodified in forms and images that are relatively nonthreatening to this young audience and to the ancillary market of parents. Indeed, the teen idol is himself generally managed and chaperoned as an entirely dependent being throughout his entire career as a teen idol (which is invariably brief). In this way, the teen idol never appears to be autonomous and therefore is never threatening as an adult; he remains, as long as he is popular, perpetually childlike and dependent. The teen idol's image is similarly controlled and works to reinforce his lack of full independence.

The structure I have outlined concerning the teen idol that emerges from popular music varies somewhat with each incarnation. One can see that often the organization of the popular music star centers on the individual's relative autonomy. The less autonomous and independent the star, the more he is structured purely as teen idol. In the 1950s and 1960s, Elvis Presley surfaced as a popular music star of enormous influence and market appeal. However, unlike "pure" teen idols of the same era, Presley cultivated a clearly sexualized image, which constructed a code of independence, adulthood, and autonomy in his celebrity sign. In contrast, stars like Fabian, Frankie Avalon, and, to a degree, Pat Boone represented nonthreatening types of personalities that were constructed to present a harmless form of sexuality. Their predominant musical form was the ballad; Presley's original claim to fame was his raucous treatment of rock and roll songs.[31]

The question that arises from this delineation of type with the larger structural type of teen idol is, Why do these differentiations exist? The teen idol's image is structured to be ambiguous, particularly with reference to rebellion and sexuality. What must be remembered is that the teen idol is a transitional commodity that must in some instances appeal to parents' sensibilities as well as represent the youth culture and its spirit of difference and sometime opposition to parent culture. For example, there is an ambiguous quality in most teen idols' representation of sexuality. First, there is the clear structural division between predominantly male performer and young female audience. The male performer, though more often than not a young adult and therefore somewhat older than the younger female audience, is constructed not to be an adult. In terms of image, the obvious signs of puberty are underplayed, so that the male performer is seen as a "representation-ally removed" image of maleness. The male teen idol is overcoded to have a baby face, on which the absence of facial hair is significant in its articulation of nonmasculinity. The Beatles' bobbed long hair, lack of seriousness, and clean, hairless faces when they became famous can be seen as once again a play with sexuality, as they represented male-ness and nonmasculinity simultaneously to their young female audi-ence. Similarly, teen idol pop stars of the 1970s, such as David Cas-sidy, Leif Garrett, and Shaun Cassidy, possessed these same qualities of prepubescent maleness; they were physically slight and possessed boyish looks and wore hairstyles that resembled the predominant fem-inized fashion of the period.[32] Serious transgressions of these ambigu-ous codes of nonmasculinity/masculinity would remove the teen idol from the circulation of commodities aimed at this transitional market.

New Kids on the Block built on these patterns of the teen idol mu-sic star. The industry operates as the cultural memory of what is ef-fective in this construction of the transitional commodity. The Beatles, the Monkees, the Jackson Five, the Osmonds, and the Bay City Rollers provided the structural framework for the development of the con-cept of New Kids. It is interesting to see that most types of commodi-ties that were associated with New Kids had been previously tested and marketed for these precursors. Like the Beatles, New Kids had their own Saturday-morning animated television series. The animated series also indicated that these musical groups were positioned to en-tertain children, and, when defined as commodities, they moved be-tween toy products and promotional products of the recording indus-try. Their level of rebellion, then, was somewhat muted. The marketing of New Kids produced a plethora of products aimed at school-age chil-dren. Folders for school notes, lunch pails, T-shirts, dolls (which came in several sizes and materials), concert videos, television shows, games, and comic books made New Kids into a sign that served to sell a host of commodities beyond their music. The group also expanded into new techniques for reaching specific audience groups. For example, in 1989, 100,000 fans were calling a 900 number each week to hear their fa-vorite New Kid reveal a "secret."[33] A sales estimate for the 1990 New Kids line of merchandise was put at $400 million. Over and above this figure were concert earnings and video and record sales.[34] From 1989 to 1992, New Kids were constantly on the covers of preteen magazines in the magazines' efforts to ensure high sales. Their ubiquity through their attachment to a host of commodities made New Kids the most financially successful pop group ever.[35]

Partly because of this ubiquity, and partly because of New Kids members' appeal as clear pop stars, the popular music press has generally considered the group to be the epitome of inauthenticity.[36] Teen idols are therefore significant not only in terms of their core audience, they are also extremely relevant in establishing the authenticity of other forms of music and performers in the music industry. New Kids on the Block established the domain of the authentic in their obvious commerciality, their overt appeal to children, their studied and controlled rebellion, and their generally nonthreatening masculinity. These qualities provided the binarism that operates throughout the music industry between pop music and rock music, between the banal and the serious. New Kids were declared a contrivance and a marketing scam, the ultimate example of pop music's commercialism and superficiality.

New Kids' emergence does provide virtually all of the appropriate markers to indicate that they were a marketing invention that had been fabricated to be teen idols. There is a subtle distinction being made here. In popular music that is usually called rock, the audience is believed to be independent and therefore able to discern what is good music from bad or contrived music. The performers are likewise independent thinkers and creators. In contrast, the audience of groups like New Kids is considered to be manipulated, duped by marketers and promoters. It is for this reason New Kids appealed only to children; anyone else would have recognized the marketing scheme and identified the inauthentic nature of the group. Like their principal audience, this argument goes, New Kids themselves were controlled and managed by a team of marketers and coaches.

The verity of most of these claims is borne out in any study of the group's formation. But what is missing in such an analysis is that New Kids itself was used as a foil for the legitimation of other forms of music that appear to be less contrived and, in comparison with New Kids, less commercial. In the entire field of popular music and popular music meanings, these comparisons are useful to define the various markets and market fragments that use music to define their social identities.

Briefly, here is the now overcoded story of the emergence of New Kids from the position of a discourse of authenticity. Maurice Starr, a moderately successful singer-songwriter and former member of the group the Johnson Brothers, had by the 1980s begun developing and

Figure 6. Managing the commodity. As is indicated by this still from a *Billboard* advertising supplement, New Kids on the Block were surrounded by production and concert promotion companies that allowed for the internationalization of the audience. Both Dick Scott and Maurice Starr are pictured here, which serves to emphasize their Svengali-like roles in shaping their teenage stars. The formation of a recognizable audience through personalities is a powerful way to create a commodity that attracts a cluster of related interests.

managing popular singing groups. In the early 1980s, he had conceived and developed a young black group called the New Edition. In the popular press, the New Edition was immediately compared with the Jackson Five of the late 1960s and early 1970s. Songs were organized around the lead vocals of the youngest member of the group, whose voice had not deepened. Starr composed and produced virtually all of the New Edition's songs, managed their promotional tours, and helped choreograph their stage shows; the members of the group were purely performers. The group was moderately successful. In the mid-1980s, Starr, in association with Boston talent manager Mary Alford, attempted to produce a similar group with white boys.[37] He scoured the racially mixed Boston inner-city schools for white performers who had some interest in black dance and rap music. Starr held auditions for six months before he constructed the right blend of personalities. From that search, he chose the members of New Kids on the Block (originally called Nynuk). The average age of the performers at the beginning, in 1985, was about fifteen. The youngest, Joey, sang lead vocals for the first recordings in a high soprano voice. Once again, Starr wrote and produced all of the group's original songs. He also developed the group's highly choreographed concert show. New Kids on the Block, much as the Monkees were originally nonplayers in the 1960s, did not play instruments, and occasionally in their performances they used taped vocals so that they could continue their choreographed dance routines without interruption. However, the use of taped segments in their programs led to a steady stream of criticism in the press and from some parents of fans, who claimed either that they were too manufactured or that they were not really the singers.[38] After an initial album that did poorly, their three follow-up albums all sold multiplatinum.[39] The group toured for months on end, hence their appropriated slogan, "the hardest working act in show business."

As is evidenced by this standard history of New Kids, which has been reproduced in magazine profiles, fanzines, and books, they possessed all of the qualities of illegitimacy: they didn't write their own songs; they didn't play their own instruments; they were chosen in a talent search and didn't develop independent of the music industry apparatus; they made a great deal of money; they appealed to preteens; and they were managed very carefully. All of these truths about New Kids underline their illegitimacy in rock music. Their emergence, then, was more clearly in line with the show business origins of singing stars like Frank Sinatra and—to a lesser degree—Elvis Presley than groups like the Beatles, the Rolling Stones, or R.E.M. What makes them doubly cursed is that they had the appearance of being a group that had come together on its own, when in fact its origins were highly planned. The irony of the entire discourse of authenticity that envelops rock and popular music is that it is dependent on the existence of such examples for the maintenance of the mainstream of what rock means for other audiences. New Kids on the Block operated as a highly successful scapegoat that maintained an equally fabricated sense of purity of the authentic in other examples of popular music.[40]

Building Difference:
Music Celebrities Embodying Subcultures

In the construction of social identities among youth, music figures prominently. Likes and dislikes are represented through one's musical taste, which betrays a series of connected tastes. A celebrity who arises from the popular music industry is thus positioned by both the industry and the audience to represent aspects of difference and differentiation. It is a system of celebrities, where each celebrity sign is partially constructed in opposition to, in contradistinction to, or in relation with other popular music celebrities. New Kids on the Block, much like other groups, established a close rapport with their audience through differentiation from other performers. They made their public identities valuable social markers for their audience. Although not entirely synonymous, the fans of New Kids constructed a series of codes based on these celebrity figures that resembled the structures of meaning of a subculture. The level of commitment to New Kids, the level of what is often called fanatical support, determined the level of understanding of the various codes and histories. This loyalty to and solidarity with New Kids among their fans was expressed in a number of ways, most prominent among which were buying their records and videos, knowing the words to all of their songs, attending their concerts, collecting their images in posters and magazines,[41] buying "officially" produced and authorized New Kids paraphernalia, knowing the "personalities" of all members of the group, and defending their music and its integrity from attackers. The depth of a fan's commitment to New Kids could be determined by how well she knew the codes.

Although I have generally spoken of the image as being the key variant in the meaning of New Kids, this image must be contextualized in terms of the kind of music they performed, because the music establishes a clear form of delineation of audience groups. The full meaning of music is difficult to conceptualize. It is embedded with the affective associations of the listener, which makes any reading of its meaning a game of searching for commonalities in idiosyncratic decoding. Nevertheless, music does have social contexts worked into its rhythms, its musical notation, in the words and phrases and topics that are part of any group's repertoire.[42] New Kids drew principally from three sources: dance music, which has part of its origins in the Motown sound; Western love ballads; and rap/hip-hop music. Each of these origins had a great deal of significance to the sound and meaning of New Kids.

New Kids' use of dance music indicated that they were not attempting to appeal to some intellectualized aesthetic. This is music for the movement of the body. In their concerts, the performance was very much focused on dance and movement. The group moved often in unison through a song, in the tradition of black groups of the 1960s such as the Temptations and the Four Tops. No doubt this expression of black dance music had been orchestrated to a large degree by their songwriter and manager, Maurice Starr. The use of young white boys to work through music that arose in African American culture has been a common technique of the entertainment industry of the twentieth century, and New Kids furthered this tradition. Like Elvis, the Beatles, the Rolling Stones, and the Bee Gees, New Kids used this resource to extend the reach of a certain type of music to a suburban American and youthful population. In the biographical details that appeared in the teen magazines, biographies, and various interviews New Kids members gave, there was an emphasis on their intimate connection to black culture or the music of the street, as they often referred to it.[43] Their Boston accents were identified in *People* as "coming from the wrong side of the tracks." Donnie Wahlberg, the recognized leader of the group, has said that he thought of his music as being like basketball, because it kept him away from the dangers of the street. There was a degree of celebration of working-class roots that allowed for the public representation that they came to this form of music honestly: once again, the discourse of authenticity is articulated in the meanings of any popular music celebrity. Four of the five members of New Kids went to the same elementary school, and their humble beginnings as children of large, poor Irish Catholic families reinforced their legitimate right to sing music of the street.

The incongruity between their black dance style and song construction and their white American looks was also used to discredit the New Kids. The group was used to articulate various sentiments about the realm of the authentic and the inauthentic. New Kids' complete commodification buttressed the rock discourse of musical rip-off and sellout of black musical culture. Moreover, their virtual lack of involvement in the writing of their songs made them vulnerable to accusations of the same kind of rip-off that Chappell and Garafalo have chronicled concerning black performers in the 1950s.[44] The vociferousness of the attack on their credibility served not only to galvanize some fragments of youth culture and popular music criticism against them, but to construct a siege mentality among their fans and the ancillary teen press that supported them. The intensity of the discourse of authenticity worked to establish much clearer uses of popular celebrities for the articulation of social identities and distinctions.

The second source of New Kids' music presented a different line of demarcation for the use of audiences. The popular ballad, which formed one of the three sources of musical style in their recorded and concert performances, follows in the tradition of the Broadway and movie musical love song and is firmly ensconced in Western European popular music. It identifies a line of demarcation in terms of the principal audience's gender.

Susan McClary has done some work on the way in which music is defined as masculine or feminine that is relevant to the current discussion.[45] *Feminine ending* is a term used in music criticism to describe a weak or softened conclusion to part of a composition. Principally, the term has been used in a negative sense. Although McClary begins her discussion with an exploration of the way patriarchy inflects the meanings of classical musical texts, she adapts it successfully to the organization of popular music in her treatment of Madonna and Laurie Anderson.[46] Similar readings can be made of the love ballad, although with much greater emphasis on its social uses than on its textual configuration. The feminized popular musical text has been constructed as the love song, which, in its softened sound, its entreating (male) voice, and its romantic construction of love, works to construct a female listener. Paralleling the development of the romance novel and the soap opera, the female listener has embraced the love song text in a proprietary way. The New Kids' core audience of young adolescent and preadolescent girls took the love song and not only incorporated its general message into their own lives and everyday experiences, but also constructed a close connection to the artists themselves. The bedroom shrines of New Kids images that many female fans created indicate that the celebrity figure himself has been thought of directly as a romantic possibility. In their choice and performance of these love songs, New Kids on the Block were playing within these social constructions of a feminized text. The love song was a willful acknowledgment of their own fans and a way in which to "talk" to their fans' fantasies directly.

Implicit in the relationship between female fan and the boys of New Kids on the Block was the play with proximity and distance. The love song, in its direct appeal to another individual, is an intimate decla-

Figure 7. The idealized New Kids fan's bedroom. The paraphernalia available for the fan to further affective investment in the group seemed endless. Because of the group's appeal to preteen girls, the nature of the goods crossed between toys and leisure products. The bedroom itself represented the private sanctum for the true fan—a shrine to her devotion. The bedroom was a natural (and previously tested) site that allowed for the close association between the presexual (comfort) devotion and the relatively nonthreatening sexuality of New Kids to coexist comfortably in the imaginary.

ration and an indication that the fan is hearing the personal and private realm of the singer. Popular music works quite specifically in the affective realm, where sentiments and feelings are conveyed. In this sense, the New Kids love song broke down the distance between the pop star and the individual audience member at the very least in the level of fantasy for the audience member. Simultaneously, the emotion and intimacy that the song expressed was being conveyed to thousands, if not millions, of other core audience fans. The subjective experiences that developed from listening to the love song, although not

Figure 8. Jordan's kiss. The fanaticism of New Kids fans replicated scenes in our cultural memory of adoring girls flocking around Sinatra, Elvis, and the Beatles. The sense of connection and solidarity of performers with their audience is part of the myth and representations of popular music. The distinction between fan and performer is at least symbolically broken down through gestures. The close connection is the power of the popular music celebrity. The concert entrance fence intensifies the desire for the divide to be broken down, a divide ritually disintegrated through the touching of a fan. (Image from the video *Step by Step*; CMV, 1990.)

identical among all the fans, would be correlative in the play with the fantasy of intimacy and the reality of distance. For the young female fan, the distance from the personal maintains the pop icon as a nonthreatening personality. The sexual innuendo is real at the emotive level but perfectly impossible at the level of the real. It is this wonderful combination of the feeling of intimacy and the structure of distance that makes the teen idol so powerfully appealing at the level of fantasy.

New Kids members typically presented themselves as personally open and intimate while objectively distant and unknown, except through their images and sounds. The bedroom shrine discussed above articulates the way in which intimacy was connected between the images of the teen idols and the private world of the fan's bedroom.

The music, then, was coordinated with the various other sources of information the fan could collect about the members of the group. One of these, a glossy photo album of the band members peppered with their commentary on their feelings, provides the typical play between accessibility to the group members' intimate world and the impossibility of fully entering that world. In this publication, various "bedroom" pictures are juxtaposed beside performance images in the thirty-page section devoted to each member. Superimposed on an image of a performing, shirtless Jordan surrounded by fans' hands trying to reach out and touch him is the question, "How do you feel about all the girls reaching out to touch you at shows?" His reply maintains the possibility of his fans' possessing him: "If I know they can't reach me I love it. I feel in control of the situation, but sometimes I'd like to get attacked. It seems like it'd be fun."[47] The anchoring text for an "intimate" photo of Jonathan in a terry bathrobe invites the audience to complete the romantic sentiment in fantasy: "I think romance is very sweet. I don't think there's too much of it out there these days. Men try to be too macho."[48]

Whereas the love song was central to the maintenance and organization of the New Kids audience, its construction as a feminized and preadolescent discourse also served to delegitimate the group in the eyes of others. Heavy metal music, which, it could be argued, is a celebration of the masculine text and is talked about in masculinized terms of power and hardness, operated as the antithesis to much of New Kids music. Rock music in general also functions as a masculinized discourse that in its self-criticism often tries to purge the feminized love song from the lexicon of what constitutes good popular music. Derogatory terms such as *bubblegum* and *teenybopper music* are used to separate the female-constructed popular music audience from the mainstream of male rock culture.

What surfaces from this type of audience differentiation is the kind of identification that is central to each audience group. With New Kids there was an emphasis on what I would call a *completing* identification: the audience did not identify with the group members directly, but rather in relational terms. The performers were male and the audience primarily female, and thus the normative discourse that underplayed this organization was heterosexuality, which in this construction was played out at the level of a fantasy of intimacy. In contrast, the heavy metal performer, the punk rocker, and the thrash metal idol work to construct an emulating identification with audience members. These kinds of performers are predominantly male, and their primary audience is also predominantly male. The performance is meant to empower, so that audience members see themselves as if they were the performers. In a sense, both forms of identification are the invocations of a normative discourse of patriarchy. The relational completion form of identification proffered by New Kids established that social power is derived from the male figure; the emulative form of identification establishes, first, the bond between the male audience and the male performer and, second, that empowerment flows along these gender lines.

A different layer of meaning was constructed through New Kids' use of another musical/cultural source that was simultaneously built on their relational form of identification with their fans. Through the adoption and adaptation of rap music and hip-hop into their performance, New Kids on the Block established a connotational connection. The general social context connected to this type of music — that is, urban street culture and black ghetto culture — provided two principal meanings for the construction of the celebrity signs of New Kids on the Block: authenticity and contemporaneity.

With the use of black urban forms of music and dance, the New Kids underlined their own humble origins and thus their own claim to a discourse of the authentic. As well, the musical form connected a social text of populism and nonelitism to the members' positions as public personalities. Drawing on the conventions of current street music was a way of connecting to the audience and indicating that there were no barriers to the music and meanings they conveyed through song and dance.

Second, rap music provided a social context of currency and contemporaneity. To position New Kids as in fact something unique to their cultural moment and thereby distance their constructed sign from previous popular music idols, the new currency of musical expression ensured their status as a contemporary phenomenon. In this way, New Kids and popular music have continued to fill the role of constructing a discourse of change and transformation. And each new phenomenon represents a celebration of change itself. Not only does this celebration of change aid in the circulation of new commodities connected to new social constructions of signs, it also works to reconstruct peripheral cultural phenomena as economically valuable forms of innovation for the mainstream of a cultural industry. Thus, New Kids' sign operated as a signal of the successful integration of popular cultural forms previously marginalized as now aesthetically manipulable cultural commodities.

The Meaning of the Group

On one level, New Kids operated as a cohesive moniker for public identity. As with other popular music groups, New Kids on the Block was a brand name for a commodity. Although there were five members in the group, there was a concerted effort to maintain the cohesiveness and solidarity of the group behind the group's name. The name stood for their distinctive sound and, by implication, a particular audience. Maintaining consistency around the name ensured a degree of brand loyalty among music consumers. Thus, one of the meanings of the group identity was to organize the popular music market.

On another level, group identity for New Kids grafted them onto a tradition of rock music. At least in the romantic connotations, the musical group is a collective, where the various interests of each band member contribute to the musical sound. As mentioned in the analysis of popular music formations above, the group identity also represents a democratic solidarity among the artists and ultimately the fans. New Kids, even though the group was orchestrated in its formation by a manager, connected itself to this collective spirit of rock music. Instead of an emphasis on the individual, group identity became paramount.

New Kids, however, operated under another tradition that often works in contradistinction to the meaning of the group: that of the highly individualized and mediated teen idol or pop star. In fan literature and printed interviews, the members of the group were presented as possessing individual though very typecast personalities. There was Joey, the youngest member, chosen for his youth, to attract younger audience members.[49] Jordan represented the leading boy-man and was constructed as the best-looking member of the group. Donnie, who frequently appeared in the tabloid press—in 1991 for alleged arson— was constructed as the rebel. Jonathan was the quiet introvert, and Danny represented the more mature masculine personality. Photographs and texts reaffirmed and reinforced these constructed categories for the play of relations with their fans. For example, Danny was fre-

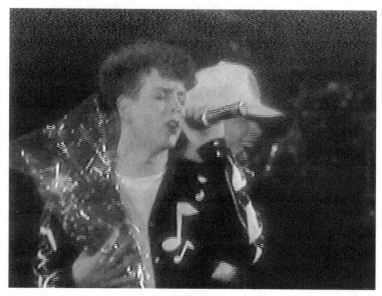

Figure 9. Choosing favorites. Joey sings a love ballad and serves to individualize himself and his coterie of fans. The personalization of the group members was a strategy of their agents and managers and also fit into the pattern of affective attachment of their young fans. Here Joey imagines himself as a young Frank Sinatra, which shifts him out of the codes of rock music and into the gentler and feminized patterns of attachment to the singing star in pop music. (Image from the video *Hangin' Tough*; CMV, 1989.)

quently depicted as a bodybuilder, thereby evoking a connotation of hypermasculinity. In contrast, Joey was desexualized; in at least one book (and in a network TV special) he was represented as a young performer in the mold of Frank Sinatra, and with the image of Sinatra as pop icon, Joey established his own image as something that predated and circumvented the overt sexuality of the entire history of rock music.[50] In sum, what was constructed was a series of rather simplistic caricatures of boy-types that could be reread and distinguished for use by their predominantly young female audience. Extensive personal information about each New Kid was presented to help audience members choose their favorites. In making the choice of a favorite, the female fan played with the conception of a greater intimacy and empathy with that particular member. The meaning of the constructed heterogeneous group, then, was not only to establish a brand name and a connection to the romantic tradition of popular music, but also to construct a series of celebrity signs within the group that allowed for fans to play with the notion of a more personal attachment to one of the members.[51]

Conclusion: Dissipation of Celebrity Status

More than any other form of celebrity, the popular music celebrity, and in particular the celebrity who emerges from the adulation of a preteen or young teen female audience, demonstrates the rapidity of dissipation of the power and influence of a public personality. The reason for part of this dissipation is the way in which the popular music industry has helped to construct itself as a symbol of change and transformation. Thus, each new popular music star represents virtually simultaneously the moment of innovation and the moment of replacement. In popular music's reconstruction of a youth culture, the succession of apparent new images and sounds constitutes the representation of change that is often used by the culture at large as a representation of the vitality of the entire culture.

To explain the particularly rapid dissipation of teen idols, one needs to consider the way in which the audience has been constructed by the various cultural industries. As mentioned above, the audience of the teen idol is considered to be irrational, in a frenzy of devotion to the idol. The fan's relationship to the teen idol can be thought of as built on an incredible level of emotional intensity. Thus, the economic power of the pop star is configured around affect. However, the challenge of affective power is that it is very difficult to maintain; it is by its very nature subject to dissipation. Because the recording industry has organized itself around the momentary capturing of expansive affective power, it is also organized around losing the ability of any given commodity to produce that affective power. The industry's solution to its own construction of successive waves of affect is to produce new commodities that allow for the containing of collective affect. The pop music celebrity, then, is the convertible personality who can capture youth's affective intensity.

What we can conclude about New Kids on the Block is that they achieved through the industry the status of a powerfully affective commodity. Their sales worldwide of albums alone were truly staggering and indicate the economic clout they wielded. However, we can also conclude that New Kids on the Block's power as a commodity has dissipated. The group has been succeeded by new so-called phenomena that maintain the discourse of change that is at the center of the popular music industry and the culture in general. Indeed, by all indications the performer known as Vanilla Ice led many fans of New Kids to pull down their shrines, although he has now disappeared from public consciousness. For a moment, several of the characters from the television series *Beverly Hills 90210* overflowed the preteen magazines, while New Kids occupied only the mail-order pages. In 1994, New Kids attempted a reincarnation as a young adult group with varying degrees of facial hair, more hip-hop music, and extensive writing and producing credits on their music to indicate their new autonomy; however, their new album, *Face the Music,* and their new image disappeared rather quickly from the charts and were virtually shunned both by radio stations fearful of stigma and by music magazines aware of the ever-present backlash to the group's seen-to-be-illegitimate success.[52] The succession of the play with affect continues with the young and temporarily loyal female fan as it migrates to cluster around new identities produced by the entertainment industries.

7

The System of Celebrity

In each of the three preceding chapters, I have outlined the institutional structures that have historically organized the development of celebrities in the film, television, and popular music industries. I have conducted a dual hermeneutic that charts the construction of celebrities in each of the entertainment industries; in the historical preambles and in the specific genealogical interpretations of individual celebrities, a hermeneutic of intention and a hermeneutic of reception have been combined. In terms of resources, this dual hermeneutic has been massaged from the various readings of stars detailed in both the popular press and industry trade journals. In congealing these two elements, I have developed the way the celebrity is an embodiment of his or her industrial/institutional setting as well as the expression of an audience/collective that attaches meaning to the public figure. The form of attachment that is intensively worked upon by the industry and also embraced by the audience is affective. The concept that public forms of subjectivity represent the organization of collective affect is central to an understanding of the power of the celebrity. Also, the representation of affective power that runs through the array of public figures provides the unifying thread that links entertainment celebrities to other public personalities and indicates that a system of public subjectivity operates in contemporary culture.

In this chapter, I will indicate first how each apparatus constructs particular forms of celebrities and how there are in operation subsystems of a system of celebrities. What I will emphasize here is that the celebrity system presents a structure for the organization of public personalities as well as a structure for the models of modern subjectivity. The celebrity system principally addresses the organization of concepts of individuality and identity for the culture. This chapter identifies, then, the various privileged constructions of subjectivity and affective attachments that are fostered in our current system of celebrity.

Two primary insights can be drawn from the preceding discussion of the formation of the celebrity in the various domains of the entertainment industry. First of all, the formation of the celebrity in the entertainment industry is not couched in the language of rationality and reason, either in its articulation by the industry or in its rearticulation by the audience. As opposed to the political sphere of leadership politics or the rational rhetoric that envelops business discourse, the entertainment industry celebrates its play with the affective, emotional, and sentimental in its construction of public personalities. Because of this open and avowed relationship to the irrational, a study of the entertainment industry permits an entry point into the way in which affect is housed in public personalities.

Second, the study of entertainment celebrities has allowed us to see two levels of celebrity construction in operation and thereby to identify subsystems within a larger system. Each industry produces a range of celebrity types that not only are constructed to have distinctive qualities when compared with other celebrities within that industry, but are differentiated from the production of celebrities in each of the other domains of the entertainment industry. This double layering of construction of public subjectivity describes the way in which the larger system of celebrity formation operates. The active play with affect by the strands of the entertainment industry is also an attempt at producing viable differentiated categories of popular taste. The work on distinction and differentiation is the industrial construction of audiences or markets; viability of a celebrity can be translated as the celebrity's capacity to appeal to an audience through a specific array of commodities or services. The various social constructions of taste intersect with the industrial construction of celebrity figures to produce a system of "functioning" public personalities and forms of subjectivity.

As outlined in the previous three chapters, each of the entertainment industries organizes its production of celebrities around particular characteristics. These characteristics within each industry work to form types of binarisms that operate to distinguish the formation of personalities within their particular industry and among the industries. My intention in this summary chapter is to use the principal characteristics of the celebrity sign that have emerged from film, television, and popular music and relate them to the categories of identification that Hans Robert Jauss has developed to identify the "modalities of reception" that define types of identification of heroes in fiction.

Celebrities, like fictional heroes, do not often figure in only one modality of reception; however, I would argue that each industry has attempted to privilege a particular formation for reception that can be correlated to the binarisms that operate in the cultural production of celebrities to emerge from each field/domain.

Identification with the Film Celebrity: Auratic Distance

Autonomy figures centrally in the formation and solidification of the film celebrity. In the historical/institutional reading of Tom Cruise, one can discern that the film star works to create a distance from his or her audience. There is active work on controlling information concerning the nonscreen meanings and representations of the screen star. There are two realities of film stars proffered in the public sphere: their representations in films, where the heroes they portray are fixed images, and thus relatively fixed conceptions of their identity can be made; and, in contrast, their supposed "real lives," the private and intimate as well as the various public lives, which are less obvious, less explicit, and much more controlled than those of celebrities in other entertainment industries. The fictional presentations generally determine the nature of the identification of the film star. In order to gain autonomy from these screen images, the screen star invokes a number of codes to indicate his or her ultimate independence. The code of acting, the active reworking and then publicly performing his or her private life for public consumption, and the playing of "serious" or against-type roles all work to concretize the star as a more permanent sign of the public sphere.

The way in which this autonomy from the screen image and the fictional representations is achieved determines to a high degree the modality of reception that inscribes the film celebrity with significance for the audience. The screen image provides an aura for the film celebrity that constructs a form of *admiring identification,* to use Jauss's terminology, to envelop their celebrity sign.[1] From these images the audience can construct the "perfect hero," where the star's actions serve as exemplary models for a particular community. Film stars are constructed in this first order of identification in a manner that has not changed significantly from the inception of narrative cinema: the star is born through the playing of a leading (that is, central to the narrative), generally sympathetic character. Although there has been little change in this organization of stardom, there have been transformations in the construction of the film star that indicate how the industry has repositioned itself through the public representations of individuality. The film star has become progressively more representative of artistic practice. An aesthetic distance is conveyed even in the most entertainment-oriented stars, such as Arnold Schwarzenegger, Billy Crystal, and Steve Martin. These stars have achieved film stardom through their emergence in other industries or other cultural forms. The celebrity sign of the film star that they now embrace and embody is made to be superior to those celebrities of other technologically mediated performance arts. The careers of performers like Crystal and Martin are coded with the connotation of progression from live comedy performance, to television, to the ultimate form of film. Film signifies through its performers/stars the pinnacle for the expression of one's metier, one's own individual creativity and genius. The conception of a serious aesthetic to emerge in film is substantiated in a number of ways. The development of the art film and the associated audience have become established since the 1940s and since the 1910s in Europe. The appearance and growth of film departments in universities that have courses that look specifically at the aesthetics of films also indicate the institutionalization of film as a legitimate form of cultural practice. Many of these departments emerged from literature departments and use the constructs of genres, periods, and authors as models for the study of film. Finally, an entire avant-garde cinema practice has paralleled the development of the Hollywood movie industry in a number of settings. All of these practices have worked to solidify film as a legitimate form of cultural expression. The stars of film are associated in the expression of these artistic pretensions.

To achieve celebritydom in the context of film also connotes the pinnacle of the individual star's commodity value. With the demise of a studio system in the 1950s, stars' salaries came to reflect their central value for the profitability of production. Currently, most major film stars receive not only guaranteed salaries of millions of dollars, but also some percentage of the box-office receipts.

The star thus possesses within the film industry two forms of capital that, because of their correlative power, begin to determine the direction of film production: cultural capital, because each star is one of the key representatives of individual creativity and artistic practice;

and economic capital, because the star emerges as the economic center of any production. The industry, it must be made clear, has not fallen victim to this increasing power of the celebrity. Rather, it has been an instrumental accomplice in this construction of a public personality. Within the cultural industries, the film industry has attempted to maintain its preeminence in the organization of an entertainment culture by establishing film as ultimately more significant than other entertainment forms, specifically television. Since the 1950s, it has worked to construct its celebrities to maintain this "larger-than-life" persona, to differentiate them from the everyday celebrity constructions of television. The film star's appearance in other settings, either in person or on television, is constructed as a significant event—in essence, a change from the everyday. The film star is the special guest of the talk show. Films are treated with a certain reverence on television, whether in the form of promotional clips or in their full presentation, which, when they premiere on broadcast television, may preempt the regularity of the television schedule.

One can see in this objective of differentiation how the various celebrities are part of a loosely defined system of celebrities. The generally "admiring identification" that contains a certain aloofness and distance has been constructed for the film star in contradistinction to the meanings of the television celebrity. The admiring form of identification entails a distance from the audience. This aesthetic and "larger-than-life" distance is intended primarily to maintain the film industry as the center of cultural capital. Of course, the intention is to parlay that form of cultural capital into economic capital. The film industry attempts to maintain its preeminence by constructing its production environment as the main source of creativity and ingenuity. Through this form of creative hegemony, the industry can generate revenues from the various types of releases and spin-off productions that can come from a successful film production. A successful film, such as *Batman*, can produce for the industry a number of sources of revenues, for example, through the sale of exhibition rights; the release of the film on videocassette and videodisc; the sale of pay-television exhibition rights and network broadcast rights; the sale of an album sound track; the marketing and sale of toys, games, and apparel associated with the film's characters; the production of a sequel; and the production of a television series and/or an animated series based on the film. Being at the origin of such a proliferation of commodities and

different sources of revenues to emerge from the same original commodity is the central impetus for the film industry to do what it must
to maintain its hold on cultural capital. The particular development
of the aura of the public personality of the film star is part of this
general industrial strategy.

Devising the Television Celebrity: Identification with the Familiar

As I have mentioned above, the loose system of celebrity is
built on differentiation. The key differentiation that operates in the
construction of the television celebrity is in relation to film. Whereas
the film celebrity exhibits a great deal of control over his or her celebrity sign and thereby constructs distance, the television celebrity works
to break down those distances and to develop a conception of familiarity. In my discussion of Oprah Winfrey, I identified several ways in
which television has constructed this discourse of familiarity; there is
no need to elaborate here on that discussion, other than to connect
those features to a form of identification by the audience. In terms of
Jauss's categories of heroic identification, the television celebrity is generally organized around a *sympathetic identification,* where "there is
a solidarity with the personality" and "we [the audience] place ourselves in the position of the hero."[2] Again, I should add the caveat
that other forms of audience identification are part of television's construction of the celebrity and indeed can occur within the same celebrity. What I am emphasizing is that television tends to privilege a form
of sympathetic identification that makes it distinctive from the production of audience identification in film.

With the television celebrity we are drawn to think of the talk-
show personality or the news anchor as standing in for us or representing our interests. The celebrity's interests are painted as if they orig-
inate from an audience. In the talk-show format, a style of television
production that dominates the televisual universe, the host constructs
familiarity with the studio audience setting and the continuous touring
of the audience for questions and comments for the assembled guests.
In the case of Oprah, this familiarity leads to a sympathetic form of
identification and is buttressed by occasional program episodes that
have personal relevance to her life. Occasionally, episodes of her show
have focused on themes directly related to her "private battles" con-

cerning her history as an abused child or, alternatively, her battle with diets and weight loss. Oprah as hero is presented as vulnerable and subject to weaknesses that others suffer. Audiences are thus constructed to be loyal and therefore regular viewers of her program; they are drawn to her candor, which allows her to move seamlessly from the public sphere to the private in her presentation of self. There is a virtual public acknowledgment that her audience is aware of her "private battles"; her private life, in general, is not constructed as a separate and private realm and is unified with her public performances. Her power as a sympathetic hero is dependent on her presenting herself as both honest and open.

The specific case of Oprah reveals some general features about the construction of the television celebrity that relate to television's difference as a medium. The familial feel of television and its celebrities is also a play with verisimilitude. The construction of a news reality and the various forms of live and simulated live television that dominate the television schedule are all aspects of television's efforts to represent a truer-to-life form of cultural expression. Whereas film has moved to the fictional and sometimes an aesthetic construction of its meanings, television concentrates on representing the real. Even in much of its special dramatic programming, an often favored formula is the docudrama, where a specific and topical issue is tackled in a fictionalized way. Although these special programs tend to be moralistic and heavy-handed in their presentation of right and wrong, they are also exemplary of how television often eschews the presentation of an aesthetic code and attempts to move to the nonfictional and the newslike. Indeed, the generally acknowledged flatness of television images is often placed in contradistinction to the depth and richness of the filmic image. The television image can be seen as less embellished and less crafted and therefore closer to the real and the everyday. One can see television's different play with the real through the soap opera's generally poor production values and the continuity of story lines so that they resemble everyday life. In situation comedy, the general familial feel of the stories and casts also makes them closer to the everyday. Both sitcoms and soap operas are constructed to fit into the rituals of everyday life through the regularity of their presentation. Again, these features of regularity and their fit into an audience's leisure and consumption patterns are examples of how television constructs its strength of connection and proximity to reality.

The implication for the television celebrity is that he or she is structured to reinforce the feeling of close proximity to the real and the familial. The TV celebrity is more accessible than the film celebrity. He or she is seen on a more regular basis, in the serial format of television programs. The auratic distance is less central to the television celebrity. The pretensions of an aesthetic abstraction are also underplayed. The codes of acting are replaced by the similitude of the television character with the television star's supposed real life; the break that defines the independence and autonomy of the film star is less significant in the construction of the television celebrity.

This difference between the television celebrity and film celebrity, however, is also constructed as a hierarchy of public subjectivity. The successful television celebrity, like the film star, is rewarded through an incredibly generous (and incredibly inequitable) system of remuneration. In different periods of the past decade, two television stars, Bill Cosby and Oprah Winfrey, were considered to be the highest-paid entertainers, each earning in excess of $40 million in a single year.[3] Thus, like the film star, the television celebrity begins to accumulate economic capital and associative power. Both Oprah Winfrey and Bill Cosby have their own production companies, which are involved not only in the production of their own programs but also develop other cultural productions. The difference between television and film celebritydom lies in the organization of power through cultural capital. The film celebrity evokes aesthetic conventions in the production of his or her public image. These aesthetic conventions, as I have detailed elsewhere, are essential to the larger-than-life meaning of the film star and the film commodity in general. The celebrity casts a large shadow of artistic significance and thus, in comparison with the television celebrity, constructs a hierarchy of culture through the difference in meanings of the celebrities that emerge from the two industries. The distinctions demarcated by this difference in celebrity formation maintain the aura of film as a significant event and television, in contradistinction, as a form of routine consumption. The stars of television — and here I mean network television in particular — are working toward the construction of a mass and relatively undifferentiated audience. In contrast, the stars of film are positioned to construct more specific taste cultures and more differentiated forms of audiences, where specialized knowledge may be essential for decoding their significance. Although both film and television are certainly popular cultural forms, they have constructed a form of differentiation that resonates with the categories of high culture and middlebrow culture. Celebrities are the industrialized products of this subtle differentiation in cultural form.

Celebrating the Community: The Popular Music Celebrity and the Claim to Authenticity

Where film and television have developed a dyadic industrial relationship that is reflected in the formation of their celebrities, popular music's construction of public personalities tends to be modalized around intrinsic differentiation as opposed to extrinsic distinctions. The key characteristic of popular music and its construction of subjectivity that leads to these intrinsic differentiations is the claim to authenticity. To adapt this conception of popular music's claim to authenticity to Jauss's categories of identification, one would have to conclude that popular music celebrities are centrally involved in an articulation of *associative identification:* "The barriers between audience and actors are broken and there is a celebration of active participation."[4] The crowd and the reactions of the crowd are a central metaphor of the meaning of popular music. It is a collective celebration, a celebration of a community that considers the representation of specific performers and their music significant. The concert is the ritualization of this claim to authenticity and this associative identification with the audience.

The expression of the close proximity of performance to audience is one of the principal ways popular music has established its authenticity. As I have mentioned in the institutional study of popular music celebrities in chapter 5, the various incarnations of popular music since the Second World War have attempted to reclaim a solidarity with their audiences that has been lost with previous forms of music. Thus, mid-twentieth-century folk music, with its simplicity in dress and performance, worked to fabricate a community where the performer and the audience were virtually inseparable. Likewise, punk rock, with its simplicity of expression, celebrated the virtual inseparability of performers and their audiences. Even current dance music, with its clubs using primarily recorded music, makes a claim to authenticity for the eschewing of the importance and significance of star performers in favor of the dance, rhythm, and movement of the club patrons.

Thus, popular music plays out a tension between artifice and authenticity in its construction of celebrities. In the example that I have used, New Kids on the Block, this tension is vividly displayed. According to some conventions, New Kids was entirely fabricated and therefore possesses no "authentic" value whatsoever. For the group's supporters, the members' youthfulness, sincerity, and contemporaneity were their legitimate claims to authenticity and stardom. Other performers actively assault the canon of rock authenticity through a demonstrative and flamboyant display of artifice and transformation. David Bowie and Madonna are examples of popular music celebrities who build on the authentic soul of popular music. They transform and transfigure themselves, and through these reincarnations present a moving subjectivity and ultimately an enigma about their authentic selves. Their enigmatic quality is reinforced by the centrality of authenticity to popular music discourse. Their play with identity and image is often an ironic modality to the claims in rock for authenticity. Indeed, their claim could be construed as an appeal to an aesthetic in which the performer has the "genius" to transform like the brilliant actor. The key to their continuing appeal is the continual deferral of the resolution of the enigma; the authentic self is never revealed completely.

Within this tension between artifice and authenticity, the audience is drawn to particular performers and their expressions of this tension. What is characteristic of fans of popular music performers, no matter how they deal with this tension between artifice and authenticity, is their loyalty. Through this loyalty, a representation of community develops around the popular music celebrity composed of those people who are committed to the celebrity's music and identity. This close connection to their audience is what makes popular music celebrities so attractive to advertising agencies: in the past decade, the use of popular music performers has been one of the principal advertising strategies for both Coca-Cola and Pepsi. As well, most major concert tours are sponsored by beer or soft drink companies. The popular music celebrity offers advertisers an entrée into an audience that has made a commitment to a certain entertainment product; the advertisers want to piggyback that loyalty so that their products are seen in a cluster around the particular celebrity and his or her identity with definable audience. Each popular music celebrity who moves into marketing other products is selling his or her capital as a kind of brand loyalty to the advertising company. The advertising company then is searching for a resonating wave of brand loyalty that provides a liaison between the celebrity and the advertised commodity.

To summarize the forms of power that are held by the popular music celebrity, the close connection of the performer to the audience demarcates this celebrity's power from other celebrity forms. Whereas television has its regularity of serial performance *broadcast* to each individual home, popular music has the *physically live* communal ritual of the concert to provide concrete evidence of the audience and the audience's support. Although film has the concrete evidence of box-office and audience numbers, it denies the possibility of interaction between performer and audience. The close connection and apparent commitment of the audience in popular music bestows on the popular music celebrity a connection to the power of the crowd, or, more accurately, provides for the public sphere a representation and embodiment of the crowd and the crowd's power in contemporary culture. The frenzy of the rock concert, the active play in the realm of sentiment and affect, makes the rock star an alluring representative of cultural power. Apart from the performer, there is a reduction of the individuals of the crowd into some organized collective force.

The popular music celebrity possesses other forms of power as well, although these forms of power are connected symbolically to the representation of the solidarity and unitary strength of the concert crowd. He or she can achieve a certain amount of artistic freedom through the selling of massive numbers of recordings and thereby begin to construct economic capital to fit certain ends. For instance, the Beatles established their own recording company, Apple Records, to manage and produce their own artistic adventures and those of others. Madonna has organized an entire managerial team of hand-picked female executives to run her complete operation. On a much more basic level, successful performers often set up their own recording studios in their homes to facilitate their creative and productive processes. All these examples underline the way in which the celebrity reorganizes the flows of capital in the popular music industry to suit particular objectives.

Close association with his or her audience also has impressed on the popular music celebrity a certain amount of sensitivity that he or she is representing something, however vague that something might be. In some instances the conception of what the celebrity represents may be just that of a large group of people; however, often popular music celebrities are constructed to represent a generation of interests. On occasion, this representation of a group of interests manifests itself more directly as a form of political power. The celebrity figure/sign operates as a way in which discourses about interests are focused and shaped by opposing groups. The close connection of performers to specific political causes in the 1960s, for instance, can be understood as the manifestation of how issues and interests of different groups of people are represented in the public sphere in the form of public individuals. The celebrity serves a simplification function, not only in his or her message, which is channeled through the indirect form of a song, but also in the way a collective formation of will can be better comprehended and positioned when it is housed in particular public individuals.

The expression of this political power has continued to operate at the center of popular music for the past thirty years. In some instances popular music celebrities are positioned in the public sphere as threats; Elvis in the 1950s embodied a moral panic along generational lines in the United States. Other popular music stars, like Mick Jagger or later incarnations of the Beatles, have been similarly constructed as public threats. The connection between popular music and youth culture has also often been articulated as a threat to the established order. The celebrity, then, represents the potential for societal transformation or even the catalyst for its breakdown. The discourse of the threat, if it can be so labeled, works not only to formulate and focus the established position, but also to congeal a community of interest that is opposed to the established position. Popular music, in its constant reformulation into new songs (which may or may not resemble past forms), represents change itself and the chaos that change can potentially produce. The popular music celebrity, then, is often the public representation of change. The large crowds that are associated with the performance of popular music celebrities (here we can think of the massive crowd at Woodstock and its many reincarnations since 1970) serve to substantiate the organization of power behind these representatives of change.

It is this relationship to the crowd that continues to foster political ambitions and formulations by rock stars. In the 1980s, the world witnessed a proliferation of popular music events that were organized around specific issues and concerns. Bob Geldof's Band Aid and the subsequent Live Aid were intended to focus world attention on and to garner support and food for the people in drought-stricken regions of eastern Africa. To marshal that support, various pop stars performed in front of massive crowds in both London and Philadelphia; the concerts were watched simultaneously on television by an audience estimated to be in the hundreds of millions. Similar concerts, tours, and albums were produced in support of other causes: Farm Aid was organized to raise money to prevent foreclosures of American family farms, Rock against Apartheid/Racism Sun City organized to help raise public support for resistance to the South African regime, Sting and others organized political action to save the world's rain forests, and Amnesty International was benefited by a tour featuring Peter Gabriel and others. In every city in North America, smaller benefit events have been and still are being organized by popular music celebrities to focus attention on a variety of social issues. The celebrities of popular music have been used as the way to organize a clear link between entertainment and issue politics. They are used both to extend the reach of the political message and as a source of funds for particular causes.

To conclude, two valuable components of the popular music celebrity demonstrate the form of power that is part of this celebrity's public subjectivity. The amount of capital that circulates in and around the popular music celebrity establishes the celebrity as powerful; however, the symbolic power that this celebrity possesses is equally significant. More than other entertainment celebrities, the popular music celebrity is close to a living audience — and not only a living audience, but one that is committed to the celebrity's persona and music. The popular music celebrity, then, represents the physicality of affective power of the people. In countless commercials, the popular music celebrity is used to rearticulate this affective power, as the image of crowd and its adulation is juxtaposed with the image of the celebrity and the image of the product so that the celebrity's sway over the crowd is connected to the product. The use of music itself reinforces this concentration on the affective realm of performance and crowd. The appeal of the celebrity and his or her music is not to the rational but to the emotive and the passionate.

Conclusion: The Concept of a System of Public Subjectivity

In the preceding summaries of the formations of celebrities and the ways they represent forms of power through audience identification, I have focused on three types of celebrities that I have connected to specific domains, technological and cultural, of the entertainment industry. The relatively close relationships among these three forms of celebrity construction have allowed me to emphasize the differentiations and distinctions that are at play in the emergence and sustenance of any celebrity sign.

The complexity of the celebrity signs that emerge in the entertainment industry is difficult to unravel. I have attempted to provide clues to the ways celebrities are differentiated and thus to convey different representations of public subjectivity through a study of what kind of audience identification is privileged in each of the technological forms. In general, what has been revealed is that the three entertainment forms construct different predominant channels through which affective power is housed in the public individual. The film celebrity is organized around distance and a relatively controlled text. The television celebrity is constructed around a conception of familiarity. The popular music celebrity represents variations on the themes of authenticity and communality with the audience. Within each of the technological forms a range of celebrity identifications are offered; nevertheless, all are organized in relation to these three types of identification.

My objective in working through these specific formations of celebrity has been to develop the conception that a system of celebrity is in operation in contemporary culture. I have emphasized the process of differentiation in terms of specific types of technologies and industries of dissemination. Each cultural form can be thought of as establishing a way in which the public individual is constructed; as well, each entertainment industry's construction of celebrities provides an interconnected subsystem of public individuals that works to form a system of entertainment celebrities. My privileging of the entertainment celebrity system is not to say that other forms of celebrity construction do not operate in contemporary culture. It is quite evident that sports celebrities, business celebrities, political celebrities, and other public figures emerge and disappear with equivalent regularity. However, the emergence of any celebrity depends on the various technologies of dissemination for its connection to a massive audience. For instance, both the sports celebrity and the political celebrity are at least partially constructed as significant public signs through television coverage. Entertainment celebrities provide examples of intense connections to these technologies and industries and allow us to identify most clearly the way in which public subjectivity is articulated through these forms. Certainly, the forms of public subjectivity that I have identified do not provide an exhaustive archive of the way in which public personalities are formed in contemporary culture, but I have uncovered their construction in a domain that is unfettered by appeals to rationality. The entertainment celebrity plays intensely in the world of affect and affective attachment of an audience to these public signs of the individual. Where other forms of celebrity are rationalized into the disciplines from which they emerge (i.e., into the structure of rationality of business, science, or politics), the entertainment celebrity allows us to see the workings of affect in the relation between a public and a celebrity.

The following chapter establishes the way in which the structures of public subjectivity that I have identified as emerging in the entertainment industries inform the production of political leadership and political culture in general. Through this extension of the construction of public personalities into the political sphere, I hope to demonstrate that leaders perform functions similar to those of other celebrities; they are means and methods of housing affective power. The three categories of affective power that I have identified at work in the construction of entertainment celebrities will be mapped onto the organization of politics and political leadership.

Part III

The Embodiment of Affect in Political Culture

For the sake of presumed clarity of analysis, it is the usual course of research to separate cultural activities into categories that are believed to operate autonomously. Thus, it is rare to see the domains of politics and entertainment linked in any fundamental sense. What I plan to identify in this final chapter are the linkages that exist between the political and entertainment spheres. One of the critical points of convergence of politics and entertainment is their construction of public personalities. In politics, a leader must somehow embody the sentiments of the party, the people, and the state. In the realm of entertainment, a celebrity must somehow embody the sentiments of an audience. These functions construct celebrities and political leaders that identify a general system for the construction of public subjectivity and conceptions of subjectivity. They are representations of the individual in contemporary culture; they do, however, represent a peculiar form of individual and individuality because of their active construction and deployment in the public sphere.

The Convergence of Public Identities in Capitalist Democracies

I have argued that there are public forms of subjectivity that are privileged in contemporary culture because they are connected to particular ends and interests in the organization of power. Within that argument, I have avoided the conception that this organization of public subjectivity is somehow a master scheme for the subjugation of the people. What I have tried to identify is that there has been intensified interest in the disciplining of the mass or, in its metaphorical construction, the crowd in the past two hundred years. This intensity has worked to produce a system of celebrity that is positioned as a means of comprehending and congealing the mass into recognizable and generally nonthreatening forms. Simultaneous to the emergence of the popular will and democratic constructions in government was the building of means and methods of understanding and controlling the expression of that popular will. The system of celebrity is one of the ways in which the crowd/mass is housed/categorized and understood.

To categorize politicians as celebrities is to include their activities in a more generalizable project of constructing public subjectivities to house the popular will. The celebrity category also permits looking at the meaning of the politician, or identifying his or her "affective function" in the organization of interests and issues. I am not asserting that this is the political leader's only function in politics, but it is a principal function. The affective function is also difficult to ascertain in the political sphere because of the layering of other forms of rationality that are connected to the actions of leaders. For instance, the election is constructed as a rational expression of the people's will and is positioned as such for the sake of the legitimacy of democratic governments. Without this representation of the political campaign and the electoral process as rational and therefore legitimate, the very authority of democratic regimes would be severely undermined. The affective function, although a central component of the political leader's campaign to gain and maintain power, is obscured in the final meaning by a shroud of rationality.[1]

This paradox of political rationality is made abundantly clear in the way political campaigns are presented for the public. Television advertisements for political candidates, as Diamond and Bates have chronicled, are often organized around the emotions of an issue rather than the development of rational debate.[2] As well, political campaigns employ polls more often than not to help create a bandwagon effect, where success of the candidate is used as a kind of affective leverage to encourage others to follow with their support. Ginsberg has attempted to describe the very action of political polling of all sorts as a technique for the expansion of power and jurisdiction of government itself, because results of polls can be used to indicate, with quantitative legitimacy, that a massive number of people are supportive of any particular issue, position, or leader.[3] In their active attempts to contain the mass in various messages and images, political leadership campaigns can be thought of as intense efforts to connect to affective power so that it can be expressed through the individual candidate.

The two layers of political rationality of leaders — reasoned, rational legitimacy and a form of affective consensus building — describe the organization of contemporary political campaigns and elections. This double system of rationality has emerged in concert with another double system of rationality, the framework of consumer capitalist culture. The linchpin of legitimacy in consumer capitalism is the consumer. The centerpiece of contemporary political culture is the citizen. In contemporary culture, there is a convergence in subjectivity toward the identification and construction of the citizen as consumer. This convergence entails a reinforcement of the dual system of rationality in politics. The citizen becomes reconfigured in political campaigns as a political consumer who, like any consumer, must make purchase choices among several different commodities. On one level, the consumer is constructed as ultimately rational: the entire legitimacy of the organization of markets and the discipline/science of economics is built on the conception of the rational consumer and his or her capacity to make rational selections depending on a variety of variables. Simultaneous with this conception of the consumer as ultimately rational is the complementary organization of the consumer through advertising as motivated by irrationality. According to historical research conducted by Leiss, Kline, and Jhally, there has been an expansion in the use of irrational and emotionally charged imagery in display advertising, and a diminution of rational argumentation.[4] The product advertising campaign provides the underlying model for the political election campaign. Both instantiate the prominence of the irrational appeal within a general legitimating discourse of rationality. Both are attempts to establish resonance with a massive number of people so that connections are drawn between the campaign's message and the interests of consumers/citizens. The central objective of the advertisement is to provide some form of connotative connection; likewise with forms of promotion featured in an election campaign. The effort to provide cultural linkages between a candidate/ product and a massive public is an intense play in the realm of affective power. The cultural linkages or forms of connotation that momentarily make sense are appeals beyond the domain of the rational consumer to the realm of affect, which is perceived to be a more powerful and expansive way to influence decision making. Enormous capital expenditures are made to create and disseminate the images and forms that can at least momentarily encompass the affective power of the mass public.

The convergence of a consumer capitalist discourse and the forms of political discourse transforms the types of subjectivity that are constructed for both political leadership and citizenry. The leader is reconstructed as a commodity to some degree as he or she enters into an election campaign couched in the discourse of consumption choice. Also, the citizen's subjectivity is reconstructed to be a variant of the consumer, that is, simultaneously constructed as a rational individual and irrational collective. The meaning of political choice is also transformed in this link between the worlds of consumption and politics. Consumption is also allied with the connotation of the expendability of the commodity consumed; the political commodity is either consumed, used up, or, in some instances, constructed as only momentarily useful and easily superseded or replaced. The supposed telos of this infinite manufacture of commodities and the images that surround commodities works as one of the foundations of the system of economic growth: new commodities and the consumption of new commodities provide for the circulation of capital, which is equated with increasing prosperity. With the absorption of the commodity structure into the political system, there is also acceleration in the production of the images of politics. There is a concurrent production of political leadership and production of new ways of presenting that leadership that parallel the circulation of commodities in other spheres. Politics through leadership is constructed as a game of product differentiation and the establishment of market share in the electorate. It is also constructed through the commodity structure as a system that affords a surplus of political images and leaders; in a sense, there is an overproduction of political forms even though the variations in these political forms may be within a limited range. Thus, part of the contemporary political process is the expendability of positions, issues, and, ultimately, political leaders.

Two institutions of contemporary political culture, press agencies and public opinion polling, have been involved in the proliferation of a political discourse that conflates the exigencies of capitalism/the marketplace and the organization of a democracy. By looking at the origins and functions of these institutions as they relate to organizing public forms of subjectivity, we can identify the links between other systems of celebrity, which are more obviously connected to consumer capitalism, and the political celebrity.

The press agent's primary function is to prepare the politician for public consumption. He or she attempts to massage messages and meanings so that they are interpreted favorably by the media first and then the public itself. Press agents are involved with the organization of public appearances of the political leader, the construction of media events, and the reconstruction of events and issues in ways that augment the authority and legitimacy of the political leader. Some agents now have very specific titles that describe their roles in handling the proliferation of a discourse that is seen to affect the power and prestige of the leader. The particular function of press agents to handle the "spin" or general direction and news angle of given issues has come to be called spin doctoring.[5] Agents also operate as a shield for the political leader; instead of the media being permitted to talk directly to the leader, the press agent interprets the position of the leader for them. Such practices may act to dissipate the threat of certain issues for the leader.

The press agent role articulates efforts to control the image and representation of a political leader. The extensive development of this industry of control in the twentieth century also identifies the centrality of the political image in definitions and meanings of legitimacy in politics. As well, in a kind of binarism, the effort to control the image betrays its opposite: that the image in its play with affect could produce uncontrollable consequences in the mass public. One of Canetti's metaphors concerning the nature of the crowd is apt for explaining the threat perceived by political consultants in the play with affect: the "wrong" message can easily spread like a wildfire through the public sphere.[6] In the age of democratic politics, where legitimation is established by a representation of public interest through elections, the industry of public relations has grown to inhabit the political sphere and to provide a layer of meaning that envelops most political discourse and particularly the discourse that informs the construction of political leaders.

The origins of this layering of political discourse with a form of public relations and press agency have been connected to the development of the publicity agent for the entertainment industry in the late nineteenth and early twentieth centuries. Most histories of public relations identify this direct link between the craft of the press agent and the publicity agent. Indeed, public relations tries to distinguish itself from the practice of press agents while acknowledging their fundamental link in terms of beginnings:

> Most texts on public relations make a clear distinction between public relations and press agentry, the former being a sober effort to inform the public and create good will, and the latter involving flamboyant and exploitative events designed to achieve space in the media with no thought of truth or sobriety. Yet, while tawdry press agentry is hardly to be condoned, the press agent was clearly the precursor of the professional publicist, and some of these publicists have been responsible for the creation of interesting and frequently entertaining and contrived news events.[7]

In the American setting, the acknowledged forerunner of the profession of public relations and the press agent is P. T. Barnum, who in the nineteenth century constructed a series of "media events" to corral attention for his museums and/or circuses. Public relations proliferated from this origin. The craft involved, in its nascent form, two forms of knowledge that were seen to be valuable for both corporations and governments: knowledge of the codes and practices of the media, particularly the news media, and knowledge of the means and methods that could be used to attract the public's attention. The discipline of public relations can be understood as the bridge for both industry and government to use media forms in containing the expression of the affective power of the mass. The publicists of the entertainment world were seen to have an intuitive capacity to *know* their audience and to know how to affect their audience. The form of knowledge they were seen to possess was translated into a structure that both industry and government could use: by the 1950s, public relations departments became standard appendages of all political parties, government departments, and large corporations in the United States.

A number of factors have been identified as stimulating investment in the form of knowledge of the public sphere that public relations offered. For the industrial sector, the Pennsylvania Railroad disaster of 1906 resulted in the first full-fledged public relations campaign. Ivy Lee, the virtual father of public relations, organized the campaign; instead of suppressing information, Lee transported reporters to the wreck site with railroad company funds.[8] In this way, the company was able to control the information released, because the public relations division was able to establish the "reality" of the event before other sources could establish credibility. The success of this campaign in mitigating negative publicity about a human disaster caused by a corporation has been read in retrospect as the stimulus for the expansion of the profession of public relations. By the 1920s, corporations such as AT&T were quick to establish in-house public relations departments to shore up their legitimacy as virtual monopolies.[9] Other large corporations followed suit, either establishing their own public relations departments or hiring consultants to manage crises of public confidence. For governments, the setting up of propaganda departments during wars led to the institutionalization of public relations in the daily control of government information. In the United States, George Creel set up the Committee on Public Information, which served as "the first bona fide government communications program."[10] Individuals involved in this World War I communications program formed the nucleus of the first generation of public relations consultants for industry and government. Finally, Franklin Delano Roosevelt was instrumental in constructing the legitimacy of public relations practices and techniques in American presidential politics and image making. In the inexorable proliferation of techniques, Dwight D. Eisenhower's 1952 presidential campaign is considered by many to be the first that was dominated by press agents and public relations: $80 million was reportedly spent in the campaign, and after Eisenhower's election, public relations consultant Walter Williams became a permanent staff member of the White House.[11]

The integration of press agents and public relations into political discourse identifies the dissipation of disciplinary boundaries among various domains of the public sphere. The entertainment sphere operates as an originary source for methods of shaping public interest in other industries and politics. Moreover, distinctions between the requirements of business and industry and those of politics and government in terms of communicative strategies and efforts to control the flow and meaning of information have been dissolving as the discursive strategies of public relations have become universally applied. The public personality constructed in one sphere is informed by the methods and manners used to construct a public personality in another public sphere because of the commonality of discursive strategies that has emerged with the general rise of public relations. Political leaders, along with other public figures, are part of a general system of constructing public images that are intended to reply to the people's position as a collective power. Press agents and public relations firms have developed expertise in reading the affective power of the populace and providing the symbols that will contain that power within current institutions.

Public opinion polling is similarly an elaborate way to understand the mass and place their interests within the bounds of existing institutions. It provides scientific evidence of what the people think and is an authoritative counterbalance to the less scientific craft of public relations in establishing a symbolic link between political leadership and the people (the mass). Ginsberg's work on the origins of public opinion polls identifies their function as intimately connected to two political agendas: the expansion of state power and the institutionalization of conservative elites as natural holders of political power.[12] The progressive enfranchisement of the population not only gives the concept of consultation of the people in the form of elections, but also legitimates the expansion of the domain of the state. Elections, as Ginsberg notes, are designed as representations of democratic will that channel political action into one of the more passive constructions of involvement. The vote works to diminish the development of active dissent, which could manifest itself in a number of other forms. The sheer number of participants in the process of voting allows governments to consider that they, in fact, represent the will of the people. Elections also serve to delegitimate other forms of political action. Historically, elections can be read as formal consultation with the crowd or the masses that works to diminish the threat of violence and other forms of civil disobedience that have traditionally been the shape of resistance of the underclasses.[13]

Public opinion polling is an extension of the process of "domesticating" the concept of the mass and the power of the mass. It has been used extensively since the early part of the nineteenth century to survey the desires of different groups of the populace to determine their needs and interests. On many occasions, opinion surveys have been used to provide evidence that various labor leaders and working-class representatives have not been representing the interests of union members. In the American presidential election campaign of 1896, the conservative *Chicago Tribune* polled fourteen thousand factory workers to prove that 80 percent of laborers were in favor of the Republican candidate, McKinley, as opposed to the Democrat, Bryan.[14] The practice of surveying "the people" on a regular basis expanded beyond newspapers and magazines in the nineteenth century to include governments and numerous large corporations in the twentieth century. From the early to mid-twentieth century, virtually all of the clientele of the principal pollsters — that is, George Gallup and Elmo Roper — were aligned with the conservative end of the political spectrum.[15] There are two reasons opinion polls of that time were significant in the politics of the conservative elite of both business and government. First, elites' knowledge of nonelites and working classes was limited. Without polls, and with the organization of modern politics around the representation of the masses, conservative elites knew very little about the rest of the social world, and they needed such knowledge to be able to construct common symbolic ground for the maintenance of power. Second, polling served to undermine the power of the labor leaders, as different polls gave clear, quantitative evidence that union members had different interests from their leaders. Because industry and government funded these various polls, the questions asked were geared to produce responses that could be used favorably by businesses against labor organizations and by governments against organized opposition movements.[16] In terms of political leadership, the objective of many polls was to separate the support for a given political leader from any specific issue that might harm the support of that political leader. The ultimate achievement of this dissociation of interest and policy desires that were diametrically opposed to the political leader's position from overall approval for the leader occurred in the Reagan presidency: for several years, a massive proportion of the American public opposed virtually all of Reagan's major political positions, and yet an equally massive proportion supported the president. An overriding link between the political leader and "the people" had been established, so that unpopular policies did not necessarily threaten the politician's power and did not substantially threaten the execution of the unpopular policies.

In general, opinion polls provide a categorization of the mass, so that the unknown quality of the mass can be reconfigured into something quantifiable and concrete. For instance, George Gallup's polling service has spanned the needs of business and politics. For the Hollywood film industry, polls were used originally to determine the attractiveness of certain film titles to the mass audience.[17] The company was instrumental in maintaining the connection between the entertainment industry and its audience. This service of providing the reading of the mass audience was also used in the political sphere: Gallup's services were commissioned by parties and media outlets to determine the popularity of political leaders. The statistical accuracy of the reading—its framing of the affective sphere into quantitative, verifiable categories—established a conception of the mass that was more real and more expansive than any interest group representation or its leadership. Polls therefore work to reinforce the politics and leaders already in positions of power while working simultaneously to subvert the power of politically active groups.

The combination of opinion polling and public relations has produced an entire specialized industry called political consultancy, which services the legitimation needs of political leadership. Political consultancy is the maintenance system of modern capitalist democracy; through various scientific techniques of polling and unscientific means of reading the mass public, the consultant attempts to help establish the "cultural frames" for the election of the politician. The term *cultural frames* is drawn from Leiss et al.'s assessment of the function of modern advertising. These authors conclude that advertising helps to situate the cultural reference points for the consumption of products. The ad works to surround the product with images of well-being and of connections to culturally embedded values and desires to make the product resonate with the lives of its target audience.[18] Similarly, the political consultant constructs a frame for selling a political candidate to the electorate through the attachment of culturally embedded meaning to a particular issue or to the particular personality of a candidate. The cultural frames are the support structure for the establishment of the legitimacy of any candidate's claim to represent the mass public(s).

The expansion of political consultancy, along with its sister professions of opinion polling, press agentry, and public relations, describes the development of a layer of mediation between institutions and the public. Fundamentally, it is a proliferating interpretive discourse; it operates as a sense-making apparatus/technology for the organization of a capitalist-based democracy that depends on knowledge and inclusion at some level of the entire public. Integrated into the discourse is the organization of social and political reality into the conceptualization of the marketplace. Thus, part of the interpretive discourse of political consultancy, and public relations in general, is the organization of identities into the structure of commodities. The citizen is reconfigured as a political consumer; the candidates and leaders are reconstructed as political commodities. The interpretive discourse of political consultancy provides correlations between these two spheres of the political market by establishing a language of common interest.

To extend further the significance of this reconfiguration of politics, political consultancy also identifies the intense work that is pursued in contemporary culture to maintain a connection between political and cultural hegemony. If political hegemony can be characterized as a moving consensus among various institutions and groups in society to maintain power, cultural hegemony can be thought of as the symbolic structures that are in place or developed to provide a commonality among the various groups in the society. The nation and nationhood, the family, folksongs, and culture are the most obvious examples of symbolic structures that operate as the bases of cultural hegemony. These universal experiences within a culture are used to provide linkages among disparate groups and interests. Fundamentally, these symbolic structures are techniques for establishing the very existence of a particular polity. Cultural hegemony is institutionalized in the political process at the level of leadership. Cultural hegemony is another connecting fiber for the housing of the mass public in the political process. The leader must be structured continually to correlate with this cluster of universal cultural sentiments. The leader, although institutionally an element of the political sphere, must work to embody what is perceived as universal interest or common experience, which is defined primarily in the realm of cultural life. These are mass experiences and general sentiments that cannot be seen as evidence of divisions or forms of cultural distinction. The political leader in capitalist democracies functions to wed the political hegemony to a successful characterization of cultural hegemony.

The political leader thus actively works at a form of cultural legitimation that is perceived as the means to establish contact with the mass public, which is not generally part of the ruling political hegemony. Political consultants are primarily involved with servicing this aspect of the leader's public personality. They rework cultural sentiments so that they can be integrated into the constructed *character* of the leader.

The political leader, in terms of function and as a form of political legitimation, is constructed in a manner that resembles other public personalities that have emerged from a variety of cultural activities. First, the political leader, like the celebrity, is produced as a commodity. Second, the symbolic content of the political leader as commodity arises primarily from the similar groundwork of common cultural sentiments. Entertainment celebrities, like political leaders, work to establish a form of cultural hegemony. The meanings of masculinity and femininity, the meaning of family, and the definition of common cultural identity are the various territorial domains upon which popular cultural celebrities navigate in their formation of public personas. Popularity, or the temporal establishment of a connection to a significant configuration of cultural symbols, is essential for both the politician and the celebrity.

In the following sections, I will establish linkages between the forms of celebrity developed in the entertainment industry and the forms and functions of political personalities. The central constructions of public subjectivity developed in the film, television, and popular music industries will be mapped onto the organization of political culture and specifically the organization of political leadership. In contrast to the previous analyses of celebrity, these sections will begin from the forms of identification and construction of celebrity types that have emerged from the entertainment sphere and then will read constructed political events as techniques for the development of these forms of identification. The examples I will use for this survey of the political construction of affective forms of identification are drawn from recent leadership campaigns and elections in the United States and Canada. This is not meant to be an exhaustive or all-inclusive survey; rather, it is meant to indicate the way in which these forms of affective power are rearticulated in the construction of the political leader.

The Construction of the Familiar and Familial Leader

Television provides for the political leader a site through which a politics of familiarity can be developed and constructed. In terms of Jauss's categories of hero identification, television privileges this cathartic identification. I have mentioned previously the regularity of television, its serialization of characters and its construction of familiar faces structured into a pattern of repetition. On one level, the political leader must enter this system of familiar faces and familiar narratives in order to establish his or her continuing legitimacy with the mass public.

The Political Leader as News Form

Within the television apparatus, news programs are the primary location for the production of the celebrity of the political leader. The determination of what airs as news on television is shaped by several criteria that may or may not conform to the exigencies of the politician. One of the central criteria for the production of news is the identification of something new. Wars, natural disasters, and fires are all events that are naturally newsworthy, because they provide obvious representations of the extraordinary and appear to be something new.

The media event, constructed by both aspiring and established politicians, is a technique intended to constitute the politician as news. Boorstin has described the media event as a "pseudoevent," that is, an event that is fabricated to attract the news apparatus for the sake of attaining airtime.[19] Because of the prefabrication of media events, television news is often quite compliant in covering them in newscasts; instead of conducting an investigative search for televisual stories, it is often much simpler to take what is provided by politicians, material that is organized to conform to the codes and conventions of what constitutes a news story. For example, Bob Graham, while campaigning for the governorship of Florida in 1978, constructed a series of events that maintained the interest of the media. In an announced attempt to understand the people of Florida, he worked in various settings around the state, as a construction worker, a police officer, a farmer, and so on. As well, this campaign constructed each of the work sites where he engaged in labor as a media event. Not only was the campaign constructed into an image and slogan of an advertising campaign (slogans included "Bob Graham Worked Here," "The Story of the Man Who Worked for Governor," and "Bob Graham: Working with People"), Graham and his media consultant, Bob Squier, were also successful in establishing the candidate, a virtual unknown before the campaign, as a legitimate contender for election through massive exposure on the nightly news.[20]

Established political leaders do not have to resort to the construction of media events nearly as often as do unknowns. The prime minister of Canada or the president of the United States, for instance, can rely on the institutional weight of the office to produce a guarantee of a certain amount of coverage. Also, the organization of television news leads to the institutionalization of reporters and camera crews to cover the leader in power. The press that is directly connected to covering a president or a prime minister is a complementary institution that leads to the production of news stories that are centered on the political leader. For reasons of cost, simplicity, and the perceived news status of the incumbent, the political leader achieves a seriality in newscasts, where his or her image and comments are almost assured to be presented every night. As a television performer, the incumbent political leader enters the community of familiar public personalities constructed by the continuous flow of television. He or she is an integral element in the continuous narrative of news.

Opposition leaders can also be part of the seriality of political performance on television. In terms of the codes of objectivity, the Canadian political opposition leader is often used as a means of providing objectivity in the newscast. If the words and image of the prime minister are part of a story, they are often balanced by the words and image of the leader of the opposition. The two images of leaders often become the way in which an issue is constructed and reinforce the very limitations of the debate.

There is a further construction of the incumbent political leader that differentiates him or her from this simple televisual seriality of an organized binary opposition concerning issues. The incumbent leader can also represent a form of neutrality that allows him or her to be constructed as above the game of politics and involved with the larger symbols of the nation-state. This symbolic function of leadership can best be observed in what are thought of as largely ceremonial affairs: a political summit, the official government welcome of a royal visit, and the touring of a foreign state are all examples of how the incumbent leader is positioned into a domain of perceived and constructed neutrality. Television news is very accommodating in presenting the "drama" of these ceremonies and the performance that attempts to embody the nation and its people.[21]

The Familial in the Construction of Political Leadership

The invocation of the familiar is presented in terms of deeply embedded cultural categories of legitimate power and authority. These categories of authority are genderized and placed within a familial context. The presentation of leadership often becomes represented in politics as a masculine trait. Layered onto the construction of leadership as a form of masculinity is the division of power in the family itself. The political leader, then, is generally painted as the father figure for the nation and its people. This is an authoritarian presentation of leadership that invokes a form of paternalism in the organization of politics. Ronald Reagan's familiarity was variously described as avuncular and grandfatherly. In Canadian politics of the 1950s, there was an active public relations campaign to construct aging Prime Minister Louis St. Laurent as "Uncle Louis," so that his childless and bureaucratic life could be reconstructed within familial boundaries of representation.[22]

Positioning the political leader in the family context must be understood as working in concert with the meaning of masculinity in contemporary political discourse. Masculinity continues to connote power, control, and mastery. Political leaders must demonstrate these qualities of masculinity to establish their legitimacy. In George Bush's final thirty-minute campaign film shown on all three national networks on election eve, November 7, 1988, this combinatory construction of masculinity is presented. In the opening scenes, Bush is seen as a military leader, first as a World War II hero, then as a leader reviewing the American troops in a vaguely defined Middle Eastern setting; then, in a later sequence, his militarism, which can be defined as evidence of his masculine power, is contextualized with a lengthy series of edited clips involving Bush and his children, grandchildren, and wife participating in a family picnic. Within Bush's specific campaign, the combination was to reveal that Bush would be "strong," to counteract perceptions of his "wimpiness" or effeminate posturing, yet compassionate, to provide evidence that he would attempt to foster a "kinder, gentler America" than his predecessor, Reagan. The family operates symbolically in this construction of political leadership as an acceptable feminized version of masculine power. To put it crudely, the family patriarch is represented as the benevolent leader whose power is tempered by his responsibilities for others. The family represents the citizens of the United States and is correlated with the father figure representing the natural form and style of the president. The homologous relationship between the familial and the nation, the father and the political leader, is a form of affective transference: the acceptability and the "warmth" conveyed by a "good" and "strong" family structure become a legitimate model for structuring the organization of the political sphere.[23]

There are countless other examples in the construction of political leadership of attempts to organize the representation of power and benevolence through codes of masculinity and codes of the family. The various members of the Kennedy family of Massachusetts who have run for political office in the United States are constructed as simultaneously virile but connected to a strong family. Indeed, although John F. Kennedy has been dead for more than thirty years, his constructed image as a youthful, virile, and sexually attractive leader who was also part of a strong and cohesive family has remained an archetype of what contemporary leadership should embody.

In the Canadian context, the 1968 election of Liberal leader Pierre Trudeau implicated an extensive construction of the code of masculinity through youthful virility. Trudeau's representation of leadership was positioned in clear contrast to Conservative leader Robert Stanfield, whose image of power was hampered by his comparative lack of athletic grace and representation of youth/virility. However, in subsequent years, Trudeau's constructed image was seen to be not contained within the conception of the familial and the family. The homology of family to nation was never clearly established in the Trudeau image. Over time, Trudeau never embraced the familiar and familial constraints of representation and was thus accused of arrogance, insensitivity, and lack of connection to the people.

Summary

Virtually every politician surrounds him- or herself with family at the close of any election campaign. It is an image that seems simultaneously nostalgic and contemporary. As well, the clichéd representation of the politician kissing babies is yet another evocation of the manner in which the familial is central to the affective construction of the populace through the political leader. Although these connections to the familial appear to be natural, they must also be seen to be techniques that provide the sentiment of a common bond with the people. The unknownness of the electorate is shaped with these rather simple symbols of commonality to a certain political meaning that is connected to the meaning and significance of the leader. Power becomes articulated through a masculine code that is positioned in terms of national interest through the family structure.

Similarly, familiarity is essential for the politician who hopes to achieve and maintain power. The regularity of news coverage and the seriality of the leader's image ensure that the leader becomes the focal point for the organization of political sentiment. The television apparatus symbolically embodies the electorate in its audience construction. The mass television audience may not be identical from moment to moment, but its symbolic representation as the mass and thus the public sphere is continuous. The leader's regular appearance in the structure of the flow of television establishes, at the very least, a semblance of connection to this massive citizenry and, at the very most, commonsensical status of legitimacy as a public personality who represents the political sphere.

The Political Leader and the Construction of Solidarity

The political leader's image must also be attached to representations of the people in order to legitimate the conception of mass embodiment. In the preceding analysis of the production of popular cultural celebrities, this connection to the crowd, in all its physicality, is privileged in the organization of popular music celebrities. Politicians are similarly involved with representations of intimate connections with a fragment of the mass that is affectively deeply involved with the candidate and the candidate's message. One can see this construction of solidarity in a number of settings in the display of the political leader. In televised images of the campaign, there are attempts to shape the images so that daily scenes of crowds of people attempting to shake hands with the candidate are ever present. Once again, these images often become clichés of campaigns and lose their affective power to establish the conception of massive support: the candidate shaking hands and talking to workers at the factory gate; the ubiquitous image of the candidate addressing a hall of supporters; the persistent attempt to construct an intersection of a campaign stop and a crowd scene organized by another event or setting, such as a county fair, a crowded shopping mall, or a popular sporting event. Neverthe-less, at a symbolic level, all these settings work to establish the con-nection that the leader has to the "common" people.

In contemporary politics in North America, the political conven-tion serves as one of the best examples of how the leader attempts to establish a message of solidarity with a group of voters. At a number of levels, the convention provides symbolic evidence of committed sup-port. What follows is an analysis of the political convention and its significance in the construction of the legitimacy of the democratic political leader.

The Significance of the Participants: The Remaking of the Power of the Crowd

The participants in North American political conventions are a highly constructed representation of the public sphere. Each party has an elaborate process for the selection of delegates. In the United States, delegates are selected through presidential primaries and are thus committed to specific candidates before they arrive at the con-vention site. Canadian political parties, although several are currently reevaluating and transforming their processes of electing party lead-ers, select delegates at the riding association level who are forwarded to the national or provincial convention. Unlike their American coun-terparts, Canadian delegates are not committed to any particular can-didate; rather, they are committed to the institution of the party it-self. In all cases, the delegates represent the mass, the people, and the people's will in a highly partisan and committed fashion.

Convention delegates collectively are the representation of an ac-tive democracy. Whereas the election represents the formation of in-dividual decision making through the isolation of the vote and the protection of anonymity in the casting of the vote, the convention is a celebration of a collective commitment to a candidate/leader and of blatant forms of support. It is the invocation of the crowd as a sym-bol of massive support and democratic will. The convention is also an attempt to channel the crowd's power into leadership; the uncon-trollability of the crowd's affective power is directed toward the lead-ership candidates, each of which houses the emotion, commitment, and affection of different groups on the convention floor. The convention thus operates as an institution that represents the rationalization of the potentially irrational democratic polity.

The symbolic function of convention participants is ultimately a constructed spectacle of participation. Ostensibly, the focus of the television cameras is on the stage of the convention, where leaders present their speeches and the votes of each ballot are announced; however, this would represent a nonsensical level of staging without the convention crowd. Thus, the television text of the convention is a series of shot-reverse shots between the stage and images of the delegates. Members of the convention crowd are the arbiters of support. The television commentators work to decipher the meaning of the crowd through the size of demonstrations, the number of signs, the volume of applause, and support for each candidate. It is a competitive game of competing collectivities of the crowd, who attempt to establish the overwhelming mass of support for each candidate. The delegate demonstration for each candidate in Canadian conventions is highly orchestrated. At the June 1990 federal Liberal convention, several of the candidates employed bands to lead the entourage of enthusiastic supporters. At the center of these convention-floor spectacles, where the sound, images, and movement of the supporting delegates would occupy up to thirty minutes, the candidate him- or herself would slowly make his or her way to the stage and podium. Indeed, the size and length of each of these demonstrations of support would become the focus of television commentary to determine resolutely the relative levels of support for the various candidates.

In these moments of massive crowd support, the actual candidate is subsumed by the representation of the power of the crowd. In a sense, the separation between the crowd of supporters and the candidate is for the moment indiscernible. The leader is constructed to emerge from this massive support to assume its mandate in his or her arrival at the stage. This unity of the crowd and the political candidate, the momentary lack of separation, is similarly constructed as a form of public subjectivity in the popular music industry. The convention supporters can be translated into fans. The loyalty for the particular performer parallels the sensation of blind loyalty to the particular candidate at the convention. The crowd in both instances is part of the meaning of the public personality. The use of a particular music to herald the arrival of the candidate at the convention hall also is a signal of the momentary movement of political legitimation to this realm of affect and emotion. For Steve Langdon's campaign for the NDP leadership in 1989, Tracey Chapman's "Talking about a Revolution" was adopted as the theme song. Whenever Langdon was about to speak or had just finished speaking, the song was played, so that an indissoluble union was established between the emotive song about social change and Langdon's campaign.

Within the parameters of the convention hall, the various stylized and emotively overt demonstrations of support serve the function of establishing the credibility of the candidate as popular and capable of engaging the general public in this competitive game of collective sentiment. It has become a distinction of leadership to be able to generate a form of hysteria that can be controlled and channeled into an image of a particular leader. Max Weber would have called these elaborate rituals of establishing the legitimacy of leaders a form of institutionalized charisma.[24] In any case, the displays of the convention crowd are displays of strength as they are manifested in these signs of numbers, volume, and apparent commitment of people.

The meaning of the convention crowd for the general political culture is specifically one of democratic spectacle. The images of the convention are mediated by television and television news to be constructed into narratives of the operation and function of democratic politics in contemporary culture. Two forms of identification are placed before the television viewer. First is the identification that the convention delegates actually represent the various groups and interests of the society. Various policy programs have been in place in several of the parties in North America to ensure that a cross section of members of different ethnic groups, genders, and races are represented in the pool of delegates chosen. The television cameras survey these constructions of difference and distinction and display quite effectively the representation of diversity in their images of the convention delegate crowd. The party convention thus works symbolically to represent the people. In this symbolic representation, there is also a defined performative act of the people: the people as convention crowd are situated to present their significance in terms of displays of affect and emotion. The politically active convention crowd is constructed to respond not so much in a rational way as in an emotive way. The convention crowd's reaching for a consensus in the choice of a political leader is a collective reaching for an emotional gestalt; the chosen leader embodies the features and characteristics of leadership that are teased away from the issues and political positions so that an intense form of legitimation of leadership *in and of itself* can be enacted. The convention crowd as the representation of the citizenry/electorate, then, is called on to perform a very isolated function in the political process: to define leadership and elide the concept of leadership from other forms of issues and rationality.

Second, the television audience is called on to identify with the leader, specifically the leader who is chosen. In Canadian political leadership conventions, where a greater number of candidates usually appear on the convention ballot than in the American system, the process of selection is a progressive series of eliminations of the weakest candidates, until one candidate receives an absolute majority of delegate votes. The televisual spectacle establishes the domain of choice for the viewer among these candidates and thereby structures for the period of the political convention that the array of choice represents the political spectrum. The difference between the highly selected party delegates and the general population is temporarily backgrounded while the competitive spectacle of the leadership candidates is foregrounded to define political difference. The interest of the audience is once again transposed in the televisual presentation to an intense focus on the defining characteristics of leadership. The narrative is structured to solve the enigma of who will actually win the leadership, and the viewer and the panels of experts and pundits employed by the television networks attempt to decipher the most likely choice.

American mainstream political conventions, in contrast, are rarely forums for the production of competitive political spectacles. The system of election primaries works to eliminate contenders until, by the time of the convention, the outcome is virtually assured. The convention spectacle, then, tends to move quickly to the establishment of unanimity. The integration of former opponents into the orb of the chosen leader, the establishment of consensus through images and scenes of rapprochement (through the selection of the vice presidential candidate), the invocation of a historical tradition of leadership, and the integration of the current leader into a form of legitimate succession of leadership are all examples of the active attempt to represent a forming consensus. The convention crowd and the television audience are positioned to be witnesses of the significance of the presidential candidate by their sheer numbers. The convention delegates are again the representation of the people and are used to express in the most visible and graphic way that the chosen presidential candidate commands the adulation and support and emotive commitment of a massive number of people. The crowd's solidarity with the message of the political convention and the message of the leader, their virtual unflinching devotion to the chosen one, stand in for an active citizenry.[25]

To summarize the meaning of political conventions, they are principally involved in the establishment of the affective solidarity between a leader and the people. Unlike other representations of the legitimacy of the leader, the convention is structured to underline this link between the crowd and the leader. The physical presence of support, the proximity of the leader to the crowd, and the emotive outpouring from the convention crowd for the leader are all significant in establishing this fundamental connection between the modern political leader and his or her audience. This capacity to house the crowd is the very core of the legitimating process of political leadership. The leader works to embody in the convention what could be described as democratic sentiment. The leader's form of public subjectivity must project this capacity for affective attachment.

The control of collective affect that emerges from this process of the legitimation of political leadership also works to define the parameters of power of the political leader. The democratic moment is defined as affective and is organized as such; as a result, this primary construction of political representation of leadership is partially elided from the rational and, in its connection to the democratic, is increasingly defined by the irrational. For the organization of government, the leader establishes a social bond with the people. The basis of choice in the bureaucracy that supports the government is built on a system of rational selection on the basis of merit. The articulation of the democratic moment in terms of affect and sentiment makes the selection of the leader susceptible; the selection process escapes the rationality of a meritocracy. Thus, the solidarity that the leader establishes works simultaneously to deflate his or her power expressly because it is separated from the ideology of rationality that forms the basis of value in contemporary culture. The ideology of rationality expresses itself in human form in the concept of merit. The organization of leadership conventions and their connection to collective sentiment challenges the basis by which merit is established for individuals. The convergence between the celebrity's power (particularly that of the popular music celebrity) and the political leader's power can now be identified more directly. The modern celebrity is constructed on the basis of a relationship with the people and is dismantled because that relationship to the people is seen to be disconnected from merit, skill, and what are perceived to be traits of individual value. In their election to be public personalities, the political celebrity and the entertainment celebrity are structured to be perpetually vulnerable.

To understand this vulnerability, it is useful to connect public subjectivity to a hierarchy of cultural value that is generally described as "taste."[26] The forms of mass culture and mass entertainment are positioned at the low end of the hierarchy of taste and value. Individuals who emerge from these domains, then, are tainted with the construction that they are unsophisticated individuals whose appeal is to base and undeveloped tastes. Their appeal is not to some level of abstraction or an aesthetic, but what may be described as verging on raw sentiment and affection. In contrast, the organization of the higher arts of serious musical, artistic, or intellectual production produces identifiable artists, geniuses, and innovators; in this sphere the characteristics of individuality are established as universally valid. There are demonstrable standards, levels of skill and expertise that must be met or in evidence for an individual to achieve public status in these domains. However, in the domain of popular cultural production the same criteria are not in place to establish clear-cut evidence of the superiority of the chosen public individual. The exalted position of public personalities results from their capacity to win the affection of a crowd or an audience, a form of skill that is believed to be unrelated to individual superiority. Likewise, the politician's legitimacy as a public personality is expressed in this same capacity to sway the mass audience. Neither form of public subjectivity, because of this connection to the mass, is naturally or automatically connected to the higher values of individuality.

Thus, the capacity of a political leader to be solidly connected to a crowd is a circumscribed construction of power that resembles the forms of power that the popular cultural celebrity possesses. To expand beyond this construction of embodying the crowd/electorate, political leadership must actively invest in connecting to these higher qualities of individuality. The following section attempts to unravel the way in which the leader must also construct an aura and a distance to sustain legitimacy as a political leader and to sustain his or her right to human agency.

The Profilmic Text of Political Leadership: Establishing the Aura

As I have discussed in previous chapters, the film star is constructed to be at the pinnacle of the celebrity hierarchy. The clear distinction in types of celebrity is the form of binarism between the television star and the film star. The television star, because of his or her familiarity, is constructed as more common, more related to the everyday. The long history of stardom surrounding the film industry, its establishment of a canon and a recognizable aesthetic criticism, and its attempts to differentiate its production of celebrity from that of television have led to a production of stars who have a greater distance from their audience. Their power is partially constructed through the fabrication of this distance between their image and personality and their audience. I have previously attached to this form of celebrity construction the term *aura*, as Benjamin has used it. In addition, I have linked this celebrity construction to Jauss's heroic emulatory identification to describe the way in which audiences are structured to read the various texts that surround the film celebrity.

This construction of aura and distance that is embodied in the film celebrity category is the form of public subjectivity that is also invested in the political leader. Not only must leaders embody the crowd, they must also attempt to distance themselves from that embodiment in order to legitimate their differentiation from the crowd, the mass, or the public. In political culture, the hierarchy that the film industry actively works upon to create is at least partially in place. Political leadership implies hierarchical relationships in which authority and responsibility can be thought of as progressively moving up a pyramid to its apex. The pyramid's apex represents the leader, the ultimate point of decision making and power.

However, in the structure of legitimation in a democratic polity, the concept of leadership is a permanent problematic. Without going into great detail about this paradox of democracy, it is quite obvious that leadership entails inequality as opposed to equality. The leader has more power, more influence, and more resources than other people. One of the key symbolic processes that must be accomplished in the organization of a democratic political culture to maintain its rationality is that the institution of leadership itself must be legitimate and permanent. Political leadership not only embodies the crowd, but also must embody simultaneously a virtual authoritarian legitimacy of difference that is deserving of its status. An element of this transfer of power to specific individuals can be understood in the Weberian sense of the institutionalization of charismatic authority: the office of the president or prime minister carries a certain aura that, because of its connection to an institution and tradition, can be transferred from one individual leader to his or her successor. In symbolic terms, the president, for example, becomes an instantiation of the presidency, the office and the tradition. The institution of the presidency carries the semiotic weight of connotations of past presidents, which helps establish new presidents as "presidential," where presidential refers to their legitimacy to exercise power. There is a great deal that is embedded in the symbolic construction of the presidency or prime ministership as an institution that helps connect the connotation of leadership to a consideration of the people. There is also a great deal embedded in the sign of the presidency or prime ministership that celebrates the institution's ultimate power. Each individual leader negotiates the two terrains of legitimation of leadership. The leader must provide evidence of familiarity while providing evidence of exceptionality and hierarchical distance. A successful model for these apparently contradictory representations for political legitimation is provided in the construction of the film celebrity. The film star provides evidence that he or she is in fact connected to the audience: box-office returns and fan mail help to quantify this connection. At the same time, the film star, as I have detailed, has constructed an aura through distance from the audience. Similar strategies of constructing a public personality are in operation in the construction of the political leader.

Constructing Narrative Distance

The relationship between the narrative of film and the star is emulated in the construction of the political leader. Part of the film star's public persona is contained within the film narrative and the film's character. The film characterization essentially has a certain closure and distance. There is a tension and a resultant enigmatic quality to the film star in the separation between character and the "real-life" star. What is fundamentally constructed from this tension is a play with information and knowledge about the film personality. The distinctive quality of the film star is built on the control of knowledge about the star beyond the filmic text and, within the audience, a desire to know more. The political leader is often constructed to express this narrative distance in public appearances. One of the most common patterns for establishing this distance that works to separate the audience/citizenry from the activities of political actors is found in televised images of what could be described as the silent leader. In attempting to cover the news of the president or prime minister, television news often presents the image of the leader without his voice, and in its place a reporter's narration of events. The constructed "private" consultations with foreign dignitaries are presented in this silent form: we see the leaders conversing, but we are not permitted to hear their conversation. There is a separation of their role as political actors and agents and the audience's role as viewers and witnesses. A hierarchy of significance is reinforced by the use of silent images of actions and conversations, where what we cannot hear is believed to be of ultimate significance and consequence. The silence also establishes an enigmatic quality to the leader's persona; the reporter's voice-over is then an element in attempting to solve the enigma of the leader's actions. Viewers are drawn into attempting to solve the occulted domains of political action in the same way the audience is drawn into the film narrative by the enigma and mysteries of the plot and character. Finally, the silence establishes in the name of security that there is a private world of action in the public sphere of political leader, a domain that is impenetrable to the citizen viewer.

The apparent impenetrability of the leader's private world of decision making is the driving force behind two types of narrative construction. News reporting on political leaders can be interpreted as the constant quest to solve the enigma of political action. In television news in particular, the reporter's narration is the layering of coherence on the images of the leader, which often on their own cannot present coherence in the context of a thirty-second or two-minute story. A narrative of political action is at least partially resolved in each of these news stories into a simple code of action. A description of the actions of the leader is presented as the facts of the day's events as the leader is used to embody the sphere of politics for television news. The sound bite, which can be described as the moment in the structure of leadership reporting on television (or radio) when the leader's silence is broken, becomes the object of intense investigation, editing, and work. The managers of leaders actively attempt to orchestrate what is chosen as the sound bite in order to control the public image of the leader; television news gatherers are on a similar quest of discovering the moment that provides the most revelatory utterance of the meaning of the political leader or the meaning of his or her political actions. The sound bite, then, operates as the momentary conduit between the public and private spheres of political action. In its status as the revelatory agent and in its brevity, the sound bite also maintains the enigmatic quality of the separate and hidden sphere of political leadership and the constant effort to reveal the machinations of political power.

The second form of narration that is driven by the impenetrability of the private sphere of political actors and agency is the reconstruction by the audience/viewer. Television news provides the material for establishing a narrative of politics. Political leaders, in this reconstruction, become leading characters in a continuously unfolding drama. Indeed, leaders provide the base upon which the narrative is constructed. The audience members, in relationship to televisual texts of leaders, can be thought of as voyeurs who recognize the inability or possibly the absurdity of crossing into the text as (political) actors. The distance of the actions, the employment of the code of action, and the maintenance of the aura of the private sphere of political action work to position the viewer/audience as witness and not participant. Television news and its focus on political leaders is positioned like the film narrative. The audience watches the news with the hope that there will be some resolution of the dramatic tension that will emerge immanently and not actively engage the viewer in action. In a sense, this relationship of the audience to politics works to maintain the aura and legitimacy of the various political actors.

There are other events and situations that also work to establish and maintain the aura of the leader through a sealed narrative. Inaugurations, political summits, formal speeches given at the close of political conventions, and national television addresses all establish the distance and distinction of the office and the event into the meaning of leadership. Televised news reports, at least in their live versions, are overwhelmed by the constructed narratives of the events or ceremonies themselves. The chaos of the press conference is eliminated in these ceremonial narratives. The leader is permitted to adopt the conventional code of leadership, unencumbered by interventions and interruptions of the public or the crowd.[27]

The Controlled and Constructed Leader: Campaign Films and Advertisements

The most obvious source for the construction of the aura of leadership is the campaign advertisement. From the point of view of the production of political leadership, the advertisement allows for the greatest control of the meanings of a political leader and eliminates mediation of those meanings by news reportage.[28] The advertisement is a sealed visual and oral text that provides a coherent frame for the meaning of a particular candidate. It is a constructed vehicle for the containment of political messages about an individual candidate, where the candidate is circumscribed within a refined and defined text. These qualities of the contained leadership text make the function of the political advertisement resemble film's functional construction of the film celebrity.

The staging of the political advertisement often demands that the political leader "act." In the first series of televised American presidential campaign advertisements, Eisenhower had to play the role of himself responding to the questions of the people. In the mise-en-scène, the questions were of course predetermined; indeed, the questioners were also chosen to "represent" the electorate. Eisenhower's responses needed extensive retakes and editing. In the final versions of the ads, Eisenhower appears to be responding instantaneously to the posed questions.[29] The significance here is not that there is an integration of acting and therefore falsification of what or who the candidate really is. At some level, political rhetoric has always possessed a dramaturgical component. What is more important is that the television advertisement feeds into the proliferating discourse of the identification of the authentic "private" person. The constructed nature of the image, the distinctiveness that is encoded into the image of the candidate, works to intensify debate around the aura and attempts to break down the aura of leadership. The modern politics of aura and distance is drawn into the constant search for the politics of the personal and the intimate, so that the portrayed image can somehow be matched by the "real" activities of the individual candidate. In the same way the film celebrity is constructed between his or her filmic aura and how that intersects with his or her everyday behavior, the political leader becomes the object of scrutiny not so much on policies but almost in terms of personal habits. The momentary breakdown of the aura of the president allows for the transgression of the "presidential," which is read in this new politics as a moment when the "individual" surfaces and reveals his or her true self and the way in which he or she governs. The principal difference between the film celebrity and this transgression into the personal and the politician and his or her revelations of the private sphere is that the politician must maintain the conception of a continuity between the public presentation of self and images of the private self. On the other hand, the film celebrity, in order to establish his or her distinctiveness from the apparatus and to concretize his or her ultimate form of autonomy, must transgress the type he or she has established. In contrast, the politician is overcoded into type. The politician's autonomy and power are built on his or her ability to establish the similitude of the meaning of the office with his or her meaning and demeanor in the private sphere: the politician's individuality must be compatible with his or her public role and persona to the point where there is a natural link made between the individual and the office.

In the development of television political advertisements of political leaders in North America, a gradual concentration on the establishment of an individual character profile of the leader can be identified. The advertisements have been organized to present connections between an idealized representation of the leader and utopian conceptions of a society, or, alternatively, in negative campaign advertisements, an entire dystopian vision is created of the other candidate and the other possible future world. Both types of advertisements represent intense investment in the construction of the political character and personality. From those constructions, the personality profile has become the primary means to assess the future actions of the candidate. The indeterminacy of the future is temporarily positioned through campaign advertisements into the vague affective categories of hope and faith in the leader.

The form and format of campaign advertisements vary a great deal. For instance, their length varies from thirty- and sixty-second spots that can be inserted into the normal flow of commercial television in the United States and Canada to the two standard longer versions of four minutes and twenty seconds and half-hour profile advertisements. The spot advertisements are generally used to establish linkages and connotations between a candidate and a particular sentiment concerning an issue. Tony Schwartz's classic 1964 "daisy" advertisement, for instance, sought to link the general fear of nuclear war to the apparent trigger-happy candidacy of Republican presidential candidate Barry Goldwater. Without mentioning names or using images of recognizable people, and by using a voice-over of President Johnson, the ad attempted to resonate with the cultural trepidation that followed the Cuban missile crisis. The ad begins with an image of a young girl with a daisy and ends with the mushroom cloud of a nuclear explosion. This technique of providing a form of cultural resonance in the structure of brief advertisements has been emulated in countless generations of spot advertisements. The ads link a candidate to a particular sentiment and in this way attempt to solidify the support of significant portions of the electorate.[30]

The longer versions of political advertisements, which Devlin identifies as "profile" ads, establish very clearly a filmic code of character for the candidates. Bush's 1988 election-eve half-hour film, shown on the three principal American television networks, provides an excellent example of the way in which the filmic code of the control of the public personality is engaged in the political sphere. I will use this text to summarize the construction of filmic aura for the politician.

To begin, the quality of the image of Bush's final commercial message of the 1988 campaign sets it apart from the organization of live television and news television, the normal places a presidential candidate is seen. Two-thirds of the thirty-minute commercial were recorded on film as opposed to video. As a result, the images appear to be richer, the colors deeper and more luxuriant than the "flatter" feeling of the videotaped image. In terms of form alone, the advertisement is a deeper image, the same way that the film star through reproduction on film is a richer image than the videotaped television star. The significance of this technical differentiation of image for the political candidate is similar to its significance in the organization of the entertainment industry: the filmic code of production connotes quality and in that evocation of quality also establishes a hierarchy with the televisual image. The filmic code of quality, then, is used in the campaign film to establish a legitimacy and a significance for the political candidate. To establish "presidentialness," the connection to the most superior technological form is desirable because it places all other representations as inferior and therefore of questionable legitimacy. The election is a form of competition; in the United States it is constructed into a clear binarism in presidential elections. Cultural linkages between the candidate and other representations of distinction and quality aid in this game of product distinction.

The filmic code, as discussed above, is a permissible site for the shaping of reality into a narrative. In contradistinction to television news, where narratives are supposed to match conceptions of reality in terms of time, space, and causality, the filmic code allows for the more active and open shaping of a message and reality. For the campaign film, the shaping of reality entails constructing the political character from a wide variety of sources and contexts that do not necessarily follow causally or temporally. The organization of the political image of the candidate is subject in this form to massive amounts of editing. Bush's film is a collage of various images of Bush that are edited to provide not information concerning Bush's position on the issues, but rather a feeling for the man and his integrity. The film is organized into three segments: the first provides background on the man, the second focuses on the campaign, and the third eliminates the filmic and is simply a televised and apparently live address to the nation.

A montage effect is used in the opening profile segment. However, it is not a montage where the meaning is left to float aimlessly, to be situated by the audience; rather, a rich male voice-over narration works to guide the viewer through the various highly edited segments. The narrator, specifically because he is not the presidential candidate, functions also as a complementary voice, providing material that would be considered to be too immodest for the candidate to say himself. Indeed, the opening segment is a carefully developed film that establishes the personality of the candidate, first through a series of stills and action shots of Bush in various roles—as a military hero, as a family man, as a statesman reviewing foreign troops—and then builds on these narrated segments through various testimonials of family members and anonymous citizens about his integrity. Family members are constructed as the witnesses to the true and real George Bush. We learn from George Bush Jr., as his wife sits passively supportive beside him, that his father is "the most thoughtful person I know.... He's famous for writing letters and phoning. This is true George Bush."

He concludes his revelation of his father with a vignette: "I can remember campaigning in Cooperstown, New York, and the night bellman of the hotel walked up to me and said I have a memento that I treasure and it was from Dad, that said thank you for getting a suit pressed at an unusual hour, and George Bush is that way."

Another son, Jeb, reaffirms that Bush "can be very nice" and then goes on to explain, "But in a competitive setting no one is going to outhustle him or outwork him. He is just tenacious, extremely tenacious." The testimonials continue at what appears to be a family picnic: Neil Bush explains the importance of getting the "families together" once a year and that the gathering, with "Gampy" (Bush) driving the wedges and building the tent, is "a tradition that is really special." Doro Bush Le Blond provides further evidence of Bush's caring in another family anecdote:

> I was sitting at home and just watched this fiery interview with my dad and I'll never forget it because I was on the edge of my seat and I couldn't believe it and the phone rings and it's Dad and he says, "Doro, I just had to call you—Is your car okay? I heard your car broke down"—and I said, "Dad! You just had this wild interview!" But that's typical of my father because he doesn't think of himself; he thinks of other people at times you know he has the most pressing things on his mind and the whole country is watching and crazy over it and he thought of me.

His wife, Barbara, provides the ultimate explanatory narrative about the candidate Bush that pieces the affective dual attachments surrounding the Bush candidacy—gentle yet firm: "It's a wonderful thing to have your husband behave like that [talk warmly about their 'strong family' in the presidential candidates' debate]. He doesn't get furious, or, it's not to say he doesn't get mad or his adrenalin doesn't flow, because his adrenalin flows." In an earlier segment, Barbara explains that "I think the reason he has done so very well is he's not a fella who reacts to things; he acts. He doesn't get upset. He is a quiet man and he does hear people and then he makes up his own mind. And I think that's what people are seeing."

Barbara Bush is positioned in the film to provide the final and thus most intimate and complete portrait of Bush the candidate. The other family members give the audience various character profiles that connect to Barbara's ultimate assessments of the man. In these edited sequences what is constructed is a sensation of a growing accord about the man from the various sources that is unified through the seamless construction of family images, slow-motion pictures of a smiling and warm Bush, the smiling faces of various archetypally displayed Americans, and the overcoded display of the "innocence" and thus faith of the Bush grandchildren in George Bush.

Functionally, and in the best possible light, the information provided by these character profiles is intended to help the audience/citizenry to understand the way in which decisions will be made by the future leader. Although the audience learns about Bush through these testimonials, the film ensures that there is a certain elusiveness to the man. Our contact is through these various intermediaries, so that the image of Bush remains above these witnesses; his actions are ultimately more significant. When Bush does speak, it is framed most frequently in the standard forms of public address; we see the beginnings of a speech, fragments of a candidates' debate, a carefully edited sequence of Bush answering citizens' questions. In all of these forms of address, the public Bush is maintained. Within the structure and meaning of the film, the testimonials are used to connect the private and public spheres of Bush to establish that there is continuity between them. The family members operate as "witnesses" for the audience as to what Bush would be like as president, when and where much of the political process will be hidden and veiled behind such concepts as national security. It is a filmic reconstruction of the process of witnessing that is essential to the construction of democratic politics. The film works, therefore, to provide revelatory moments about Bush while simultaneously sustaining the heroic distance of the man from this everyday world—his public image and character are buttressed through these momentary private revelations.

Much like the narration, the ad's music provides signposts for the organization of the meaning of the filmic text. The use of a virtually continuous background/foreground musical sound track also establishes the clearly filmic quality of the construction of character; it is a break from the way in which news presents personalities. In contrast, the music helps to link the presentation of the political personality to the building of a leading film character. It washes over the various commentaries in the campaign film to establish the fundamental interconnectedness of the comments, the images, and the candidate. Where a great deal of visual editing has been carried out in the production of the film, the musical sound track sutures the narrative into something that gives the sensation of a seamless fabric.

There are moments when the music builds to a dramatic crescendo; from the sparse, high-register piano accompaniment of most of the commentaries, an occasional crash of a full orchestral wave punctuates the heightened affective moments of the text. In the most rhetoric-filled sound bite culled for the film, the orchestral wave builds simultaneously:

> I say it without boast or bravado: I've served, I've built, and I'll go from the hills, to the hollows, to the cities, to the suburbs, to the loneliest town on the quietest street to take our message of hope and growth for every American to every American moving forward, always forward. This is my mission and I will complete it.

The music makes the meaning, providing the tension and the resolution of the phrasing so that its emotive impact is heightened. In concert with a series of images of smiling Americans, the campaign film attempts to provide an emotive connection between the nation, the people, and the candidate. The music moves to its resolution and, as Bush evokes his "mission," we are visually guided through a series of sepia-toned images, of suburban Americans; various ethnicities are faded in and out, sequentially building to idyllic scenes of children. The music, in concert with the images, is meant to provide an inclusive space within the meaning of the presidential candidate. Bush can embody the various desires and aspirations of all Americans, for those aspirations are all fundamentally the same.

To express the speed and energy of campaigning, the music abruptly moves from the relatively serene piano music to frantic-paced fiddle music. The use of American fiddle music (orchestrally produced, however) evokes the folk quality of the candidate, his innate connection to the people. The fiddle music constructs the scenes of Bush trying to shake hands in the classic main-streeting fashion. What these musical and film sequences emphasize is the accessibility of the president, the lack of distance of the public individual from common people. The massive security that usually surrounds a presidential candidate is virtually absent in these carefully culled silent images of a smiling Bush.

Music also becomes foregrounded in the final two minutes of the film. In fact, an entire country and western patriotic song is played over images of the candidate campaigning and being presidential. "I'm Proud to Be an American" attaches the Bush candidacy to several

forms of affective attachment. First, country music connotes an in-
digenous form of popular culture that is seen to be authentic to the
values of American family culture. Indeed, the lyrics of the song emphasize the importance of family and its centrality to American values.
As well, the song evokes the authenticity of country music as genuine
to American emotions. The song is an attempt to establish cultural
linkages between the recent past in the construction of the symbolic
president and the current incarnation in the presidential candidate
Bush. The populist simplicity of Reagan is echoed in the declaration
of the song:

> I thank my lucky stars to be living here today,
> Because the flag still stands for freedom and they can't take
>   that away.
> And I am proud to be American for at least I know I'm free!
> Because there ain't no doubt about it
> God Bless the U.S.A.!

Here the song is used to speak the continuity of the form of populism,
nationalism, and conservatism that allowed Reagan to maintain the
support of the working-class electorate. It is the formation of an affective alliance that Hall describes in the British context as national
populism.[31] The song allows the emotions to be expressed through
association; Bush uses these signs to help reinscribe a form of hegemony established by the Reagan candidacy since 1980. The work of
elections is to sustain mass support for conservative policies through
an expression of nationalist sentiment and patriotic pride. For Bush,
the song allows for the expression of this patriotic emotion to be spoken for him through its emotive coding in a popular song. The work
of the song for the construction of the Bush presidential character is
to reassure his continuity with the Reagan legacy.

The song is connected to a series of edited images that establish
the presidentialness of the Bush character. In several sequences, still
images of Bush beside foreign leaders such as Thatcher and Gorbachev
are framed inside a television screen in individuals' homes; these still
images are transformed into images that come alive as the television
screen dissolves into the actual footage of these meetings. The televisual image is used to establish the legitimacy of Bush's position on the
national and international stage. An entire narrative is constructed
to present the candidate as presidential; he is depicted in a crowd (of

children) as towering above his supporters. The closing sequence pictures Bush raising his youngest grandchild into the air; the connotation is one of emotive uplifting and hope for the future.

What must be kept in mind is that the variety of techniques and edits in the campaign advertisement are there to construct a recognizable character that is connected to a series of affective positions that can be embodied in the cultural definitions of leadership. It is a controlled series of images and sounds that allow for the affective message of the candidate to be best expressed. The tone of the character-building film is not one of information. In fact, whenever the discussion of Bush in the narration or in the testimonials veers toward identifying an exact position on issues, the filmic code of establishing the aura of the political character steers a wide berth. It is not until the last five minutes of the ad that a specific issue is even mentioned. When an issue is broached in Bush's final direct address, it is framed visually in the simple style and videolike format of a presidential address to the nation.

The campaign film privileges the code of character to the point where all other types of information are either neglected or structured into the code. The political character code in the Bush film is built on affect. The affective structuring of the meaning of the Bush political character is designed to appeal to the audience of voters without placing possible forms of information that could lead to a negative affective linkage with the candidate. The image, then, is ultimately a controlled representation of idealized conceptions of what constitutes a leader; a good father, a strong family man, and an international statesman are all configured in the constructed image of the Bush political character. Into this mix of providing positive affective linkages for the audience, the film is structured to reveal the candidate only partially in order that the presidential aura of difference and distinction that is elemental in conveying the conception of leadership is maintained. The audience is offered glimpses and testimonials that serve to establish the authenticity of the aura without eliminating the evocation of distance. In this way, the knowledge of character is limited to a play with the intersection between the private and the public individual. The political character is modeled in campaign films to convey only this type of affective information. What the audience is left with is not the kind of information needed for rational decision making; rather, the audience is inundated with affective messages that are there to provide for an instinctive feeling about the candidate that resonates with the construction of the individual's feelings around the judgment of character. This controlled image of the presidential candidate constructs a political character devoid of clear articulations of ideology and political position. The audience/citizenry works on establishing a normative gestalt about the integrity of the political character. The political sphere is constructed, then, in the way in which we relate to the construction of identification with filmic heroes.

Conclusion

In this review of the way in which the political sphere is configured into the system of public subjectivity so well established in the entertainment industries, I have attempted to provide examples of how various codes of public subjectivity that have been privileged in television, film, and popular music have been reused and reformulated in the domain of politics. My categorization has the limitation that there are overlaps in the ways in which political characters are constructed; political events and political forms do not naturally and neatly fit into the structures of the system of celebrity. Nevertheless, the three forms of celebrity privileged in the three entertainment industries functionally identify the ways in which public personalities are used to embody the mass or, in its visceral incarnation, the crowd. Inscribed into the meaning of any political leader are the three forms of affective association I have outlined above. Political leaders are woven into the fabric of public subjectivity in contemporary culture so that through their reconstruction as what could be described in shorthand as *legitimation commodities,* they resemble other representations of active human agents in the culture. The political dimension of the political celebrity implies a symbolic layering of the meaning of the leader with the representations of democratic culture. A connection to the mass must be established and reinforced, and the connection to the mass must also function as a technique for controlling the mass. In terms of control and embodiment, the political leader can be expressed as an amalgam of the construction of solidarity with the mass or crowd, the expression of familiarity with an audience, and the expression of an aura of distinction and differentiation. These three forms of constructing a functioning form of public subjectivity and a political celebrity identify the way in which power has been housed in contemporary culture into individualized representations. What is privileged in the construction of public personalities is the realm of affect. Affect moves the political debate from the realm of reason to the realm of feeling and sentiment. It is the basis of the formation of a cultural hegemony in contemporary culture; where disunities are obvious, the leader affectively is used to stitch together a functional unity. The political leader functions as a legitimating apparatus for the symbolic representation of the people. What I have attempted to reveal in this chapter is this operation of affect and the irrational in the organization of contemporary political culture. Modern political leadership campaigns can be read, then, as intense sites for the organization of affective power of the mass/crowd/public into recognizable symbols of public subjectivity. The apparent agency of the crowd/mass/public is repositioned into the individualized agency of the political leader. The fields of public relations, press agentry, and opinion polling, which flourished originally in the entertainment industries, now provide the models and mediating discourses for the organization of contemporary political culture, in which the political leader attempts to embody the mass public *affectively*.

Conclusion: Forms of Power/Forms of Public Subjectivity

I have attempted in the preceding chapters to highlight connections between what are often perceived to be unrelated phenomena. The concept of the celebrity, I have maintained, is a modern idea that is very much linked to the development of mass democracies and concerted efforts to contain the power of the mass in those democracies.

The underlying fiber that establishes a connection between popular cultural figures and the realm of politics and power is their common ground in the formation of public personalities. I have argued that the public personality or celebrity is the site of intense work on the meaning of both individuality and collective identity in contemporary culture. It is the capacity of these public figures to embody the collective in the individual, which identifies their cultural signs as powerful.

Symbolically, democratic culture, as it has been articulated in the large modern Western democracies, such as the United States, Canada, and Britain, is represented by two sometimes contradictory representations of the people and conceptions of personal power. First, there is the underlying ideology in the democracy that all individuals have equal amounts of power and can express that power in the most rational fashion. There are two avenues for the exercising of rational action by the individual: as a consumer, the individual makes market choices; as a citizen, the individual makes rational choices concerning who will best represent his or her interests in government. Second, the democracy elevates the significance and importance of the mass as a politically potent force that can direct change in society and in the polity. The conception of this collective will is expressed in the organization of nation-states and their attempts to embody the common will of a people. The collective will has a number of representations that indicate that it is not clearly aligned with the rational organization of society. In fact, the conception of the mass, in its var-

241

ious representations as the people, the crowd, the group, and the mob, is generally linked with the nonrational, the emotional, and the domain of sentiment.

These contradictory representations of mass democratic culture have produced specific apparatuses that attempt to resolve the contradiction between the rational and the nonrational, the meanings of the individual and the collective. I have presented the three entertainment industries as apparatuses that construct a privileged discourse about individuals as well as provide sites for the organization of collective sentiments. Through a hermeneutic reading of particular celebrities as texts, I have identified that these apparatuses, in their intense construction of individuals, highlight specific types of individuality. These types of individuality also demarcate domains of human agency in contemporary culture. The celebrities who emerge as stars in these entertainment industries work to form "audience-subjectivities," a term I have used to describe the constant negotiation of their identities through both individual and collective representations by particular audience groups and particular culture industries. At any one time there are clusters of celebrities in each entertainment apparatus that provide avenues for the development of audience meaning through identification of the individual celebrity's subjectivity. The meaning, significance, and power of the celebrity therefore is constructed from a double rationality; the various cultural industries help manufacture and elevate individuals to stardom, while the audience rereads, rearticulates, and sometimes rejects in its own efforts to rationalize their quotidian with this public sphere of presented personalities.

It is important to realize that the development of the apparatuses of public personalities in these entertainment industries is historically linked to the development of mass democracies. The celebrities articulate agency and activity in democratic culture. In their often "unique" — or perhaps idiosyncratic — personalities and in their attempts to achieve autonomous status, one can see the work of active human agency. The celebrity, then, is the public representation of individuality in contemporary culture, where their movements and personality transformations are significant.

Moreover, the celebrity figure is constructed by these apparatuses to contain the public — in effect, to represent the public. Unlike with television programs or films, where the audience as a mass is temporarily contained as a distinct audience, the celebrity allows for some continuity between these discrete cultural units. Celebrities thus work to organize the markets of the cultural industries to provide some degree of stability.

Thus, what cannot be overlooked is that celebrities are *attempts* to contain the mass. The mass is the site par excellence of affective power, a kind of power that is seen to be very volatile and dangerous but also very desirable if it can be effectively housed. In the culture industries, celebrities are then aligned with strategies for the connection of cultural commodities to this volatile affective power.

What has unified the domains that are often constructed in our contemporary culture as relatively unconnected is the organization of affect and the perception of affect as a form of power. In politics as well as popular culture, the capture or containment of affect is central to the manner in which political leadership is determined and critical to the organization of risk and risk capital in the culture industries. In this book, I have identified the development of a mediating discourse that has migrated from its first home in the entertainment industries to envelop the organization of our political culture. Techniques for surveying and appealing to the masses — from press agentry, public relations, demographics, and psychographics to social psychological research, opinion polling, and political consultancy — are also discourses for comprehending and containing the mass through representations in the public sphere.

There are several insights about contemporary culture that can be discerned from a study of celebrities and the various integrated systems that develop types and categories of celebrities. I want to conclude by highlighting these insights and thereby identify some future directions for research. The ubiquity of celebrities, as well as their intangible nature, makes them difficult to define, and thus it is difficult to establish their material impact on a culture. In this book, I have attempted to locate that intangible quality in terms of their various functions in contemporary culture. The comments that follow identify the functions of the celebrity and the celebrity system.

The Celebrity as Human Agent

The celebrity is both a proxy for someone else and an actor in the public sphere. To describe this dual role, the celebrity can be defined as an agent. The term *agent* expresses a tension in meaning and significance that is homologous to the meaning of the celebrity. On one level, the proxy of the celebrity relates to his or her close proximity to the institutions of power and his or her dependence on those institutions for elevation to the public sphere. The politician arises out of the institutions of political parties, whereas the entertainer is dependent on the institutions of the culture industries, which are connected to the institutions of a capitalist economy. From this proxy, the celebrity's agency is the humanization of institutions, the simplification of complex meaning structures, and a principal site of a public voice of power and influence. On another level, the celebrity expresses the more radical conception of human agency as it has developed in the Marxist tradition. There are limits to this conception of revolutionary force that is expressed through these public personalities; nevertheless, where the economy is believed to operate in an autonomous fashion, where technology is often organized ideologically as developing a telos that is entirely self-contained, the public personality or celebrity conveys the meaning that his or her actions both are significant and can produce change. Celebrities, because they emerge from a legitimation process that is connected to the people, and because their emergence is not necessarily purely associated with merit or lineage, represent active elements of the social sphere. They are the proxies of change. Celebrities, then, often define the construction of change and transformation in contemporary culture, the very instability of social categories and hierarchies in contemporary culture. They are the active agents that in the public spectacle stand in for the people. The assuming of this secondary agency role has led many stars to become spokespersons for political causes and issues. Their activity can be seen as the site of agency and activity in a culture; their limited success allows one to discern the circumscription of agency in the culture. The agency of the celebrity is more often reduced to a privatized, psychologized representation of activity and transformation—it rarely moves into a clear social movement.[1]

The Celebrity as a Stable Configuration of Collective Formations

Collectivities in contemporary culture are inherently unstable. In North American culture in particular, the development of consumer culture has led to layers upon layers of cultural meaning that have clouded the fixity of social identity. Class distinctions are unclear in the development and fostering of a composition of a mass society of consumers. Ethnicity is weakened in favor of collective formations that are defined by consumer identities where a clustering of consumer choices establishes a recognizable pattern. The patterns of consumer culture indicate the way that marketing and advertising have reconfigured meaning and significance of collectivities in the social sphere. With the consumer economy constructed to permit variability, transformation, obsolescence, and cultural fatigue of products and their significance, there is a correlating fluidity in consumer identity.

Celebrities, in this fluid construction of identity through consumption, represent flags, markers, or buoys for the clustering of cultural significance through patterns of consumption. In consumer culture there are other stabilizing devices that parallel this celebrity function. Brand names are attempts to structure continuities in consumer culture, where a sense of trust and security is indicated by certain symbols and companies. The celebrity operates as a brand name for the organization of production and consumption of cultural commodities. The celebrity functions as a semistable identity and cultural icon that runs through several cultural forms and establishes an identity through which an audience can estimate the cultural forms' relative value. Consumer culture's persistent use of celebrities to endorse products positions their function between commodities and collective formations of the social world. The celebrity endorsement provides a cultural pattern for products that can be seen as the integument between the world of goods and the world of individuals using those goods. Celebrities function in consumer culture as a connecting fiber between the materiality of production and culturally contextualized meaning of consumption and its relation to collective identity. The celebrity, then, is a commodity that possesses in its humanness and familiarity an affective link in consumer culture to the meaning that is bestowed on consumer objects by groups.

For instance, Michael Jackson was employed by Pepsi to help stabilize the meaning of Pepsi in the realm of consumption. For a time, he provided an affective code of attachment that can link the Pepsi product to an audience to the point where collective identities of these two cultural commodities were melded into a significant meaning system for a cultural group. With his troubles over both substance abuse (an addiction to painkillers) and, more seriously, allegations of indecent acts with children, Pepsi gave up its association with Jackson. It is less significant to know whether this specific example of linkage actually was successful for the advertiser than it is to realize that celebrities function generally at the interstices between commodities/products and collective patterns of meaning and identity in consumer culture. Other celebrities continue to operate for Pepsi at those intersecting points.

The System of Celebrity as a Spectacle of Individuals

There is an ideological function that is also part of the functioning of the celebrity system. The interactions of celebrities as reported on television and radio and in magazines and newspapers establish a code of individuality that is central to the meaning of any celebrity. Generally, celebrities' behavior is representative of the expression of individual preferences and desires and the acting on those preferences and desires. The celebrity is the independent individual par excellence; he or she represents the meaning of freedom and accessibility in a culture. The close scrutiny that is given to celebrities is to accentuate the possibility and potential for individuals to shape themselves unfettered by the constraints of a hierarchical society. Celebrities are icons of democracy and democratic will. Their wealth does not signify their difference from the rest of society so much as it articulates the possibility of everyone's achieving the status of individuality within the culture. As a system, celebrities provide a spectacle of individuality in which will itself can produce change and transformation. The spectacular quality of the code of individuality that is enacted by public personalities works ideologically to maintain the idea of continuity between wealth and the disenfranchised rest of society. Celebrities reinforce the conception that there are no barriers in contemporary culture that the individual cannot overcome.

Celebrity and the Defining of the Private and Public Spheres

I have argued that celebrities are manifestations of the organization of culture in terms of democracy and capitalism. They are the privileged form of what I have called public subjectivity. Their privilege is partly related to their capacity to act as discursive vehicles for the expression of such key ideologies as individuality or new consumer collective identities. In that capacity to house a discourse on individuality, celebrities, as I have noted, are intense sites for determining the meaning and significance of the private sphere and its implications for the public sphere. Fundamentally, celebrities represent the disintegration of the distinction between the private and the public. This disintegration, as represented by celebrities, has taken on a particular form. The private sphere is constructed to be revelatory, the ultimate site of truth and meaning for any representation in the public sphere. In a sense, the representation of public action as a manifestation of private experience exemplifies a cultural pattern of psychologization of the public sphere. The formation of a public subject is reduced to various psychological motivations, pressures at the micro level, the expression of family interest and personality traits.

The celebrity is the avant-garde of this movement to vivisect public action by identifying the originary private experience. It functions as a discursive vehicle that reduces the cultural meaning of events, incidents, and people to their psychological makeup. The celebration of affective attachment to events and moments is represented by the celebrity, where further cultural connections are dematerialized. The celebrity can be seen as instrumental in the organization of an affective economy.

The affective economy, where there is reduction of meaning to psychological motivations, has become central to the way in which our politics and culture operate. Daniel Bell's famous expression of the end of ideology in the late 1950s can be reread as the rise and celebration of affective meaning.[2] Similarly, the end of the Cold War can be reread as the end of the effort to fabricate social meaning and the elevation of the moments of feeling that are provided by an affective economy.

Celebrities, as the affective economy's construction of public individuals, are sites for the dispersal of power and meaning into the personal and therefore universal. They represent the reorganization of collective identities into the affective economy of the contemporary capitalist democracy.

Coda: *George,* Celebrities, and the Shift in Political/Popular Culture

George, the American magazine launched in late 1995 ostensibly about "not just politics as usual" (a slogan that serves as its trademark insignia), identifies and actively celebrates the transformations in what constitutes public discourse and what conveys political import. On the inaugural issue cover, the supermodel Cindy Crawford vogues her way into a George Washington pose with stylized eighteenth-century garb combined with de rigueur exposed midriff.[1] Published by John F. Kennedy Jr., whose celebrity status no doubt helped convince financial backers of the viability of the concept, *George* looks like a fashion magazine, with its collection of advertisers such as Uomo, Clinique, Calvin Klein, Chanel's Egoiste, Donna Karan, Lagerfeld, and Guess Jeans. Its articles comfortably blend political with entertainment celebrities into a system of stars and intersecting lifestyles, interests, and issues. Kennedy acknowledges this orientation in his first "Editor's Letter": "Political figures are increasingly written about as the personalities and pop icons they have become. Politics has migrated into the realm of popular culture and folks can't turn away."[2] *George,* Kennedy explains, is not just a political magazine; it "is a lifestyle magazine with politics at its core, illuminating the points where politics converges with business, media, entertainment, fashion, art and science."[3] Thus, Madonna's "If I Were President" article comfortably coexists with an interview with the former governor of Alabama, George Wallace.[4] Kennedy's interview with movie star Warren Beatty about politics and other matters can occupy quite naturally the central article position of the second issue, which also includes an interesting summary of a survey conducted to find out how people's presidential preferences and political alignments correspond with their media tastes.[5]

The blending and blurring in *George* of what used to be separated into distinct categories and discourses can be identified as a sign of a

248

general shift in political culture that is not nearly so new as the magazine; in fact, it has been developing over at least the last half century. Although it is not immediately obvious, the publication closest in lineage to *George* is *Playboy*, which first appeared in 1954. In *Playboy*, serious articles and significant fiction rub shoulders with "pleasurable" interludes of photo spreads of naked women. What links these magazines is not just the juxtaposition of the serious and the seductive (which ultimately is the reason people buy the magazines), but a fundamental acknowlegment of the link between personal style and general political position. Sex and sexuality, once the domain of the private and the personal, through *Playboy* become markers of an engagement with something public. Celebrity, fashion, and lifestyle, once the domain of women's magazines and tabloids and seen to be insignificant, through *George* become acceptable ways of engaging with and reading the public sphere.

Intersecting with this new blended discourse is a cultural politics that has developed through feminism and has proliferated into other identity politics. The generalized slogan "The personal is political" describes a different intersection with the public sphere and a new engagement with areas of life formerly unheard, hidden, or devalued. Celebrities have represented one of the channels through which the personal has been discussed and debated, both prior to its overt politicization and since. As I have noted previously, celebrities are human agents in the public sphere who act as proxies. In a very pervasive way, the reading of politics openly in terms of celebrities articulates the transformation of politics.[6] The older patterns of what constitutes politics are permeated by the proliferation of political action, interest, and discourse that emerges from different sites and institutions. *George* acknowledges that shift and actively caters to this new affective politics, albeit for the limited American middle-class readership of magazines such as *Vanity Fair* that have made celebrity gossip legitimate.

On a very simple level, *George* cloyingly tries to represent the decline of some binarism in the representation of power and politics between something considered, in some vague, nostalgic way, "normally" masculine and something considered classically feminine. The binarism of women's magazines connected to consumption and men's magazines connected to production is certainly not so clearly delineated on the contemporary magazine rack, and *George* therefore is not alone in this almost mainstream trend. What is indicated in this blend and blur is an appeal to a postmodern construction of a consumer and, by implication of the content, a citizen/voter.

Ultimately, then, what *George* identifies and chronicles to some degree is the acknowledgment of how public individuals are invested affectively by audiences. Publicists and press agents have been booking politicians regularly to appear on afternoon talk shows, on MTV, on *Saturday Night Live,* and on other forms of entertainment programming over the past four years.[7] The system of celebrity and the process of affective investment in public personalities is now much more continuous between spheres. We see emerging through this continuity a different construction of where politics and the political arise; that difference is an interesting shift that makes the study of public personalities and the discourses that develop around them an important area for further inquiry, both to assess the limits of this form of politics and to measure the possibilities for expansive proliferation.[8] The celebrity embodies this very tension between the ephemeral and the invested, the floating signifier of value and the attribution of meaning and significance within contemporary culture.

Notes

Preface

1. The relationship between the image and exchange value is a topic in itself, as it describes a hierarchization of value in its implicit denigration of the image to surface, nonmateriality, and nonproduction. This categorization is as severe as the classical divisions between high culture and low culture. For a discussion of value and the sign, see Jean Baudrillard, *For a Critique of the Political Economy of the Sign*, trans. Charles Levin (St. Louis, Mo.: Telos, 1981). For a discussion of the (advertising) image, exchange value, and use value, see Sut Jhally, *The Codes of Advertising: Fetishism and the Political Economy of Meaning in Consumer Society* (London: St. Martin's Press, 1987). The critique of the image as false value is not exclusively the domain of Marxist-inspired criticisms; it is endemic to most conservative critiques of society as well. The celebrity as manifestation of the antithesis of the work ethic is exemplary of a culturally conservative approach to the significance of celebrities.

1. Tracing the Meaning of the Public Individual

1. Marlon Brando, with Robert Lindsey, *Brando: Songs My Mother Taught Me* (London: Century, 1994).

2. Michael Jackson, *Moonwalk* (London: William Heinemann, 1988), 12.

3. Kirk Douglas, *The Ragman's Son: An Autobiography* (New York: Simon & Schuster, 1988).

4. Richard Dyer, *Stars* (London: British Film Institute, 1979).

5. *Individualism*, as an English term, first appeared in Henry Reeves's translation of Alexis de Tocqueville's *Democracy in America* in 1862. See J. S. McClelland, *The Crowd and the Mob* (London: Unwin Hyman, 1989), 157.

6. A term that I develop in succeeding chapters that captures the relationship of the celebrity to modern collective and social forms that are expressed through particular individuals in the public sphere is *public subject*. This melding of conceptions of the collective and the individual and individuality is most accurately expressed in terms of this public subjectivity. *Public subjectivity* is synonymous with the term *celebrity status;* the critical distinction is that *public subjectivity* is an analytic term and tool for unraveling the organization of modern subjectivity and the role that the celebrity plays in that organization. For further discussion of public subjectivity, see chapter 3.

7. Leo Braudy, *The Frenzy of Renown: Fame and Its History* (New York: Oxford University Press, 1986), 434.

8. Ibid., 437.

9. Thomas Carlyle, *On Heroes, Hero-Worship and the Heroic in History* (New York: Ams, 1969 [first given as a lecture series in 1839]).

10. The continuation of this tradition of establishing difference in greatness can be seen if one traces the history of biography and autobiography from the nineteenth to the twentieth century. Such a study is beyond the bounds of this book; nevertheless, the biography remains a rich, relatively unmined area for the development of a discourse on individuality and new conceptions of fame and significance in the twentieth century.

11. Joshua Gamson, *Claims to Fame: Celebrity in Contemporary America* (Berkeley: University of California Press, 1994), 27.

12. Max Horkheimer and Theodor Adorno, "The Culture Industry: Enlightenment as Mass Deception," in *The Dialectic of Enlightenment* (New York: Continuum, 1972), 123–71.

13. Herbert Marcuse, *One-Dimensional Man: Studies in the Ideology of Advanced Industrial Society* (Boston: Beacon, 1992).

14. Leo Lowenthal, "The Triumph of Mass Idols," in *Literature, Popular Culture and Society,* (Palo Alto, Calif.: Pacific, 1961[1944]), 109–40. An interesting application of Loewenthal's division of "idols of production" and "idols of consumption" is carried out by Barbi Zelizer, who assesses the relevance of this division in contemporary society as it relates to television journalism in general and Dan Rather's form of celebritydom in particular. See Zelizer, "What's Rather Public about Dan Rather: TV Journalism and the Emergence of Celebrity," *Journal of Popular Film and Television* 17 (Summer 1989): 74–80.

15. Daniel Boorstin, *The Image* (New York: Atheneum, 1962).

16. Jean Baudrillard, "The Ecstasy of Communication," in Hal Foster (ed.), *The Anti-Aesthetic: Essays on Postmodern Culture* (Port Townsend, Wash.: Bay, 1983), 126–34. Baudrillard develops an argument that there has been destruction of public and private spheres in the movement to pure communication and representation. He likens the modern condition of experience to that of the schizophrenic, where the loss of the attachment to the real makes every experience, every representation, so close and instantaneous that the definition of self is lost in the play of images and representations. For further development of Baudrillard's concepts of the "hyperreal," see his *Simulations* (New York: Semiotext[e], 1983).

17. Alexander Walker, *Stardom: The Hollywood Phenomenon* (London: Michael Joseph, 1970), 21.

18. Ibid., 43–56. More will be said about this in chapter 4, on the concept of the celebrity in the film industry. The key point I want to emphasize here is the genesis of a new system of value in the personality through its articulation in this industry. Also, the particular time of the integration of the feature-length film into the mainstream of popular culture identifies simultaneously the degree of societal embracement of the film star as a public personality.

19. Christian Metz, *Psychoanalysis and Cinema: The Imaginary Signifier* (London: Macmillan, 1982).

20. The debates within feminist film theory around psychoanalysis can be seen to have built from Laura Mulvey's 1975 *Screen* essay "Visual Pleasure and Narrative Cinema," which is reprinted in her collection *Visual and Other Pleasures* (London: Routledge, 1989). Other key figures are Constance Penley (for example, *The Future of an Illusion: Film, Feminism, and Psychoanalysis* [Minneapolis, University of Minnesota Press, 1989]), Teresa De Lauretis (for example, *Alice Doesn't: Feminism, Semiotics, Cinema* [Bloomington: Indiana University Press, 1982]), Sandy Flitterman-Lewis (for example, *To Desire Differently: Feminism and French Cinema* [Urbana: University of Illinois Press, 1990]), and Mary Ann Doane (in her *Femmes Fatales: Feminism Film Theory, Psychoanalysis* [New York: Routledge, 1991]), among many others.

21. John Ellis, *Visible Fictions: Cinema, Television, Video* (London: Routledge, 1982), 58–60, 96–99.

22. Edgar Morin, *Les Stars* (Paris: Seuil, 1972); quoted in Dyer, *Stars*, 24.

23. Fransesco Alberoni, "The Powerless 'Elite': Theory and Sociological Research on the Phenomenon of the Stars," in Denis McQuail (ed.), *Sociology of Mass Communications* (London: Penguin, 1972).

24. Ibid.

25. James Monaco, "Celebration," in James Monaco (ed.), *Celebrity* (New York: Delta, 1978), 8–9.

26. James Monaco, "The Mythologizing of Citizen Hearst," in James Monaco (ed.), *Celebrity* (New York: Delta, 1978), 65–78.

27. Monaco, "Celebration," 12.

28. Richard Dyer, *Heavenly Bodies: Film Stars and Society* (London: British Film Institute/Macmillan Education, 1986), 18.

29. Ibid., 2.

30. Ibid., 8–11.

31. Ibid., 15–16.

32. Another significant writer on stars who has emerged from film studies is Richard DeCordova. In an important work, *Picture Personalities: The Emergence of the Star System in America* (Urbana: University of Illinois Press, 1990), DeCordova analyzes the development of the film star system. This work establishes the intertextual nature of the conception of the star. The star is organized by his or her films, but also by the various discussions about the star that appear in the press. DeCordova details the development of this connected system to film stardom and stitches together the history of the discourse of autonomous stardom that was established in the 1920s. The transformation of the star to the status of autonomy provides a historical discourse about public "individuality" and its relationship to a culture. The categories that DeCordova has developed to describe the relative autonomy of the film star can be transcribed to aid in the determination of the power of the celebrity in contemporary culture.

33. See Serge Moscovici, *The Age of the Crowd: A Historical Treatise on Mass Psychology*, trans. J. C. Whitehouse (Cambridge: Cambridge University Press, 1985), 219–20.

34. Ibid., 289.

35. Max Weber, *Economy and Society*, vol. 3 (New York: Bedminster, 1968), 1112.

36. Ibid., 1118.

37. Ibid., 1120.

38. Ibid., 1141–46.

39. Ibid., 954.

40. Ibid., 1135.

41. Ibid., 1146, 1156.

42. Sigmund Freud, "Group Psychology and the Analysis of the Ego" (1921), in James Strachey (ed.), *The Standard Edition of the Complete Psychological Works of Sigmund Freud*, vol. 18 (London: Hogarth, 1955), 65–143.

43. Ibid., 168.

44. Sigmund Freud, "The Future of an Illusion" (1927), in *Civilization, Society and Religion*, vol. 12 (Harmondsworth: Penguin, 1985), 190.

45. Sigmund Freud, *Moses and Monotheism*, vol. 13 (Harmondsworth: Penguin, 1985), 381–83.

46. I am drawing this elaboration of Freud from Moscovici's analysis in *The Age of the Crowd*, 300–302.

47. Weber's and Freud's analyses of leadership have figured prominently in many other studies of the leader in the twentieth century, and have provided grand theoretical parameters for continued work on the concept. However, in much of the research carried out on leadership since the 1920s, Freud and Weber have been used as "straw men" to emphasize the critical flaw in such grand theorizing.

There are significant exceptions to this trajectory. The work of Ann Ruth Willner is notable for its overly faithful application of Weber's program on charisma to past world leaders. See *The Spellbinders: Charismatic Political Leadership* (New Haven, Conn.: Yale University Press, 1984). Irving Schiffner's Freudian reading of specifically Western leaders also traverses a more faithful course. See his *Charisma: A Psychoanalytic Look at Mass Society* (Toronto: University of Toronto Press, 1973). Orrin Klapp's two books on public personalities, *Heroes, Villains and Fools* (San Diego: Aegis, 1972) and *Symbolic Leaders* (Chicago: Aldine, 1964), are popular psychosociological studies of public leaders. They are not written for academic inquiry; rather, they are written as bridging texts that establish in journalistic fashion salient points concerning modern symbolic leaders. Klapp's thesis suggests that there is now in place a symbolic system of public personalities that has a great deal of cultural significance (and power). He differentiates between two roles in public life: one that is obsessively focused on the practical — a "doer" — and one that is obsessed with the image of being and the dramatic weight of that image. Klapp identifies certain requirements that need to be met for any individual to achieve this second role of mythic and symbolic status. Generally, these involve the individual's ability to read and be sensitive to an audience's needs (whoever that audience might be) and then articulate him- or herself into a typification of those needs: "Every leader of a social movement, every big star of entertainment and sports, every really popular statesman or church leader, has to make this discovery [of type]" in order to move into this domain of symbolic significance (*Symbolic Leaders*, 35).

Epistemologically, the dominant movement toward a form of incremental scientific approach to leadership has been the main current of research. Oddly enough, the focus has not been on political forms of leadership. As Barbara Kellerman explains, "Political scientists have been reluctant to investigate what motivates the interactions between leaders and led, what accounts for the variations among them, or even to describe precisely the different types of leaders and leadership processes." *Leadership: Multidisciplinary Perspectives* (Englewood Cliffs, N.J.: Prentice Hall, 1984), ix. For examples of the centrality of the organizational study of leadership in leadership studies in general, see Bernard M. Bass, *Stogdill's Handbook of Leadership* (New York: Free Press, 1981). I deal with this affective or irrational form of political study in greater detail in chapter 7. The attempt to rationalize the organization of leadership is a peculiarly scientific endeavor that blends well with scientific studies of the populace in the form of opinion polls. A wealth of literature has emerged in organizational and administrative studies. In these disciplines, leadership is investigated for the purpose of making it more "effective," so that organizations may be run more smoothly. The teleological intent behind these studies denies their investigations of critical inquiry, as the prevailing form of societal organization is tacitly approved. As a result, the premise that forms of leadership could be part of a legitimated power structure is beyond the realm of inquiry. The advances made in this type of leadership study tend to be derived from the behaviorist sciences of social psychology and psychology. Small groups are analyzed in order to assess the "impact" or "dynamics" of the leader. For the current project, studies of this nature are more interesting for the way they extend an ideology of leadership and power than for their "manifest" findings and insights. In many of these cases, the scientific discourse is used to rationalize the essentially irrational nature of leadership power.

2. Conceptualizing the Collective: The Mob, the Crowd, the Mass, and the Audience

1. See George Rudé's writing on the crowd, particularly *The Crowd in History: 1730–1848* (Washington, DC: Serif, 1995).

2. J. S. McClelland argues in the opening chapter of *The Crowd and the Mob* (London: Unwin, 1989) that the new power of the crowd was similar to the crowd's power in antiquity. Within the city-states of Rome and Greece, the crowd continued to wield some power, partly because of the public space devoted to its formation, but more specifically because of the limited space and populace the city-state involved. With the expanse of empire and the construction of state power, the centralized nature of power meant that though crowd uprisings might occur at the peripheries, they did not disturb the centers of power, which were often hundreds or thousands of miles away. This

same distant authority was the preserve of the church's power throughout the Middle Ages in Europe. In conjunction with the church's traditions and rituals, which were technologies of social control, the power of the mob was stunted.

3. Jürgen Habermas, *The Structural Transformation of the Public Sphere: An Inquiry into a Category of Bourgeois Society* (Cambridge: MIT Press, 1991), 5–15.

4. See Alexis de Tocqueville, *Democracy in America*, trans. George Lawrence (Garden City, N.Y.: Doubleday, 1969).

5. Jeremy Bentham, *The Principles of Morals and Legislation* (New York: Hafner, 1948[1789]).

6. John Stuart Mill, *On Liberty* (Harmondsworth: Pelican, 1976[1859]), particularly 175–80.

7. McClelland, *The Crowd and the Mob*, 77.

8. Ibid., 74–81.

9. See Serge Moscovici, *The Age of the Crowd: A Historical Treatise on Mass Psychology*, trans. J. C. Whitehouse (Cambridge: Cambridge University Press, 1985), 61–65.

10. Ibid., 55–56.

11. Gustave Le Bon, *The Crowd: A Study of the Popular Mind* (New York: Viking, 1960[1901]), 16.

12. Ibid., 3.

13. Ibid., 184.

14. See Moscovici, *The Age of the Crowd*, 107–54. The relation of woman to the primitive through the linking of the crowd to the female is not specific to Le Bon. Gabriel Tarde may have stated the case more forcefully when he asserted that crowds of women are the most dangerous and atavistic. To see the breadth of this construction of fear and threat through the symbol of woman, see Susannah Barrows, "Metaphors of Fear: Women and Alcoholics," in *Distorting Mirrors* (New Haven, Conn.: Yale University Press, 1981), 43–72.

15. McClelland, *The Crowd and the Mob*, 10.

16. See Susannah Barrows, *Distorting Mirrors* (New Haven, Conn.: Yale University Press, 1981), 73–92; McClelland, *The Crowd and the Mob*, 138–54.

17. McClelland, *The Crowd and the Mob*, 185–86.

18. Gabriel Tarde, *La Logique Sociale* (Paris: Alcan, 1895), 98; quoted in Moscovici, *The Age of the Crowd*, 172.

19. Very few of Sighele's works have ever been translated. With the exception of my conclusion about the significance of Sighele's positioning of the crowd as a modern phenomenon, I am indebted for much of my knowledge and argumentation here to McClelland's writing on Sighele in *The Crowd and the Mob*, 155–80.

20. Ibid., 175–76.

21. For a good overview of the conservative critique of mass society, see Alan Swingewood, *The Myth of Mass Culture* (London: Macmillan, 1977), 1–22.

22. Max Horkheimer and Theodor Adorno, *The Dialectic of Enlighten-ment* (New York: Continuum, 1972).

23. Floyd H. Allport, *Social Psychology* (Boston: Houghton Mifflin, 1924), 6; quoted in Carl Graumann, "The Individualization of the Social and the Desocialization of the Individual: Floyd H. Allport's Contribution to Social Psychology," in Carl Graumann and Serge Moscovici (eds.), *Changing Con-ceptions of the Crowd* (New York: Springer-Verlag, 1986), 103.

24. Graumann, "The Individualization of the Social," 100.

25. Ibid., 100–101.

26. Allport, *Social Psychology*, 308; quoted in Graumann, "The Individ-ualization of the Social," 104, 108.

27. Allport, *Social Psychology*, 430; quoted in Graumann, "The Individ-ualization of the Social," 110.

28. Graumann, "The Individualization of the Social," 111.

29. This, as far as I know, has never been done in any systematic way and deserves further attention.

30. See, for instance, Harold D. Lasswell, *Propaganda Technique in the World War* (New York: Garland, 1972[1927]).

31. See Todd Gitlin, "Media Sociology: The Dominant Paradigm," *Theory and Society* 6 (1978): 205–53. For the connection to Columbia and to net-work research interest, see Jeremy Tunstall, *The Media Are American: An-glo-American Media in the World* (London: Constable, 1977), 205–6.

32. See Paul Lazarsfeld, Bernard Berelson, and Hazel Gaudet, *The Peo-ple's Choice* (New York: Columbia University Press, 1948); and Elihu Katz and Paul Lazarsfeld, *Personal Influence* (New York: Free Press, 1955).

33. It was the active construction of a form of "knowledge" of the audi-ence that had discursive power—in a very real sense a rationalization of the audience into, in this case, the meaning system of television. For further dis-cussion of this construction of the audience for certain purposes, see Ien Ang, *Desperately Seeking the Audience* (London: Routledge, 1991), chs. 1–5.

34. Ostensibly, new debates about mass society occurred in the United States as uses and gratifications communication research was gaining full force. What is interesting about these debates is that in many ways they rearticu-late the early-twentieth-century debates, with only variations in what consti-tutes a mass. In *The Lonely Crowd* (New Haven, Conn.: Yale University Press, 1961[1950]), a very popular and widely read text, David Riesman estab-lishes that the anomie of contemporary society motivates individuals to con-struct their meanings from the available offerings of consumer society. Ries-man also explains that society is not made up of one mass, but a series of masses that are differentiated by taste and class. Similarly, Dwight MacDon-ald, who provides one of the more pessimistic readings of American mass culture by an American scholar, shifted positions to conform to this senti-ment that the mass is much more heterogeneous than previously conceived. See, for example, Dwight MacDonald, *Masscult and Midcult* (New York: Par-tisan Review, 1961). Riesman's writings go so far as to link popular culture to training youth, among other groups, into social roles of consumption that

allow the potential for personal fulfillment. For a reading of the way in which social scientific research on popular culture and communication conformed to the liberal ideology of the 1950s, see Andrew Ross, *No Respect: Intellectuals and Popular Culture* (New York: Routledge, 1989).

35. E. P. Thompson, *The Making of the English Working Class* (New York: Random House, 1963).

36. Richard Hoggart, *The Uses of Literacy: Changing Patterns of English Mass Culture* (Boston: Beacon, 1957).

37. See Raymond Williams, *The Long Revolution* (Harmondsworth: Pelican, 1965), 64–88.

38. Stuart Hall, "Notes on Deconstructing the 'Popular,'" in Raphael Samuel (ed.), *People's History and Socialist Theory* (London: Routledge & Kegan Paul, 1981), 228.

39. Ibid., 239.

40. John Fiske, *Understanding Popular Culture* (Boston: Unwin Hyman, 1989), 19.

41. The study of youth subcultures (particularly male ones) has produced a large number of working papers and several books by scholars associated with the BCCCS. Two early books in the tradition are Paul E. Willis, *Profane Culture* (London: Routledge & Kegan Paul, 1978); and Stuart Hall and Tony Jefferson (eds.), *Resistance through Rituals: Youth Subcultures in Post-War Britain* (London: Routledge, 1990). The most widely read book on the subject is no doubt Dick Hebdige's *Subculture: The Meaning of Style* (London: Methuen, 1979). Other useful examples are Michael Brake's two books *The Sociology of Youth Culture and Youth Subcultures: Sex and Drugs and Rock 'n' Roll* (London: Routledge & Kegan Paul, 1980) and *Comparative Youth Culture: The Sociology of Youth Cultures and Youth Subcultures in America, Britain and Canada* (London: Routledge & Kegan Paul, 1985). The latter brings in some studies of American equivalents and debates the class constructions of oppositions.

42. John Fiske, *Reading the Popular* (Boston: Unwin Hyman, 1989), 4.

43. Ibid.

44. See Hebdige, *Subculture,* 5–19.

45. See Iain Chambers, *Popular Culture: The Metropolitan Experience* (London: Methuen, 1986).

3. Tools for the Analysis of the Celebrity as a Form of Cultural Power

1. In the attempt to provide a unity of thought, Weber's work on rationality is considered by some writers to be at the center of his life's work. Others, like Hennis, have taken the concept of rationality to be secondary to Weber's concern with "the conduct of life": "Weber's deepest concern is for the survival of a 'character' or 'personality' whose life-conduct unites pragmatic rationalism with ethical seriousness." Wilhelm Hennis, quoted in Colin Gordon, "The Soul of the Citizen: Max Weber and Michel Foucault on Ra-

tionality and Government," in Sam Whimster and Scott Lash (eds.), *Weber, Rationality and Modernity* (London: Allen & Unwin, 1987), 295. In its focus on the character and the norms emerging from the character, one can see that representative personalities, like celebrities, would be instrumental components in the formation of a just and ethical society in Weber's terms.

2. See Allan Sica, *Weber, Irrationality and the Social Order* (Berkeley: University of California Press, 1988), 168.

3. See Wolfgang Mommsen, "Personal Conduct and Societal Change: Towards a Reconstruction of Max Weber's construction of History," in Sam Whimster and Scott Lash (eds.), *Max Weber, Rationality and Modernity* (London: Allen & Unwin, 1987), 47.

4. Sam Whimster and Scott Lash, "Introduction," in Sam Whimster and Scott Lash (eds.), *Max Weber, Rationality and Modernity* (London: Allen & Unwin, 1987), 7.

5. See Jürgen Habermas, *Legitimation Crisis*, trans. Thomas McCarthy (Boston: Beacon, 1975); see also Habermas's *The Theory of Communicative Action*, vol. 1, *Reason and the Rationalization of Society*, trans. Thomas McCarthy (Boston: Beacon, 1984).

6. Whimster and Lash, "Introduction," 12.

7. Weber, *Economy and Society*, vol. 3 (New York: Bedminster, 1968), 6; quoted in Sica, *Weber, Irrationality*, 205.

8. Sica, *Weber, Irrationality*, 158–60, 206–8. The preface to *The Protestant Ethic and the Spirit of Capitalism*, which Weber wrote seven days before his death, provides the appropriate evidence for Talcott Parsons to fit Weber's intellectual project into the mainstream of positivist sociology: the irrational disappears if more analysis is given to the object of study. Understanding can eliminate the irrational.

9. Weber, *Economy and Society*, 1112.

10. Ibid., 476; quoted in Pierre Bourdieu, "Legitimation and Structure Interest in Weber's Sociology of Religion," in Sam Whimster and Scott Lash (eds.), *Weber, Rationality and Modernity* (London: Allen & Unwin, 1987), 125.

11. Sica, *Weber, Irrationality*, 216; based on Weber, *Economy and Society*, 389.

12. *Irrational*, for Weber, tends to mean those aspects of a "privatized meaning which are non-interpretable and hence irrational." (Sica, *Weber, Irrationality*, 176). In his first use of the word *charisma* in *The Protestant Ethic and the Spirit of Capitalism*, Weber aligns the term as "a concept intimately keyed to irrationality." Cited in Sica, *Weber, Irrationality*, 171. Weber's discussion of "personality" indicates that he uses the term to demarcate both the rational (and therefore freedom with control) and the irrational. The rational personality is "a concept which entails a constant and intrinsic relation to certain ultimate 'values' and 'meanings' in life, 'values' and 'meanings' which are forged into purposes and thereby translate into rational-teleological action." The naturalistic personality is "diffuse, undifferentiated, vegetative underground of personal life i.e. in that 'irrationality' which rests upon the

maze of infinitude of psychophysical conditions for the development of temperament and feeling. This is a sense of 'irrationality' in which both the 'person' and the animal are 'irrational.'" Quoted in Sica, *Weber, Irrationality,* 178.

13. Bourdieu, "Legitimation and Structure Interest," 131.

14. Ibid., 130.

15. Ibid.

16. Michel Foucault, "What Is an Author?" in *Language, Counter-Memory, Practice* (Ithaca, N.Y.: Cornell University Press, 1977).

17. Roland Barthes, *Mythologies,* trans. Annette Lavers (London: Paladin, 1973[1957]).

18. See Antonio Gramsci, "Hegemony, Relations of Force, Historical Bloc," in David Forgacs (ed.), *Antonio Gramsci Reader* (Schocken: New York, 1988). My reading of Gramsci is an adaptation of his use of hegemony in the tradition of Stuart Hall, Dick Hebdige, Iain Chambers, and others associated with British cultural studies. To attach the term *culture* to hegemony makes the reading and use of cultural forms an active struggle over meaning and consensus, where the reading of cultural texts is an arena for the negotiation of legitimacy and illegitimacy.

19. Gilles Lipovetsky, *L'Ère du vide: essais sur l'individualism contemporain* (Paris: Gallimard, 1983), 82.

20. Judith Williamson, *Decoding Advertisements* (London: Marion Boyars, 1978).

21. Sut Jhally, *The Codes of Advertising: Fetishism and the Political Economy of Meaning in Consumer Society* (London: St. Martin's Press, 1987).

22. Dick Hebdige, *Subculture: The Meaning of Style* (London: Methuen, 1979), 103–4.

23. The following analysis is drawn from my previous work on the audience. See P. David Marshall, "Deconstructing Class/Constructing the Audience: Some Considerations Concerning Popular Culture and Power," paper presented at the annual meeting of the Canadian Communication Association, University of Windsor, June 1988; see also "The Construction of Difference and Distinction in Contemporary Cultural Forms: An Analysis of the Magazines of Popular Music," unpublished Ph.D. project, April 1989, chs. 1–2.

24. Ang's work on the television audience develops this idea of the epistemological categorization of the television audience. See Ien Ang, *Desperately Seeking the Audience* (London: Routledge, 1991).

25. Louis Althusser, "Ideology and Ideological State Apparatuses," in *Lenin and Philosophy* (London: New Left, 1971).

26. John Fiske, "British Cultural Studies," in Robert C. Allen (ed.), *Channels of Discourse: Television and Contemporary Criticism* (Chapel Hill: University of North Carolina Press, 1987), 259.

27. Hans Robert Jauss, "Literary History as a Challenge to Literary Theory," in *Toward an Aesthetic of Reception,* trans. Timothy Bahti (Minneapolis: University of Minnesota Press, 1982), 23; quoted in Richard C.

Holub, *Reception Theory: A Critical Introduction* (London: Methuen, 1984), 61.

28. Jauss, "Literary History," 43; quoted in Holub, *Reception Theory,* 68.

29. Holub, *Reception Theory,* 83.

30. Hans Robert Jauss, *Aesthetic Experience and Literary Hermeneutics,* trans. Michael Shaw (Minneapolis: University of Minnesota Press, 1982).

31. Hans Robert Jauss, "Interaction Patterns in the Identification of the Hero," in *Aesthetic Experience,* 153–54.

32. Ibid., 155.

33. Ibid., 166–68.

34. Ibid., 172–73.

35. Ibid., 177.

36. Ibid., 181.

37. *Hermeneutics* is used here to indicate that what follows is an interpretive reading of cultural texts. Hermeneutics, originally a term connected to exegetical work on biblical texts, has been elaborated in philosophical terms as a way of understanding experience and (possibly) reality without reducing the experiences to pure empirical evidence or putting them into philosophical terminology, into the domain of logical positivism. Hermeneutics broaches an epistemological question of what constitutes knowledge. The interpretive sciences, which are primarily those disciplines connected to the humanities, are working essentially to constitute understanding from close readings of texts and histories. Jauss's work is, by his own admission, a literary hermeneutic, where meaning and understanding arise from more than just the manifest content of the words to the contextualization of the text. The current project launches a reading of production and reception of the celebrity through an interpretive reading of the various texts that establish the celebrity as an entity. Also integrated into the hermeneutic is a recognition of the cultural context that shapes and informs the meaning of the celebrity sign/text. Jauss's work is particularly useful because he establishes an approach that moves beyond simply discovering authorial intention through a close hermeneutic of a text to working to identify a hermeneutic of reception. I am adapting these insights into a study of popular cultural forms and the subjectivity that is constructed through the processes of production and consumption. For a "reading" of the meanings of hermeneutics, see Roy J. Howard, *Three Faces of Hermeneutics* (Berkeley: University of California Press, 1982); Hans-Georg Gadamer, *Philosophical Hermeneutics* (Berkeley: University of California Press, 1976).

38. See, for example, Richard Dyer, *Stars* (London: British Film Institute, 1979); Edgar Morin, *Les Stars* (Paris: Seuil, 1972).

39. See John Hartley, *Politics of Pictures* (London: Routledge, 1992).

40. It may be worthwhile to elaborate briefly here on what Foucault understands power to be. It would wrong to interpret Foucault as, in the end, seeing power as repressive. Foucault has said that power relations are "everywhere": "Power must be understood in the first instance as the multiplicity of force relations immanent in the sphere in which they operate and which

constitute their own organization; as the process which, through ceaseless struggles and confrontations, transforms, strengthens, or reverses them; as the support which these force relations find in one another, thus forming a chain or a system, on the contrary, the dysjunctions and contradictions which isolate them from one another; and lastly, as the strategies in which they take effect, whose general design or institutional crystallization is embodied in the state apparatus, in the formulation of the law, in the various social hegemonies." Michel Foucault, *The History of Sexuality,* vol. 1 (New York: Random House, 1980[1978]), 92. Foucault, then, does not necessarily link power with the state; he considers disjunctions to be loci of power and strategies. It is evident, however, that certain discourses predominate, and an example of a predominant and thus more powerful discourse is contained in the operation of the "state apparatus."

41. See Michel Foucault, *Madness and Civilization,* trans. Richard Howard (New York: Vintage, 1973[1961]). In the above account of this organization of knowledge and madness, I have reread Foucault's earlier work through the terms and terminology developed in his later writing. His development of the concept of an archaeology of a discourse is clearly developed in *The Archaeology of Knowledge* (New York: Random House, 1972). The use of the term *genealogy,* which he considers appropriate for describing the processual development of a discourse and its relationship to a power/knowledge matrix, emerges in his work *The History of Sexuality.* For an excellent interpretation of Foucault's intellectual movement to a greater concern with the organization of power, see Hubert Dreyfus and Paul Rabinow, *Michel Foucault: Beyond Structuralism and Hermeneutics* (Chicago: University of Chicago Press, 1983), 143–82; specifically on the use of genealogy, see 104–15.

42. Michel Foucault, *Discipline and Punish: The Birth of the Prison* (New York: Random House, 1979), 202.

43. Foucault, *The History of Sexuality,* 140–44. Foucault notes: "If one can apply the term *bio-history* to the pressures through which the movements of life and the processes of history interfere with one another, one would have to speak of bio-power to designate what brought life and its mechanisms into the realm of explicit calculations and made knowledge-power an agent of transformation of human life" (143).

44. I am simplifying a great deal of research into affect. The model I have just described is generally known as the CAB model. For further discussion of this research, see Bert S. Moore and Alice M. Isen (eds.), *Affect and Social Behaviour* (Cambridge: Cambridge University Press, 1990).

45. See Cornelis Wegman, *Psychoanalysis and Cognitive Psychology: A Formalization of Freud's Earliest Theory* (New York: Academic Press, 1985), 247–49.

46. Jean-François Lyotard, *The Postmodern Condition,* trans. Brian Massumi (Minneapolis: University of Minnesota Press, 1984[1979]).

47. Fredric Jameson, "Postmodernism and Consumer Culture," in Hal Foster (ed.), *The Anti-Aesthetic: Essays on Postmodern Culture* (Port Townsend, Wash.: Bay, 1983), 119.

48. Jean Baudrillard, "The Ecstasy of Communication," in Hal Foster (ed.), *The Anti-Aesthetic: Essays on Postmodern Culture* (Port Townsend, Wash.: Bay, 1983), 126–34.

49. Lawrence Grossberg, *It's a Sin: Politics, Postmodernity and the Popular* (Sydney: Power, 1988), 42.

50. Lawrence Grossberg, "The In-difference of Television," *Screen* 28 (Spring 1987): 41.

51. Lawrence Grossberg, "Rock and Roll in Search of an Audience," in James Lull (ed.), *Popular Music and Communication* (Newbury Park, Calif.: Sage, 1987), 175–97.

4. The Cinematic Apparatus and the Construction of the Film Celebrity

1. Richard DeCordova, "The Emergence of the Star System and the Bourgeoisification of the American Cinema," in *Star Signs* (London: BFI Education, 1982), 66.

2. The exceptions to this could be seen to be Edison's films made in studios; nevertheless, the emphasis was still on the "wonderment" of the technology and the novelty of moving images. For a thorough reading of early cinema, see Charles Musser, *History of the American Cinema*, vol. 1, *The Emergence of Cinema: The American Screen to 1907* (New York: Charles Scribner's Sons, 1990).

3. For an account of the connection of vaudeville to film, see Robert C. Allen, *Vaudeville and Film 1895–1915: A Study in Media Interaction* (New York: Arno, 1980 [originally published as a Ph.D. dissertation, University of Iowa, 1977]).

4. Alexander Walker, *Stardom: The Hollywood Phenomenon* (London: Michael Joseph, 1970).

5. Benjamin Bowles Hampton, *History of the American Film Industry from Its Beginnings to 1931* (New York: Dover, 1970[1931]).

6. Janet Staiger, "Seeing Stars," in Christine Gledhill (ed.), *Stardom: Industry of Desire* (London: Routledge, 1991), 6–10 (first published in *Velvet Light Trap* 20 [Summer 1983]).

7. The pervasiveness of the star system in vaudeville could have operated as the crucial limiting structure on the development of film stars in the early 1900s. Allen explains that there was an economic impetus for exhibitors to move into the showing of films, because of the escalating salaries demanded by vaudeville stars. The hybrid form to emerge out of the relative cheapness of films, in comparison to mounting an entire vaudeville show, was called "small-time vaudeville"; fewer live acts appeared, and there was more emphasis on film. Small-time vaudeville played generally in smaller venues than traditional vaudeville shows, but "nicer" more "acceptable" places (to the middle classes) than the rougher and dirtier nickelodeon houses. As the power of the vaudeville stars increased, the promoters and exhibitors, and the new cultural entrepreneurs who competed with vaudeville, moved on to produc-

tions that kept the performers anonymous and cheap: films. This argument is inferred from Allen's discussion of the development of small-time vaudeville; Allen does not specifically extend his economic argument to include this point concerning the obvious impeding of the film star system. See Allen, *Vaudeville and Film*, 230–73.

8. Ibid.

9. Walker, *Stardom*, 44–45.

10. Edgar Morin, *Les Stars* (Paris: Seuil, 1972), 18.

11. Ibid., 21.

12. Walker, *Stardom*, 36.

13. Joshua Gamson provides an insightful reading of the world of the publicity agent and the so-called team that surrounds the production of a successful celebrity. In a chapter titled "Industrial-Strength Celebrity," Gamson outlines the elaborate press and publicity agent machine that surrounds the successful celebrity, where up to 50 percent of the star's income may go to these organizers of events, sitings, and so on. The goal is to make the celebrity a clear brand name. See Joshua Gamson, *Claims to Fame: Celebrity in Contemporary America* (Berkeley: University of California Press, 1994), 57–78.

14. Morin, *Les Stars*, 11.

15. See Richard DeCordova, *Picture Personalities: The Emergence of the Star System in America* (Urbana: University of Illinois Press, 1990). DeCordova's analysis of the early star system defines quite accurately this investment of the industry and the extratextual industry in the construction of the public personality. DeCordova makes a distinction between "picture personalities," who were film actors between 1910 and 1919, and "stars," who were film actors after 1919, in terms of the relative investment in a discourse of intimacy and personal knowledge. Picture personalities, according to DeCordova, are defined publicly as homologous to their roles. Stars articulate the establishment of public personalities that literally have lives of their own in terms of extratextual (i.e., outside of their films) discourse. These classifications continue to define the way in which stars are constructed in the American film industry. See the analysis of Tom Cruise, below.

16. Douglas Gomery, *The Hollywood Studio System* (London: BFI/Macmillan, 1986), 173–80.

17. The only real difference between United Artists and the major studios was that United Artists did not become completely integrated with ownership in exhibition as well as production and distribution. Also, it should be added that most of the studios arose out of the corporate culture of exhibition and distribution.

18. In 1990, Sylvester Stallone signed a multipicture deal with Carolco for between $12 and $17 million per picture. Bruce Willis supposedly received $8 million for *The Last Boy Scout* (1991). Schwarzenegger received a jet for *Total Recall* (1990) and $12 million for *Kindergarten Cop* (1990). There is an entire hierarchy in Hollywood based on actors' pay. In 1989–90, the estimated incomes of the top nine stars were as follows: Sylvester Stallone, $63 million; Arnold Schwarzenegger, $55 million; Jack Nicholson, $50 million;

Eddie Murphy, $48 million; Bruce Willis, $36 million; Michael J. Fox, $33 million; Tom Cruise, $26 million; Michael Douglas, $24 million; Harrison Ford, $22 million. Peter Bart, "Stars to Studios: Pass the Bucks — Top Talent Seeks to Break Video Profits Barrier," *Variety,* September 24, 1990, 1, 108.

Because of the financial clout of these artists, they are also able to fight the studios in the court for even greater returns. With 35–50 percent of film revenues coming from video sales and rentals, the stars and their lawyers are working to negotiate even greater revenue shares from their films. Since Charlton Heston's groundbreaking deals for a percentage of the film box-office gross in the late 1950s, other stars have moved into similar financial arrangements, which have often shifted financial power to the individual stars. It is also significant that although female stars such as Whoopi Goldberg, Meryl Streep, and Goldie Hawn may receive million-plus pay packages for their films, their earnings come nowhere near those of the highest-paid male stars. See also Lawrence Cohn, "Stars' Rocketing Salaries Keep Pushing Envelope," *Variety,* September 24, 1990, 3.

19. Costner's percentage kicks in again if and when *Waterworld,* the most expensive film (approximately $170 million) ever made, actually becomes profitable, which demonstrates the complete corporate risk involvement of a star. Jess Cagle, "Dangerous When Wet," *Entertainment Weekly,* July 10, 1995.

20. In a recent review of the power of publicists, Charles Fleming notes that publicists are increasingly interventionist in determining the editorial content of magazines that feature their clients on the cover: "The balance of power between news organizations and the publicity machine that supplies them with celebrity photos and interviews has shifted. . . . the publicist is now in the driver's seat." Charles Fleming, "Star Hungry Mags Find Flacks Flexing Muscles," *Variety,* July 4, 1990, 1, 23.

21. Richard Sennett, *The Fall of Public Man* (New York: Random House, 1974), 204–5.

22. See Elizabeth Burns, *Theatricality* (London: Longman, 1972).

23. See Constantin Stanislavski, *Creating a Role,* ed. Hermine I. Popper, trans. Elizabeth Hapgood (New York: Routledge, 1989[1961]).

24. For a fascinating account of Method acting in film, see Steve Vineberg, *Method Actors: Three Generations of an American Acting Style* (New York: Schirmer, 1991). For an account of an interpretation of the acting technique by a famous tortured celebrity, see Marlon Brando, with Robert Lindsey, *Brando: Songs My Mother Taught Me* (London: Century, 1994).

25. This could be likened to the function of the novel in the nineteenth century. The form of characterization and the investment in the personal constructed and then naturalized the conception of a kind of bourgeois individuality. Likewise film, according to Edgar Morin, actively worked to extend the bourgeois understanding of individuality to the working classes. Morin, *Les Stars.*

26. Barry King, "Articulating Stardom," *Screen* 26 (September–October 1985): 45–48.

27. Ibid., 45.

28. Ibid. King draws this distinction in relative value from Hortense Pow-
dermaker, *Hollywood: The Dream Factory* (Boston: Little, Brown, 1950), 206.

29. King, "Articulating Stardom," 48.

30. For an interesting survey of the work on fandom, see Lisa Lewis (ed.),
Adoring Audience: Fan Culture and Popular Media (London: Routledge,
1992). Also see Henry Jenkins, *Textual Poachers: Television Fans and Par-
ticipatory Culture* (London: Routledge, 1992).

31. Morin, *Les Stars*, 75–83.

32. Margaret Thorpe, *America at the Movies;* cited in ibid., 66.

33. See Pierre Bourdieu, "The Aristocracy of Culture," in *Distinction: The
Social Critique of the Judgment of Taste* (Cambridge: Harvard University
Press, 1984), 11–96.

34. Richard Dyer, *Stars* (London: British Film Institute, 1979), 43–45.

35. See Stuart Ewen, *Captains of Consciousness* (New York: McGraw-
Hill, 1976). Ewen speaks of youth as a "consumption ideal," and this idea is
integrated successfully into David Buxton's critique of rock stars in *Le Rock:
star système et société de consommation* (Grenoble: La Pensée Sauvage,
1985), ch. 3.

36. DeCordova, *Picture Personalities*, 1–23.

37. A publicity still for the Coppola film *The Outsiders* (1983) identifies
several of the principal members of the brat pack as well as some other young
actors: Emilio Estevez, Rob Lowe, C. Thomas Howell, Matt Dillon, Ralph
Macchio, Patrick Swayze, and, of course, Tom Cruise. Virtually every member
of this group established himself as a star through the construction of the
new youth-oriented film of the 1980s. The still referred to above is included
in Louis Giannetti's *Understanding Movies*, 4th ed. (Englewood Cliffs, N.J.:
Prentice Hall, 1987), 205.

38. The list of films that could be included in this general strategy of understanding that film's principal market was connected to youths and young
adults who were constructing their distinctive entertainment practices outside the orb of television is very long. It would include, to name a few, *Breaking Away* (1979), *The Outsiders* (1983), *The Flamingo Kid* (1984), *An American Werewolf in London* (1981), *Fast Times at Ridgemont High* (1982),
Valley Girl (1983), *The Breakfast Club* (1985), *Spring Break* (1983), *Ferris
Bueller's Day Off* (1986), *The Lost Boys* (1987), and *St. Elmo's Fire* (1985).

39. Walker identifies this group of actors as antiheroes in *Stardom*, ch. 7.

40. The physical reconstruction of predominantly female performers represents the persistence and dominance of the category of the physical performer in the film industry. The actual reorganization of the body to match
an aesthetic has its own genealogy, from the capping of teeth by many actors
and Max Factor's cosmetic work to the more interventionist removal of Mar-
lene Dietrich's molars to maintain her angular facial bone structure, to Jane
Fonda's and Cher's (rumored) removal of ribs, to the de rigueur practices in
the film and fashion industries of breast and lip enlargements. The intense
focus on the body and its reformulation is central to the construction of the

female star. The body itself becomes the expression of and the control of the public personality.

41. Richard DeCordova, *Picture Personalities,* particularly 50–97.

42. *Risky Business* was a profitable film. It earned $30.4 million in box-office revenues in North America alone and was number one on *Variety*'s weekly list of box-office leaders on November 23, 1983. It scored particularly well with the young adult demographic. It could also be labeled as Cruise's first film that was a "star vehicle," that is, a movie that showcased his talents. See *Variety,* November 23, 1989, 9; May 11, 1989.

43. Several articles appeared that established the first evidence of Cruise as a recognizable star, including D. Hutchings, "No Wonder Tom Cruise Is Sitting Pretty — Risky Business Has Paid Off in Stardom," *People,* September 5, 1983, 107–8; "Tom Cruise Makes All the Right Moves," *Teen,* December 1983, 54–55; E. Miller, "Tom Cruise: An Actor with Heart," *Seventeen,* February 1984, 63–64. The first article about Cruise to appear in *Rolling Stone,* the magazine most closely associated with youth and young adult culture, was coordinated with the release of *Top Gun:* C. Connolly, "Winging It," *Rolling Stone,* June 19, 1986, 36–38, 89.

44. On the structure of feeling, see Raymond Williams, *The Long Revolution* (Harmondsworth: Penguin, 1965), 64–88.

45. It is interesting to see this chronicling of a category of youth in the 1980s in Cruise's regular appearance on the cover of *Rolling Stone* from 1983 to 1990. Cruise's form of successful rebellion embodied the construction of youth that dovetailed with the editorial structures of the magazine and its advertisers. For a reading of this construction of the particular form of youth audience that *Rolling Stone* developed and honed as valuable market segment, see my "The Construction of Difference and Distinction in Contemporary Cultural Forms: An Analysis of the Magazines of Popular Music," unpublished Ph.D. project, April 1989.

46. Jeanne Marie Laskas, "Car Crazy: What's Driving Tom Cruise?" *Life,* June 1990, 71. The same detail is repeated in virtually all of the magazine stories published about Cruise and the film before its release.

47. This ability of Cruise is most graphically detailed in the June 11, 1990, edition of *Sports Illustrated,* in Kenny Moore, "Cruise Control," 50–53. Cruise has in fact raced some with Newman's racing team. Rick Hendrick, who heads a stock car racing team, is quoted as saying that Cruise almost established a race track record on nonracing tires: "He ran six miles per hour faster in that than I thought he could," says Hendrick. "He has no fear. He has the need all great drivers have to extend themselves, to drive aggressively. He'd make one hell of a race driver, and in not too long a time, either" (50).

48. Laskas, "Car Crazy."

49. DeCordova, *Picture Personalities,* 98–105.

50. Ibid., 117–21.

51. Ibid., 125–30.

52. Dyer, *Stars.*

53. "Cruise Guns for the Top: An All-American Kid Wins Over Audiences," *Newsweek*, June 9, 1986, 73.

54. Jennet Conant, "Lestat C'est Moi," *Esquire*, March 1994, 70–76.

55. "Tom Cruise and His Movie Machine," *Us*, August 6, 1990, 25.

56. *National Enquirer*, July 17, 1990, 20.

57. Ronald Brownstein, *The Power and the Glitter: The Hollywood-Washington Connection* (New York: Random House, 1990), 298.

58. Indeed, the various forms of film references in *The Color of Money* ensure that many articles treat the film and the actors in terms of an aesthetic code. The best example of this integration of the film and the actors into a canon of quality can be found in David Ansen, "The Big Hustle," *Newsweek*, October 13, 1986, 68–74.

59. Vincent Canby, "Brotherly Love of Sorts," *New York Times*, December 16, 1988, C12.

60. Ibid.

61. These two transgressor vehicles for Cruise also are able to stitch together two marketing niches for the film industry: Hollywood art/Academy Award potential film and traditional potent masculine box-office king allure. For instance, *Rain Man* received exhibition box-office revenues in North America of more than $86.8 million, which made *Rain Man* the twelfth-highest grossing film of the 1980s and the most successful film Tom Cruise film. In comparison, *Top Gun* was ranked twentieth for the 1980s, with North American revenues of $79.4 million. *Variety*, May 6, 1991. It should also be noted that "quality" films like *Rain Man* and *Born on the Fourth of July* also have second lives with their video releases following their success and the publicity they receive owing to the Academy Awards.

62. It is interesting that a previous male star, Marlon Brando, also established his film acting credentials by playing a paraplegic veteran of World War II, in *The Men* (1950). The degree of transformation is part of the acting challenge. Brando is also famous for his use of the Method acting technique, which pushes him into constructing a psychological dimension to his characterizations that aids in establishing the "reality" of the representation on the screen.

63. Richard Corliss, "Cruise Control," *Time*, December 25, 1989, 59. What is interesting about these various lengthy stories about Cruise is the way in which the oeuvre is reread to coordinate with this new autonomous stature of the actor. Causality is reinforced to establish the inevitable trajectory of the star as his film works are canonized into historical significance.

64. For an in-depth reading of performance and the construction of romantic dyads in films, see Virginia Wright Wexman, *Creating the Couple: Love, Marriage and Hollywood Performance* (Princeton, N.J.: Princeton University Press, 1993).

65. See Janet Maslin, " 'Paradise Lost' Inspires Meditation on Vampires," *New York Times*, October 28, 1993, C15, C20. See also Conant, "Lestat C'est Moi." A profile of how Cruise was dealing with the negative publicity around

the film just prior to its release can be found in Kevin Sessum, "Cruise Speed," *Vanity Fair,* October 1994.

66. Geffen Pictures advertisement, *New York Times,* October 2, 1994, 12. This ad was reprinted in the *Times* from an advertisement in *Daily Variety,* September 23, 1994, headlined "To My Readers: A Personal Statement by Anne Rice Regarding the Motion Picture *Interview with the Vampire.*"

5. Television's Construction of the Celebrity

1. For a thorough discussion of how the domestic nature of viewing shapes the way television is, in fact, used, see David Morley, *Family Television* (London: Comedia, 1986).

2. For a concise history of the precursors to television and television technology, see Roy Armes, *On Video* (New York: Routledge, 1988), ch. 2.

3. Ibid., 44–45. There was also originally a royalty in Britain on the selling of receivers, which was abandoned in 1924. The main source of financing then became an annual licensing fee.

4. Erik Barnouw, *Tube of Plenty,* 2d rev. ed. (New York: Oxford University Press, 1990), 57–58.

5. John Langer, "Television's Personality System," *Media, Culture & Society* 4 (1981): 352.

6. Ibid., 365.

7. Early television, from dramatic programming to news programming, was often presented live. This era before prerecording shaped the meaning of television in its representation of immediacy.

8. The idea of the anchor in television can be thought of conceptually as similar to Barthes's *anchorage.* Barthes refers to the way in which photos are anchored by the written captions that position the reading of the photos by the viewer. The news anchor similarly helps position the world for the viewer. Roland Barthes, "Rhetoric of the Image" (1964), in *Image-Music-Text* (New York: Hill & Wang, 1977), 38–41.

9. Langer, "Television's Personality System," 357.

10. Robert C. Allen, *Speaking of Soap Operas* (Chapel Hill: University of North Carolina Press, 1987), 117.

11. Tania Modleski, *Loving with a Vengeance: Mass-Produced Fantasies for Women* (New York: Methuen, 1984).

12. Martha Nochimson, *No End to Her: Soap Opera and the Female Subject* (Berkeley: University of California Press, 1992).

13. Mary Ellen Brown, *Soap Opera and Women's Talk: The Pleasure of Resistance* (Thousand Oaks, Calif.: Sage, 1994).

14. For further discussion of the link between feminist scholarship and television soap opera, see Charlotte Brunsdon, "The Role of Soap Opera in the Development of Feminist Television Scholarship," in Robert C. Allen (ed.), *to be continued: Soap Opera around the World* (London: Routledge, 1995), 49–65.

15. Jeremy G. Butler, " 'I'm Not a Doctor, but I Play One on TV': Characters, Actors and Acting in Television Soap Opera," in Robert C. Allen (ed.), *to be continued: Soap Opera around the World* (London: Routledge, 1995), 146.

16. Langer, "Television's Personality System," 359.

17. Dana Kennedy, "Oprah: Act Two," *Entertainment Weekly*, September 9, 1994, 20.

18. Joshua Gamson, *Claims to Fame: Celebrity in Contemporary America* (Berkeley: University of California Press, 1994), 113.

19. Gloria-Jean Masciarotte, "C'mon, Girl: Oprah Winfrey and the Discourse of Feminine Talk," *Genders* 11 (Fall 1991): 83.

20. Ibid., 86.

21. For further discussion of the audience's position and participation and ultimately its link to a contemporary public sphere, see Sonia Livingston and Peter Lunt, *Talk on Television: Audience Participation and Public Debate* (London: Routledge, 1994).

22. Foucault's reading of the development of discourses about the self and the discourse of the self in his discussion of the history of sexuality are applicable in assessing the talk show as a contemporary site for the crossover between the private and intimate and the public and social. The Catholic Church confessional allows for the revealing of the most sordid and/or intimate details of affairs "of the flesh," with the hope that absolution will follow when the prescribed penance is carried out. Similarly, the talking cure of psychoanalysis, which can be read on one level as a secularized version of the confessional, is a powerful way to implicate sexual transgressions into personal problems and solutions. Sexuality, for Foucault, becomes a discourse that through its revelation of perversion and difference also establishes the normative centers of control of a society. The talk show similarly provides the revelatory discourse in its address of problems and perversions in the social world. Oprah's program can be read as mass catharsis, a public version of the talking cure. The authority figure who works toward absolution transforms into the populist television celebrity Oprah Winfrey. The cure or treatment in this televisual transfer of therapy, of course, lacks the depth of individualization found through psychotherapy, and therefore is only a surface representation of help and a deep structure of establishing norms. See Michel Foucault, *The History of Sexuality,* vol. 1 (New York: Random House, 1980 [1978]), 17–21, 123–29. Mimi White has recently written a book about television as therapeutic discourse in which she details the multiple sites across television that are designed as public confessionals. See Mimi White, *Tele-Advising: Therapeutic Discourse in American Television* (Chapel Hill: University of North Carolina Press, 1992).

23. Oprah began hosting a very typical women's chat show in Chicago titled *A.M. Chicago* on WLS-TV in 1984. Through King Productions, it was syndicated as *The Oprah Winfrey Show* to other markets. By 1988, Oprah had usurped Donahue as the ratings winner for daytime talk shows in all of the principal American markets. Moreover, she was generally proclaimed by

1991 to be the best-paid person in show business, with estimated earnings over $40 million and possibly as high as $60 million. H. F. Waters, "Chicago's Grand New Oprah," *Newsweek,* December 31, 1984, 51; *Les Brown's Encyclopedia of Television,* 3rd ed. (Detroit: Gale Research, 1992), 604.

24. In the fall of 1993, Oprah interviewed the recently retired black superstar basketball player for the Chicago Bulls, Michael Jordan. Her presence on evening television appears to be on the rise through these one-time specials, which have produced phenomenally large national and international ratings.

25. It should be added that part of Oprah's celebrity sign is her work as an actor. Contemporaneous with her rise as a television talk-show host, Winfrey starred in Steven Spielberg's *The Color Purple* and earned an Oscar nomination. Since that time, she has been involved, as both actor and producer, in a number of other fictional productions, including the two-part television movie *The Women of Brewster Place* (1989) and a sitcom titled *Brewster Place.* She also owns her own production company, Harpo Productions, which not only produces her own program but also looks for other worthwhile stories to bring to television or film. From this perspective, Oprah Winfrey has established a certain autonomy in her construction of celebritydom; her autonomy has emerged from her overall earnings of more than $60 million a year. Whatever the sources of her income, Winfrey represents, like other stars who have channeled their resources into further capital enterprises, a potential individual subjectivity that can express her will in determining what stories are produced. Her emphasis at least to date has been on stories focusing on black culture, although she denies that she is a spokesperson for the black community: "If other people perceive me to be the representative of black people in this country, it is a false perception. The fact that I sit where I sit today, you can't deny there have been some major advances. But I'm still just one black woman." Oprah Winfrey, quoted in Richard Zoglin, "Lady with a Calling," *Time,* August 8, 1988, 53.

26. "Shocking Secrets Stedman Hides from Oprah," *Globe,* May 7, 1991, 13.

27. The most common sites for defenses of Oprah's integrity are the mainstream black magazines *Ebony* and *Essence.* See, for example, "Oprah in Her Own Words," *Essence,* June 1989.

28. "Shocking Secrets." In the tabloid press, although there is an effort to shock, the articles are often written in such a way that they appear sympathetic to Oprah's plight.

29. "Oprah in Her Own Words," 46.

30. Ibid., 102.

31. "She's Fat and Happy at Last: Exclusive Oprah Wedding Plans—'I Want to Have Two Babies,'" *National Enquirer,* February 5, 1991, cover story.

32. Marjorie Rosen, "Oprah's Vow: I Will Never Diet Again," *People,* January 14, 1991, 82–91.

33. Ibid., 84.

34. In June 1994, Oprah had a public auction of her oversized clothes as part of her attempt to bury her larger figure of the past. See *Time*, May 16, 1994, 9; and "Rack Race," *People*, July 4, 1994, 42.

35. Dana Kennedy, *Entertainment Weekly*, September 9, 1994; Robert La Franco, "The Top 40," *Forbes*, September 26, 1994, 113–14.

6. The Meanings of the Popular Music Celebrity: The Construction of Distinctive Authenticity

1. David Buxton, *Le Rock: star système et société de consommation* (Grenoble: La Pensée Sauvage, 1985), 30.

2. John Shepherd, *Tin Pan Alley* (London: Routledge, 1982), 9.

3. Buxton, *Le Rock*, chs. 1–2.

4. See Steve Chappell and R. Garafalo, *Rock 'n' Roll Is Here to Pay: The History and Politics of the Music Industry* (Chicago: Nelson-Hall, 1977). Also see Le Roi Jones [Imamu Amiri Baraka], *The Blues People* (New York: Morrow, 1963) (reissued, Edinburgh: Payback, 1995).

5. Buxton, *Le Rock*, 27.

6. Ibid., 27–29.

7. Simon Frith has recounted: "A couple of years ago I went to see Al Green in concert in the Royal Albert Hall in London. At one point he left the stage (and his microphone) and walked through the audience, still singing. As he passed me I realized that this was the first time, in 30 years as a pop fan, that I'd heard a star's 'natural' voice!" Simon Frith, "The Industrialization of Popular Music," in James Lull (ed.), *Popular Music and Communication* (Newbury Park, Calif.: Sage, 1987), 53.

8. The rapid expansion of karaoke bars in North America and Europe represents the blending of the authentic background track with the personal for the representation of performance. It is an active positioning of a cultural practice in the interstices between the authentic (and the public) and the private (and the personal). A recent example of this revelation of inauthenticity was the confession of the two young men who performed as Milli Vanilli that they did not sing their songs on record or at concerts. They were purely actors of the songs and lip-synchers. The confession resulted in the duo's being stripped of two Grammy Awards. Likewise, the group New Kids on the Block was accused on many occasions of using a great deal of pre-recorded vocals and music in their programs.

9. Simon Frith, *Sound Effects: Youth, Leisure and the Politics of Rock 'n' Roll* (New York: Pantheon, 1983), 113.

10. Buxton, *Le Rock*, 26.

11. Shepherd, *Tin Pan Alley*, 103–5.

12. Roland Barthes, "The Grain of the Voice," in *Image-Music-Text* (New York: Hill & Wang, 1977), 179–89.

13. Buxton, *Le Rock*, 33.

14. Shepherd, *Tin Pan Alley*, 97.

15. Buxton, *Le Rock*, 37.

16. See in particular ibid., 64–68; Shepherd, *Tin Pan Alley,* 135–38; and Richard Middleton's discussion of subjectivity in *Studying Popular Music* (Buckingham: Open University Press, 1990), 266.

17. It is generally acknowledged that most concert tours are money-losing ventures. Thus, in recent years, many rock bands undertaking major tours have done so with the sponsorship of beer or soft drink corporations, in order to defray expenses.

18. Frith, *Sound Effects,* 182–94.

19. Buxton, *Le Rock,* 71.

20. See in particular the development of British subcultural studies: Stanley Cohen, *Folk Devils and Moral Panics* (London: McGibbon & Kee, 1972); Stuart Hall and Tony Jefferson (eds.), *Resistance through Rituals: Youth Subcultures in Post-War Britain* (London: Routledge, 1990); Dick Hebdige, *Subculture: The Meaning of Style* (New York: Methuen, 1979).

21. See Simon Frith and Howard Horne, *Art into Pop* (London: Methuen, 1987), ch. 2.

22. Chatterton, who attempted to create a long-lost poet named Rowley from a previous century, committed suicide at the age of seventeen in the late eighteenth century when his faked discovery and his faked poet gained no attention. What makes this otherwise insignificant event one of resonance is how Chatterton's life (and death) was celebrated and relived by nineteenth-century romantic poets like Wordsworth, Byron, Keats, and even a young Coleridge. See Leo Braudy, *The Frenzy of Renown: Fame and Its History* (New York: Oxford University Press, 1986), 421–25.

23. See Robert Pattison, *The Triumph of Vulgarity: Rock Music in the Mirror of Romanticism* (New York: Oxford University Press, 1987). Pattison maintains that rock music epitomizes a contemporary version of romantic pantheism.

24. Frith, *Sound Effects,* 147. In fact, this statistic on the success of records roughly parallels the success rate for the introduction of any new consumer product.

25. Paul Grein, "New Kids Have Blockbuster Year," *Billboard,* December 23, 1989, 10; "New Kids Top Tour List," *Variety,* December 13, 1990, 52. Most of these statistics do not indicate international sales of New Kids records. Comparable levels of sales and success were recorded in the United Kingdom, Canada, Australia (to a lesser degree), Japan, and Europe. For example, see International Charts, *Billboard,* December 16, 1989, 66. Other indications of the group's "phenomenal" status include the fact that the release of their 1990 album *Step by Step* established a first-day sales record. Also, New Kids released a series of videos to coincide with their albums. Their first two music video releases became the first music videos to have sales of more than one million copies. See Ed Christman, "New Kids' *Step by Step* Sells by Leaps and Bounds," *Billboard,* June 16, 1990, 6, 92.

26. Steve Dougherty, "The Heartthrobs of America," *People,* August 13, 1990, 78.

27. Ibid.

28. Grace Catalano, *New Kids on the Block* (New York: Bantam, 1989), 5.

29. This is also the rough demographic of the audience for MTV and Much-music, two video music channels in North America. Particularly the teenage demographic is seen to be an extremely valuable commodity to "capture": the value of this audience for advertisers is one of the principal motivations for the development of these specialty channels focusing on youth culture.

30. Frith develops the significance of the distinctions between pop and rock in *Sound Effects*, 27–38.

31. In his third and final appearance on *The Ed Sullivan Show* in 1957, Presley's sexually provocative hip gyrations were not shown; only his upper body was televised. After his first two appearances on the program, in which his entire body was visible to the viewing audience, public furor resulted in the decision to photograph him only in close-up when he next appeared. His full image was thought to be too dangerous to be left uncensored for young female audience members. Alex McNeil, *Total Television: A Comprehensive Guide to Programming from 1948 to the Present*, 3rd ed. (New York: Penguin, 1991), 226–27.

32. David Cassidy, in the tradition of the early 1970s, had shoulder-length extremely straight hair; Leif Garrett, a mid-1970s teen idol, had flowing locks in the style of Farrah Fawcett; Shaun Cassidy, emblematic of the boy-man, had characteristic dimples and baby face.

33. Catalano, *New Kids on the Block*, 4.

34. Dougherty, "The Heartthrobs of America."

35. A 1990 advertising insert in *Billboard* estimated the various revenues New Kids had amassed from the spring of 1989 to December 1990. Merchandising revenue dwarfed all the other categories: $400 million of a total of $861,373,000 of earnings were derived from merchandising agreements. By comparison, the group's record sales totaled $143.8 million domestically and concerts totaled $120 million. The ad also identified the products New Kids images were connected with: "posters, t-shirts, hats, banners, buttons (the regular concert fare).... then the merchandise diversified — postcards, poster books, jewelry, baseball-type trading cards, sleeping bags, bed sheets, poster puzzles, beach towels, watches, jackets, cups, laundry bags, balloons, boxer shorts, pajamas, water bottles, rainwear, umbrellas, gloves, scarves, mittens, shower curtains, sunglasses, sunglass cords, lunchboxes, mirrors, slippers, paper tattoos, belts, socks, sweater, storage trunks, bedspreads, and of course, Hasbro Inc.'s two lines of dolls — one in concert clothes with stage set available, and one in street clothes." Karen Schlossberg, "Merchandising: The Amazing Business of Defining, Controlling and Marketing an Image Explosion" (in an advertising supplement), *Billboard*, December 15, 1990, NK-22, 32, 34. The ad supplement itself was an interesting phenomenon. It indicated, through a series of congratulatory inserts, the number of companies that had been involved in the New Kids' success.

36. Typical of such reportage is D. Wild, "Puberty to Platinum," *Rolling Stone*, November 2, 1989, 15–17. Even more typical is the general overlooking of the band in many music publications, including *Creem*.

37. Catalano, *New Kids on the Block,* 16.

38. This controversy plagued New Kids' claims to legitimacy or "authenticity." The latest claim, made in early 1992, is that they in fact did not sing major parts of their albums. So, in this latest variation not only is their authenticity of performance challenged, but their authenticity in the "official" records of their music is put under suspicion.

39. The original album, after the success of their second album, also went platinum (i.e., had sales of more than one million).

40. The age of listeners attracted to New Kids was quickly seen as a "problem" for radio programmers throughout North America. For example, Mike Edwards, a programmer for a Buffalo, New York, station, explained that "some of our research has shown burn on the New Kids and that the perception of playing too much of New Kids can be a negative for you. We have to be very cautious." Other programmers indicated that by April 1991 stations were getting a lot of hate calls about the group. Many stations chose not to play the group except during certain early evening hours. Their fear was that they were losing an older listening demographic, a demographic much more lucrative to their advertising clientele than six- to ten-year-olds. Sean Ross and Thom Duffy, "Radio Gridlock on New Kids' Block?" *Billboard,* April 28, 1990, 4, 74.

41. The female preteen magazine has a heavily overcoded structure. Operating as fantasy magazines organized around male adolescent stars, *Tiger Beat, Bop, Teen Machine, Superteen,* and others build each of their segments around full-page or two-page photo spreads of these individual stars. Thus, from 1988 to 1991, the members of New Kids on the Block individually were repeatedly the subjects of these photo features. The utility of the magazines is as sources of these one- or two-page photos for decoration of the bedroom. The magazines must reorganize themselves constantly so that the images presented are in concert with the newest stars of television, film, and popular music. In order to do so, they sponsor a plethora of contests and polls interspersed with profiles of idols. The contests represent an essential marketing technique for a magazine industry that must continually re-present fantasy materials for the preteen female audience.

42. See John Shepherd, *Music as Social Text* (Cambridge: Polity, 1991).

43. Indeed, Starr's choices of the five members had a great deal to do with their familiarity with black street culture and break dancing. For instance, Donnie's claims to fame were his dance imitations of Michael Jackson and the bravado to engage in spontaneous rap performances in the local park. Jordan and Danny were part of rival break-dance groups who would practice and perform their moves in downtown Boston every Saturday well before they became New Kids members — white kids engaged in what was an essentially black youth activity. As Danny's fellow break-dancer and friend David Harris described it: "We would select a suitable store and start breakdancing on it, with cushions in our hats. . . . We'd perform for half an hour or so then move on to another store. By lunchtime, we'd have earned around forty dollars, which wasn't bad for thirteen and fourteen year olds." Robin

McGibbon, *New Kids on the Block: The Whole Story by Their Friends* (New York: Avon, 1990), 16.

44. See Chappell and Garafalo, *Rock 'n' Roll Is Here to Pay.*

45. Susan McClary, *Feminine Endings: Music, Gender, and Sexuality* (Minneapolis: University of Minnesota Press, 1991).

46. Ibid., chs. 6–7.

47. Lynn Goldsmith, *New Kids* (New York: Rizzoli/Eastman Kodak, 1990), n.p.

48. Ibid.

49. For example, one teen magazine feature about Joe McIntyre was titled "Get Cozy with Joey," *Superteen,* February 1992, 20.

50. Goldsmith, *New Kids.*

51. According to their lawyer, Barry Rosenthal, an integral part of the marketing of New Kids was to construct them as five individuals who "have their own set of fans. Our concept was to make these kids bigger than the group so they cannot be replaced. Fan appeal to the kids as individuals was the insurance that we did for our clients." Advertising insert, *Billboard,* December 15, 1990, NK-32, 33.

52. In addition, they changed their name to just the initials NKOTB, and the first single from the album, the raunchy "Dirty Dawg," was released on a white label. Even Columbia's publicity listed the group in anagram fashion as BONK-T. They dropped their Svengali, Maurice Starr, and took on other producers who allowed them greater control to return to the musical roots they love. See Craig Rosen, "Columbia, NKOTB 'Face the Music' with New Album," *Billboard,* January 15, 1994, 10.

7. The System of Celebrity

1. Hans Robert Jauss, "Interaction Patterns of Identification with the Hero," in *Aesthetic Experience and Literary Hermeneutics,* trans. Michael Shaw (Minneapolis: University of Minnesota Press, 1982), 168–72.

2. Ibid., 173.

3. In different years in the 1980s, these two black stars were seen to have had the highest incomes. See *Fortune* magazine's regular surveys of top-income entertainers.

4. Jauss, "Interaction Patterns," 184.

8. The Embodiment of Affect in Political Culture

1. The forms of rationality that are layered over the process of decision making in contemporary democratic politics can be linked to Weber's work on types of rationality and forms of rationalization. The end point of the political process — that is, the election of a candidate to be the leader — is layered with forms of purposive rationality that become a form of technical rationality or "instrumental rationality." What is incompatible in the development of a "disenchanted" world is the affectual realm; "Action is purposive-

rational [*zweckrational*] when it is oriented to ends, means, and secondary results. This involves rationally weighing the relations of means to ends, the relations of ends to secondary consequences, and finally the relative importance of different possible ends. Determination of action either in *affectual* or traditional terms is thus incompatible with this type." Max Weber, *Economy and Society*, vol. 3 (New York: Bedminster, 1968), 26; quoted in Jürgen Habermas, *The Theory of Communicative Action,* vol. 1 (Boston: Beacon, 1984), 168. What seems evident in a democratic system is the incompatibility between the general instrumental rationality that forms the ideological base of the democracy and the forms of affective legitimation that are accentuated in political campaigns. The intense play with affect in the organization of public subjectivity, including our political leaders, could be evidence of a legitimation crisis in contemporary capitalist democracies.

2. Edwin Diamond and Stephen Bates, *The Spot: The Rise of Political Advertising on Television* (Cambridge: MIT Press, 1988).

3. Benjamin Ginsberg, *The Captive Public: How Mass Opinion Promotes State Power* (New York: Basic Books, 1986).

4. William Leiss, Stephen Kline, and Sut Jhally, *Social Communication in Advertising* (Toronto: Nelson, 1990), 281–83.

5. Here is an example of an advertisement by the political consultancy firm Smith/Williams, which specializes in spin doctoring:

> *The Wind-up*
> Your campaign or organization probably spends hundreds of thousands of dollars on paid media. But when it comes to free media, dealing with news outlets, you probably rely on a staffer. Think about it. . . . all that money to buy TV and radio, but when it comes to the press . . . it's usually catch as catch can.
>
> *The Pitch*
> Our company focuses on free media. We can do an initial set-up. We'll help your press secretary plan and implement your campaign strategy. We can help map out a press plan for an upcoming debate. We know how to handle indictments, arrest, or a candidate that simply falls down stairs a lot.
>
> *It's in the Dirt*
> Campaigns can often take unexpected turns. These turns almost always surface in the free press. Be ready for them. Be confident that you can shut them down, or milk them for all they're worth. Call us.

This advertisement appeared in *Campaigns and Elections: The Magazine for Political Professionals,* September 1991, 29.

6. See Elias Cannetti, *Crowds and Power,* trans. Carol Stewart (Harmondsworth: Penguin, 1973[1960]).

7. Charles S. Steinberg, *The Creation of Consent: Public Relations in Practice* (New York: Hastings House, 1975), 27.

8. Stanley Kelley Jr., *Professional Public Relations and Political Power* (Baltimore: Johns Hopkins University Press, 1958), 17–18.

9. Ibid., 19.

10. Steinberg, *The Creation of Consent,* 29.

11. Kelley, *Professional Public Relations*, 2.

12. Benjamin Ginsberg, *The Captive Public: How Mass Opinion Promotes State Power* (New York: Basic Books, 1986).

13. Ibid., especially 32–58.

14. Ibid., 78.

15. Ibid., 79.

16. Ibid., 75–80.

17. One of the earliest uses of Gallup's polling services was in test-marketing the title of the 1939 film *Gone with the Wind*. Another discovery by ARI, a division of Gallup, was that audiences prefer one-word titles. The studio can be seen in these efforts of polling to be trying to protect its investment as much as possible and thereby maximize the audience reach for its product. Polling and premarketing strategies for the entertainment industries are a form of investment insurance that the mass can indeed be temporarily captured. For a history of the early surveying of the audience, see Garth Jowett, "Giving Them What They Want: Movie Audience Research before 1950," in Bruce A. Austin (ed.), *Current Research in Film: Audiences, Economics and Law,* vol. 1 (Norwood, N.J.: Ablex, 1985), 19–35; on one-word titles, see 31.

18. Leiss et al., *Social Communication in Advertising*, 327–48.

19. Daniel Boorstin, *The Image* (New York: Atheneum, 1977[1961]).

20. See Kathleen Hall Jamieson and Karlyn Kohrs Campbell's analysis of the campaign in *The Interplay of Influence: The Mass Media and Their Publics in News, Advertising and Politics* (Belmont, Calif.: Wadsworth, 1983), 233–37. Graham won this election campaign and became Florida's governor in November 1978.

21. For an interesting reading of the meaning and significance of these public spectacles and the way in which they shape the meaning of legitimate culture, see David Chaney, *Fictions and Ceremonies* (London: Comedia, 1979).

22. "The Big Sell," on *The Journal*, CBC, September 1988. See also David Taras, *The Newsmakers: The Media's Influence on Canadian Politics* (Scarborough: Nelson, 1990), 135.

23. What is interesting to note is the acceptable way the wife of the president is also positioned in this patriarchal structure of authority. Mila Mulroney and Barbara Bush adopted "appropriate" roles, serving as chairs of various charities. When there is a transgression of such passive, social support roles on the part of a leader's wife, there is perceived to be a challenge to the coherence of the political leader. An example of an unacceptable wife who did not play out the mythic sign system of family solidarity is Maureen McTeer, wife of former prime minister of Canada Joe Clarke. Similarly, in the 1992 U.S. presidential campaign, questions about the "strength, brilliance, and ambition" of Hillary Clinton were constructed as threats to the legitimacy of Bill Clinton's candidacy.

24. Weber, *Economy and Society*, 954, 1141–46.

25. A good interpretation of the organization of the spectacle of American political conventions and a reading of the dual role of the convention as

a forum for establishing party solidarity and as a way of conveying that solidarity in a televisualized form is found in Byron E. Shafer, *Bifurcated Politics: Evolution and Reform in the National Party Convention* (Cambridge: Harvard University Press, 1988), 226–89.

26. My reading of taste differentiations is derived from Pierre Bourdieu, *Distinction: The Social Critique of the Judgment of Taste* (Cambridge: Harvard University Press, 1984).

27. The press scrum symbolically represents the crowd in most television news coverage. Here we have the instantiation of chaos, the expression of uncontrollable desire to know, to decipher the meaning of leadership, as well as the unabashed connection to the crowd/public and the leader. Ceremonies structurally eliminate, through the institution of protocol, this crowdlike intervention into the proceedings. They work to construct the leader as rising above the mass and operating in a narrative that is entirely distinctive from that mass. Indeed, its power as a narrative of legitimacy is tied to this separation. Interestingly, in both Canada and the United States there have been active attempts to control the press scrum and to regulate the press conference. Trudeau banned press gatherings on the steps of the House of Commons and organized news conferences on his terms. Likewise in the United States, to save Reagan from the confusion of press conferences, the audience was seated and a rough order of who would be allowed to ask questions was instituted.

28. This is not to imply that some direct path of influence is established to the viewer/citizen through the advertisement; such is not the case. The point here is that advertisements, as elements of a system of meaning, are constructed as if they could have this direct persuasive impact.

29. Eisenhower's commercials are among of the most written about in the history of political advertising. See Kathleen Hall Jamieson, *Packaging the Presidency* (New York: Oxford University Press, 1992), ch. 5; Diamond and Bates, *The Spot*, 51–60.

30. The "bear in the woods" spot used in the 1980 Reagan campaign has become famous for establishing a mood that rivals that of the daisy ad. Without using the image of Reagan, and substituting an image of a roving bear for the Soviet Union, the voice-over highlights the threat of the Soviet Union to the U.S. way of life. The ad is structured to resonate with certain cultural connotations that a weak leader would allow the Soviet "bear" to dominate the West. Reagan's strength is thus juxtaposed with the careful technocratic style of Jimmy Carter. The binarism of strength versus strength in global relations is thus linked to Reagan's candidacy. Similarly, the negative ad campaign against Dukakis in the 1988 campaign that linked the parole release of convicted killers to the softness of Dukakis could be read as an attempt to establish cultural connotations and sentiments about the relative strengths of leaders. It is interesting to note the way in which strength has been naturalized as a quality of the right and conservative politics. In contrast, the technocratic and cautionary have been constructed as symbols of leadership "naturally" from the left. For readings of these advertisements,

see Diamond and Bates, *The Spot*, 127–33, 25–30; L. Patrick Devlin, *Political Persuasion in Presidential Campaigns* (New Brunswick, N.J.: Transaction, 1987), ch. 18.

31. See Stuart Hall, "Popular-Democratic vs. Authoritarian Populism: Two Ways of 'Taking Democracy Seriously,'" in Alan Hunt (ed.), *Marxism and Democracy* (London: Lawrence Wishert, 1980). The approach is drawn from Lawrence Grossberg, *It's a Sin: Politics, Postmodernity and the Popular* (Sydney: Power, 1988), 25–28

Conclusion: Forms of Power/Forms of Public Subjectivity

1. The celebrity can be restructured and retooled to fit into the structure of feeling of a particular cultural group. Dyer's reading of gay culture's appropriation of Judy Garland, whose personal and public struggles provide for dramaturgical expression in gay subcultures, is an excellent example of the use of a celebrity sign/text within a particular social movement. Camp, celebrity impersonation, and "vogueing" by different marginalized subcultures are also examples of how celebrity signs can be integrated into sartorial elements of social movements. See Richard Dyer, *Heavenly Bodies: Film Stars and Society* (London: British Film Institute/Macmillan Education, 1986); Andrew Ross, *No Respect: Intellectuals and Popular Culture* (New York: Routledge, 1989), 135–70.

2. Daniel Bell, *The End of Ideology* (New York: Free Press, 1962).

Coda: *George,* Celebrities, and the Shift in Political/Popular Culture

1. *George*, October/November 1995.

2. John F. Kennedy Jr., "Editor's Letter," *George,* October/November 1995, 9.

3. Ibid., 10.

4. Madonna, "If I Were President," *George,* October/November 1995, 280; "George Wallace," *George,* October/November 1995, 180–87.

5. John F. Kennedy Jr., "Politics and Other Dirty Words: John Kennedy Talks to Warren Beatty about Our Favorite National Pastimes," *George,* December/January 1995/96, 180–86; "Pop Politics" 140–44.

6. Andreas Huyssen describes the particular link between mass culture and the feminine: "Mass culture has always been the hidden subtext of the modernist project ... [and i]t is indeed striking to observe how the political, psychological and aesthetic discourse around the turn of the century consistently and obsessively genders mass culture and the masses as feminine while high, whether traditional or modern, clearly remains the privileged realm of male activities." Andreas Huyssen, "Mass Culture as Woman: Modernism's Other," in *After the Great Divide: Modernism, Mass Culture, Postmodernism* (Bloomington: Indiana University Press, 1986), 47. The extension of this debate about the feminine construction of popular and consumer cul-

ture has produced considerable discussion and debate about its political import and its generalizing reach. Tania Modleski, while acknowledging Baudrillard's use of the feminine in his description of the silent masses as a positive political refusal, is wary of the political strategy of this essentialism as to what constitutes the feminine: "A feminist approach to mass culture might begin, then, by recognizing and challenging the dubious sexual analogies that pervade a wide variety of discourses, however seductive they may at first appear. And this is especially important when, as in the case of Baudrillard, such discourses masquerade as theories of liberation." Tania Modleski, "Femininity as Mas(s)querade," in *Feminism without Women: Cultural Criticism in a "Postfeminist" Age* (New York: Routledge, 1991), 34. Certainly a great deal of study of popular culture, particularly women's soap operas and romance fiction, has generated an argument of a distinct—potentially essentialist—construction of feminine representations. Nevertheless, it has to be acknowledged that gender, as Van Zoonen has underlined, "should not be conceived as a fixed property of individuals but as part of an ongoing process by which subjects are constituted often in paradoxical ways." Liesbet Van Zoonen, *Feminist Media Studies* (Thousand Oaks, Calif.: Sage, 1994). It is still useful to chart how what has generally been designated as "feminine" has migrated and moved within the culture, particularly in its rearticulation of the play of politics on the border between the private and the public. As Joyrich has explained in her study of the pervasiveness of the normatively positioned feminine form of melodrama throughout television, this may posit subversive potential, but it also steers the representations to the needs of consumer culture. Lynne Joyrich, "All That Television Allows: TV Melodrama, Postmodernism and Consumer Culture," in Lynn Spigel and Denise Mann (eds.), *Private Screenings: Television and the Female Consumer* (Minneapolis: University of Minnesota Press, 1992). Celebrities similarly embody this tension of different articulations of value within the culture.

7. Steve Forbes, a Republican candidate for the 1996 presidential nomination, hosted *Saturday Night Live* on April 13, 1996. Although Forbes had already withdrawn from the race by that time, his appearance is indicative of the willingness of political public figures to inscribe themselves within popular culture.

8. Some of the most interesting work about this transformed "public sphere," and the most advanced thinking about how it is connected to the postmodern, has been developed by John Hartley. For a revealing look at the Nelson Mandela issue of *Vogue*, see Hartley, "The Mediasphere (Equality)," in *Popular Reality: Journalism, Modernity, Popular Culture* (London: Arnold, 1996).

Index

283

public sphere, 6, 7, 8, 14, 29, 70, 71, 76,
  82, 94, 97, 126, 135, 187, 191, 196,
  203, 207, 208, 209, 228, 229, 242,
  243, 247, 248, 281n; television as, 219

quasar, 16
Queen Elizabeth (1912), 81

Rabinow, Paul, 262n
Rain Man (1988), 111, 268n
Rather, Dan, 123
rationality, 20–22, 25, 27, 32, 50, 52,
  54, 55, 199, 204, 242, 258n,
  276–77n; in politics, 204, 205, 224,
  241; substantive, 53
rationalization, xii, 20–21, 32, 39, 42,
  48–49, 52–56, 67, 68, 73, 75, 255n
Ray, Johnnie, 157
Reagan, Ronald, 19, 211, 217, 237,
  279n
reception theory, 66–71
Redford, Robert, 13, 98
reification, 10
R.E.M., 173
representative public, 29
Reynolds, Burt, 13
Rhoda, 141
Rice, Anne, 114, 269n
Riesman, David, 257n
Risky Business (1983), 98, 100, 102, 267n
Robeson, Paul, 154
Rock against Apartheid/Racism Sun
  City, 197
Rogers, Mimi, 109
Rogers, Roy, 154
Rolling Stones, 161, 173, 175
Roosevelt, Franklin Delano, 209
Roosevelt, Teddy, 16, 31
Roper, Elmo, 211
Roseanne, 130
Rosen, Craig, 276n
Rosen, Marjorie, 171n
Rosenthal, Barry, 276n
Ross, Andrew, 258n, 280n
Ross, Sean, 275n
Rudé, George, 255n

St. Laurent, Louis, 217
Saturday Night Fever (1977), 18
Saturday Night Live, 250

Schiffner, Irving, 254n
Schlossberg, Karen, 274n
Schwartz, Tony, 232
Schwarzenegger, Arnold, 13, 19, 83,
  188, 264n
Scorsese, Martin, 111
Scott, Dick, 172
screen test, 95
selective tradition, 45
semiotics, 57–60, 67, 70, 71
Sennett, Richard, 87, 265n
Sessum, Kevin, 269n
Shafer, Byron E., 279n
sheet music, 150–51
Shepherd, John, 272n, 273n, 275n
Sica, Allan, 259n, 260n
Sighele, 34, 36, 256n
signature tunes, 154
Simpson, O.J., ix, 124
Sinatra, Frank, 154, 157, 173, 178, 182
singer-songwriters, 156, 161
situation comedy, 129–30, 191
Smith, Bessie, 157
soap opera, 126–29, 191
social psychology, 32, 36–44, 49
Sony Walkman, 155
sound bites, 228–29
Squier, Bob, 215
Staiger, Janet, 80, 263n
Stallone, Sylvester, 13, 264n
Stanislavsky, Konstantin, 87, 265n
Star is Born, A, 91
stardom, 7, 12–18, 79–118
Starr, Maurice, 171–73, 175, 275n,
  276n
Steinberg, Charles S., 277n
Step by Step (1990), 178, 273n
Stewart, Jimmy, x
Sting, 197
Streep, Meryl, 83, 265n
structure of feeling, 35, 45, 101
subculture, 46, 60, 174
superego, 24
Superteen, 275n
Swayze, Patrick, 266n
Swingewood, Alan, 256n

Taine, Hippolyte-Adolphe, 32, 37
talk shows, 126; and empowerment,
  142; as talking cure, 143

P. David Marshall is director of the Media and Cultural Studies Centre in the Department of English, University of Queensland, in Australia, where he also lectures in screen analysis and media studies. Previously, he taught at the School of Journalism and Communication, Carleton University, Ottawa, Canada.